In Memorium

Toshi, the benediction of all benedictions, she, who with the warm compassion invested all things, small or big, with beauty and herself loved Kashmir with an ethereal passion and whose courageous companionship sustained in many an hour of upheaval and turmoil. She has authored various parts of the book.

Kashmir

The Nuclear Flashpoint

Kashmir

The Nuclear Flashpoint

Birbal Nath

Former

Director General of Police : Punjab
Director General : Central Reserve Police Force (CRPF)
Director General : Border Security Force (BSF)
Advisor : Ministry of Home Affairs

(with contribution from Ms. Toshi Nath)

1998

Manas Publications

New Delhi - 110 002 (India)

MANAS PUBLICATIONS
(We Convert Fighters into Writers)
(Publishers for IAS, IPS, IFS, Defence, Judges, Press etc)
4402/5-A, Ansari Road (Opp. HDFC Bank)
Darya Ganj, New Delhi-110 002 (INDIA)
Off. ☎ 23260783, 23265523, Res. 23842660
Fax: 011-23272766
E-mail: manaspublications@gmail.com
manaspublications@yahoo.com
website: www.manaspublications.in

2nd Impression 2014 (FP - 1998)

ISBN 13 Digits - 978-81-7049-097-5
10 Digits - 81-7049-097-9
₹ 595/-

Designed at
Manas Publications

Printed in India at

HS Offsets, Delhi and published by Mrs Suman Lata for
Manas Publications, 4402/5-A, Ansari Road,
(Opp. HDFC Bank),
Darya Ganj, New Delhi-110 002 (INDIA)

Preface

The book arises out of our love for Kashmir and its beautiful and affectionate people. It also arises as a tribute to the wonderful people of India and Pakistan who after the blood soaked trauma, in which 5 million people lost their lives, of partition have made reckonable progress except in the field of eradication of corruption and poverty.

We have lived in Srinagar, the heart of Kashmir Valley, for years and years. We not only loved our neighbours, the Nagin Lake and Hazrat Bal with huge ancient Chinars turning burnished gold from green every autumn but also the people young and old, the students of Kashmir University with their frequent agitations, the bent craftsmen and women.

In the process we acquired a small knowledge of spoken Kashmiri dialect to interact affectionately with our old milk vendor lady, the vendors of fruit, and sundry sales person. Toshi Nath delighted in visiting M.A. Ramzana, the Jeweller, and seeing his exquisitc jewellery but hardly anything to purchase for lack of funds.

We were in the Kashmir Valley chiefly when Khwaja Ghulam Mohd. Sadiq and Syed Mir Qasim were the Chief Ministers. We socially interacted with the politicians, state officers and their families and socially and professionaly with numerous senior army officers and their families. We are fortunate to have travelled to all the sub-valleys and hills which comprise Kashmir Valley. Professionally Mr. Nath had to visit and check the performance of the BSF anti-infiltration posts...on Pir Panjal Rajouri in Kashmir Valley axis a number of times of every year. We have warm and fond friendships with Kashmir families till date and we hope to maintain the same till our last breath.

We hope that our book will assuage the agony of innocent Kashmiri families who have lost six thousand of their dear ones since the inception of fundamentalist terrorism. We also seek to establish trust and amity between India and Pakistan in this 50th year of our Independence. Can't we convert our adversial relationship into one of normalcy if not of friendship? Do we realise that if we fail to shed our mutual distrust and hostility towards each other the only alternative is nuclear holocaust which will destroy us, our heritage and our future generation?

BIRBAL NATH

Contents

The Evolution of State of Jammu & Kashmir as on 15th August 1947

1

The Beautiful Land and the Beautiful People

On the eve of India's partition in 1947 the state of Jammu and Kashmir comprised Jammu province, the small state of Poonch, the Gilgit Agency in north-west, including Hunza and Nagar, and Ladakh and Baltistan down the lower reaches of the river Indus. The geographical entity of Kashmir, comprising the above constituent units, covered an area of 82,258 sq. miles. The area of the state and its longitude and latitude vary, though in a minor way, in old records and documents. It was inhabited by Muslims, Hindus, Buddhists and Sikhs who had not much in common. It was predominantly a Muslim inhabited area: Moslems were Hindu converts who had embraced Islam during Islamisation of Kashmir in the fourteenth century - a process which gathered momentum when Timur invaded Iran, and Saiyid Ali Hamdani and Sufis of Naqshbandi Order, numbering more than six hundred, fled their homes in Iran and entered Kashmir in 1379 to escape the ruthless persecution of their sect by Timur whose armies had, after capturing Samarqand and Bokhara, also conquered Balakh (1579), Khurasia (1369-80) and Herat in 1380. We will revert to Islamisation of Kashmir later.

Kashmir has an ancient history. It is so mentioned by Herodotus. The recorded history shows that Kashmir came under the rule of Ashoka the Great who founded the city of Srinagar near village Pandrethan which is now located at some distance away from Badami Bagh area in the south of Srinagar literally means a city of wealth, beauty and knowledge.

Ashoka built Srinagar in 3rd century B.C. Pandrethan is a corruption of *Purana Distahana* or old capital. The Mauryan Emperor actually built 500 Buddhist monasteries of which 100 were existent when Hiuen Tsang visited Kashmir 1000 years later. The discovery of Buddhist relics and edicts has led historians to conclude that Ashoka was the original founder of Srinagar. Three centuries later Srinagar passed into the hands of Kushans, and under Kanishka Buddhism once again flourished. Kanishka convened the Third Buddhist Council in Kashmir for rectification of Buddhist scriptures. Kanishka, whose rule extended to Central Asia, sent a number of Buddhist missionaries to Sinkiang, Tibet, and Ladakh called 'Little Tibet' at that time. Kanishka was of Turki descent. Under this Indo-Scythian king evolved the Buddhist doctrine of northern areas of 'Greater Vehicle of the Lord' or 'Mahayana', which he preached in parts of Central Asia.

The heart of Kashmir is Jhelum valley, also called the valley of Kashmir. The valley comprises the plains and plateaus formed by River Jhelum and its tributaries. It luxuriates in its placid lakes such as Dal, Wular, Mansabal and others. About 100 sq. miles of its area is under water. Being an oval plain, Kashmir valley is 85 miles in length and 25 miles in breadth stretching from east to west. It is sheltered by the Karakoram and Pir Panjal mountain ranges. Chengiz Khan (1162-1227), the Great Mongol ruler and warrior, who had penetrated China and Europe, had also called his capital Karakoram. Either he borrowed this name from the mountainous range, or the mountainous range had come to be so called after the name of the city of tents, formed by the Great Mongol.

In the Korakoram range in Baltistan is to be found K/2 (Mt. Godwin Austin) 28,250 feet high mountain peak, the second highest in the world.

Anyway, the state of Jammu and Kashmir is extremely mountainous. Russel Brine calls it "a land of rocks and snow"[1] whereas Lord Birdwood called it a completely artificial area, a "geographical monstrosity"[2].

However, the Kashmir valley is more than adequately fertile as it is irrigated not only by Jhelum but also by Chenab and Sindh. The three rivers have made Kashmir a place of exquisite beauty. Mughals, who had captured Kashmir in 1587, came to the valley not only to escape the heat of dusty plains but also because they were enthralled by verdant meadows and shimmering snows of the Pir Panjal and Korakoram mountains - the natural ramparts around the valley. Jahangir made his own contribution when he laid Mughal Gardens called Shalimar and Nishat near Dal lake - they have the same design as the Moghal Garden at Pinjore at the foot-hills of Shimla. Anyone, who has visited or lived in Kashmir can't help getting enchanted by the cherry-blossoms, almond trees, stretches of lush green meadows, meandering rivulets and the majestic chinar trees lining the avenues and pine and fir trees on hills rising to kiss the skies. Sir Francis Younghusband, the British Political Agent in Kashmir, wrote in 1912, "Kashmir is more beautiful than Greece ... its purple hills are on a far greater scale". Kashmir has been called a 'paradise on earth.' The panoramic beauty of Kashmir is vividly described as follows:

> The snows, reaching out to the sky and the depth of icy lakes;
>
> A riot of colour and fragrance;
>
> Flowers, blossoming spontaneously;
>
> Trees, bursting out of the verdant earth;
>
> The clouds, floating over the bosom of the sky;
>
> Darkness and light chasing each other;
>
> Rivulets dancing and singing everywhere, meandering, faltering, proceeding towards their destination;
>
> enchanting not only men but even the stones laying magical spell on each sight.
>
> *Barf Ki Oochainon Barfaab ki Gharaian*
>
> *Rang Boo ki Shokhian, Phooloon ki Beparwahian*
>
> *Sabz Qaleenon pe Deevaron ki Bazmarian*
>
> *Hanste Chalte Phirte Abar ki Parchaian*
>
> *Aage Peechhe dagdana tharkati, gaati, hooen*
>
> *Nadian Harsoo*
>
> *Kasmasati, Ladkhadati pech balkhati hooien*
>
> *Aadmi kya pathataron ko wazd me laati hooien*

Apni, Apni Manzil-e-Maqsood ko Jaati hooien
Kartijaati hain nigahon par Qamal taskheer ka
Aamion ne kehdiya Kashmir ko Janat-e-Nishan
Warna Janat mian Husan-o-Rango shaadob kahan
Kya hai Janat Chand Hooren, ik Gulshan, do nadian
Khat Zahid ki riyat se yeh Kahata Hoon Kehaan
Aalam-E-Bala peehai parto Isi Kashmir Ka

Some uninformed people say Kashmir is a shadow of the paradise. This is untrue. The paradise contains only a few beautiful damsels. One garden and two streams. Anyway, I'd make concession to the holy saints and say that the paradise is merely a shadow of Kashmir valley!

The snow-capped mountains and sparkling streams draw rapturous admiration. The Europeans sing peans to its beauty in lyrical terms; we will presently see what Francois Bernier and Sir Younghousband have to say.

However, the people of Kashmir have suffered not only at the hands of nature when incessant snows bring miseries beyond words and deprive them of essential supplies - no vegetables, no electricity, no fuel and temperature plunging below minus! Art-loving Kashmiris, who have given the world superb carpets, copper-ware, wood carved furniture, pappier machiè articles of decor, cane furniture and baskets, exquisite shawls and jewellery, lead a forlorn life during dismal winter days.

Again, the beauty of the valley and the cultivated riches such as saffron at Pampore and shawl wool in Baltistan and Ladakh have invoked successive invasions by the aliens. They have been exploited by Scythian Hindu princes, Moghuls and Durranis of Kabul, Sikhs under Maharaja Ranjit Singh and Dogras.

P.N. Bazaz sums up the beauty of the land and the misery of the people as follows: "Fortunate in having a beautiful homeland, they have, however, not been fortunate in their rulers who frequently proved to be tyrants and cruel men. Kashmir is a land on which God has showered His blessings in the making, where the earth is good and can be made to grow much fast. Yet many of its people are near starvation... a land where the finest silks and the softest wool are spun and woven into cloth, most of its people are clad in rags; a land where precious stones are to be found few of its people possess any."[3]

The first European to visit Kashmir was Francois Bernier, a French physician in the Mogul court of Aurengzeb. In his book *Travels in the Mogul Empire AD 1656-1668* he describes his journey to Kachemiere as a member of the entourage of Mogul King Aurengzeb and calls Cashmire as the Paradise of the Indies. In his epistles to the King of France he described the happenings in Hindustan and the intrigues of the Mogul court.

Regarding the Kingdom of Kachemiere he wrote:

> "Monsieur,
>
> The histories of the ancient kings of Kachmire maintain that the whole of this country was in former times a vast lake, and that an outlet for the waters was opened by a certain 'pir', or the aged saint, named Kacheb, who miraculously cut the mountain of Baramoule."[4]

Bernier also referred to the translation of *Rajatarangine* (The Ocean of Kings) of Kalhana, by the Royal chronicler of Kashmir, into Persian by the command of the Sultan Zin-Ul-Abidin of Kashmir, who named this version the *Bahr-Ul-Asmeer* or 'The Sea of Tales'. He further informed his King: "the numberless streams, which issue from the mountains, maintain the valley and the hillocks in the most delightful verdure ... meadows and vineyards, fields of rice, wheat, hemp, saffron ... vary the enchanting scene. The whole ground is enamelled with our European flowers and plants. Villages and hamlets are often seen through the luxuriant foliage."[5]

About Shankaracharya hill of Srinagar which overlooks Dal lake, he writes: "Opposite this hill (Hari Parbat) is seen another, on which is also erected a small mosque with a garden and an extremely ancient building which bears evident marks of having been a temple of idols, although named Takht-e-Suleman, the throne of Solomon. The Mohamedans pretend that it was raised by that celebrated King (i.e. Soloman) when he visited Kachemiere, but I doubt whether they could prove that this country was ever honored by his presence." The explanatory note says that the Takht-e-Suliman hill, on the top of which stands a Buddhist temple, was built by Jakola, the son of Asoka, who reigned about 220 BC[6]. Part of it was turned into a mosque at the time of the first invasion of Kashmir by the Mohammadans, about 1015 AD. The hill owes its present name to Hindu philosopher Shankaracharya who had visited Kashmir 1000 years back. In fact, Adi Shankara had meditated here in the 9th century A.D. Ever since the place is called Shankaracharya Hill.

"The Kachmiries are celebrated for their wit and are considered more intelligent and ingenious than the Indians"[7].

"You have no doubt discovered already that I am charmed with Kachmiere. In truth, the kingdom surpasses in beauty all that my warm imagination had anticipated. It is not indeed without reasons that the Moguls call Kachmiere the terrestrial paradise of the Indies, or that Akbar was so unremitting in his efforts to wrest the specture from the hands of its native friends. His son Jahangir became so enamoured of this little kingdom, that he often declared that he would rather be deprived of every other province of his mighty empire than Kashmiere"[8]. (By the way, Jehangir died on 28th October, 1627, at Charges Sarai between Rajauri and Naushahra while returning to Lahore. His death was kept a secret and declared later only when he had reached Lahore).

Sir Francis Younghusband, claiming to know Kashmir since 1887, writes that it is not the eye but the soul that sees the beauty. He referred to his enchantment with Haramukh Peak, 16,903 feet high, on his visit to Harwan, once the abode of a famous Buddhist patriarch Nagarjuna who introduced the doctrine of Shunya, or Void, in Buddhist philosophy. In ancient times, Harwan was known as the Forest of six Arhata saints[9], and has a famous Buddhist vihara built by the Khusnas in the 1st century AD. The vihara's tiles, stamped with special motifs reveal that scholars from lands like Yarkand, Kashgar and Tartar visited the place. (At present it provides the main reservoir for supply of potable water to Srinagar). However, Buddhism was to receive ruinous blow at the hands of Mihir Kula, the 'white man' whose approach people knew by noticing the vultures, crows and other birds which flew ahead, eager to feed on those who would be slain.

Younghusband described the visit of the Viceroy Lord Minto in 1906 who, on entering the valley, bid adieu to all the ceremonials and left state business behind and felt that there, at least, he was in heaven of rest and natural enjoyment.

According to Younghusband, house boats were not indigenous to Kashmir. They were introduced by M.T. Kennard in about 1888. Like the present day tourists, this political regent revelled in his visits to the two Moghul gardens, the Nishat Bagh and the Shalimar Bagh, to Achibal and Verinag and his shooting expedition to Astor for ibex and bear in Tilail and Gurais. His enchantment with Shah Hamdan mosque on the right bank of Jhelum river near the third bridge, called Fateh Kadal, because of its Norwergian type of architecture. Built in the memory of Shah Hamdan, the Persian saint who came to Kashmir in the reign of Sultan Qutub-ud-din (AD 1373-98), it is one of the most sacred of the mosques. Its wooden structure, with pointed steeple and beautifully carved eaves and hanging bells, is a marvel of beauty. On the left of the river is Pathar Masjid built by the famous wife of Jahangir, Nur Jehan.

Younghusband found the Lolab valley beyond Kupwara and the Liddar valley around Pahalgam fascinating. Lolab also has Chandigam named after Chandi or Durga, the goddess, and also the birthplace of the renowned Buddhist missionary Kumarajiva who took Mahayana Buddhism to China via Central Asia.

Sir Younghusband went ecstatic about the Martand temple ruins. He writes:

"The temple of Martand is the finest example of what is known as the Kashmirian style of architecture and was built by the most noted of the Kashmiri kings, Lalataditta, who reigned between the years 699 and 736 AD. There is about it a combination of massiveness and simplicity and of solidity and grace which have earned it fame for a thousand years. There is something of the rigidity and strength of the Egyptian temples and something of the grace of Greece ... and owes much to the influence of Gandhara, while the sculptures show, according to Marshal, a close connection with the typical Hindu work of the late Gupta period."[9]

Younghusband continues : "The temple is built on the most sublime site, occupied by any building in the world - finer than the site of the Panthenon or of the Taj (Mahal)."[10] The sun temple at Martand is said to have been dedicated to Lord Shiva. Shiva is represented as Bhairon, Lokeshwara, Nataraj and Trimurti through the four figures in the temple. A female figure, dressed for bathing, symbolises Ganga. The fanatic Sultan Sikandar is said to have destroyed this unique temple. This temple has a courtyard colonnaded with the shrine in the center. It has 84 columns—a digit sacred to Hindus. Shaivism in Kashmir has given the world the classic "Vigyana Bhairave Tantra". One can see the ruins of the temple at Mattan in south of Kashmir valley.

Mattan was inhabited by a number of poor Kashmiri Pandits who have now been made to flee the place because Muslim militants wanted to convert Kashmir into purely an Islamic State for all purposes.

Talking of beautiful historic places, one cannot help appreciating Pari Mahal (i.e. place of fairies) located on the north of Chashma Shahi and the Governor's House in Srinagar. It is a terraced garden with meditation cells facing the Dal lake. It was built by Dara Shikoh, the elder brother of Emperor Aurangzeb, who was a great scholar. He translated the Upanishads into Persian.

People

According to Younghusband, 'The inhabitants were not however always Mohamedans. Originally, they were Hindus. It was only in the fourteenth century that they were converted mostly by force to become Mohamedans".[11] He further observes that Kashmir is very generally renowned for the beauty of its women and the deftness and taste of it shawl makers ... the strikingly handsome women with clear cut features, large dark eyes, well marked eyebrows and a general Jewish appearance".[12]

"Other interesting types of Kashmiri Mohamedans are found among the headmen of the picturesque little hamlets along the foothills. Here may be seen fine old patriarchal types just as we picture to ourselves the Israeli heroes of the old times. Some, indeed, say, though I must admit without much authority, that these Kashmiries are "of the lost tribes of Israel". People are in appearance of such a decided Jewish cast. Quadians of Gurdaspur maintain that Christ had come to Kashmir and was buried in Srinagar"[13].

Mount Nobo Aishmuguam, Ishabar, Yusmarg, found in Kashmir echo names mentioned in the Bible. Aishmuguam on the way to Pahalgam, has a Asa-i-Sharif the road of Moses as per a popular legend. And a sepulchre in Mount Nobo has been called the Tomb of Moses. Verily, these are called the Biblical mysteries of Kashmir which deepen further by the fact that there is startling evidence from Tibetan, Sanskrit, Persian and Arabic sources about the life of Christ. What is being asked is—Did the Buddhists first discover the Baby Jesus? Did he visit Kashmir at the age of 13? Did he survive his crucification and came again to Kashmir? If he did not, who is the mysterious Yuz Asaf? A popular legend tells that B'nai Israel, supposedly one of the lost tribes of Israel, took refuge in the East and the Kush tribe in the valley of Kashmir. Evidently, Kashmir and Kashgar have "Kush" in common. The Israel Arabic Kush descendants of Nimrod, are mentioned in the Genesis of Bible. The nomads who roam the Yusmarg meadows still call themselves the Bani-Israel or sons of Israel. The legend says that Jesus was saved by the Essens (a Judaic sect) from crucification and came to the East in search of the lost tribes. He finally settled in Kashmir and came to be known as Yuz Asaf, the prophet of B'nai Israel. The tomb of Yuz Asaf in the heart of Srinagar city, called Rozabad, is the most controversial site in the world. That is how the present day Shankaracharya hill was known as Takht-e-Sulaiman.

Sir Younghusband found that Kashmiri Pandits were well known all over India for their astuteness and subtlety, their intelligence and quick wisdom. "They prefer priestly, literary and clerical occupations ... the Kashmiri Pandits are essentially town people and out of the total number, about half of them live in the city of Srinagar. But they are also scattered sparsely through the villages, where the visitor will easily distinguish them by the caste mark on the forehead. On the whole they have a cultured look about them and a superior bearing". "Kashmiri men are tall and well built. Kashmiri women are pretty and brave."

Kashmiris are renowned for their skill in handicrafts, embroidery and other artifacts. Their staple food is rice which is grown in good quantity in the fertile terraced land of the valley. Their language is Kashmiri which is considered to belong to Dardic group of non-Sanskrit languages. In Jammu region Muslims predominate as also in Poonch, Rajauri and Doda clusters. It is estimated that 45 per cent of the people of Doda district in Jammu province speak Kashmiri.

Jammu is the home of the Dogras who are both Hindu Rajputs and Muslims. They are of Aryan origin and speak Dogrian an admixture of Persian, Punjabi and Sanskrit. Pahari and Punjabi too are spoken in this region. Sikhs and Hindus migrated to Jammu from West Pakistan in the wake of wanton destruction of life and property, caused by the partition of the subcontinent in 1947, and with that a large number of Muslims from there migrated to Pakistan.

In Jammu region districts Rajouri and Poonch are inhabited by Gujjar Muslims who have nothing in common with their co-religionists of Kashmir valley. The Muslims in Kashmir are Sunnis with a sprinkling of Shias. They are rigid adherents of Islam.

The Gujjars are another hill people who lead a life of nomadism. They move with their herds of cattle and flocks of sheep and goats from upland pastures to lowland pastures, and vice versa according to the rigours of the climate. It is believed that they are Rajputs who had migrated from Rajasthan since their language is akin to Rajasthani. They are Muslims.

Ladakh

Ladakh means "A land of Passes (Lanophgs)". Its landscape is barren. Viewed from above, it gives the appearance of a vast monotony of three colours, the brown of the earth, the white of the snow and the black of dark shadows of the valley. It is a land of vibrant vitality. Ladakh's landscape is criss-crossed by shimmering streams. It is the land of ancient Bhuttas, followers of Dalai Lama. They are of Tibetan stock with Turanian features and are generally short structured. Mountain ranges, running from south-east to north-west, have the exotic valleys of the Indus, Zanskar, Sura, Shyok, Nubra and Dras rivers. They are tourist attractions. In Ladakh people speak Ladakhi, Balti, Budh and Tibetan languages.

Leh is the capital of Ladakh. Ladakh lies to the east of Kashmir in the Upper Indus valley. It is rugged table-land country. In the north it is bounded by the Kuen Hun range and the slopes of Karakoram and in the west by Kashmir and Baltistan. In its south are Chamba, Rampur, Bashaher and Kulu of Himachal Pradesh and on its east and south-east beyond the international boundary lie districts of Rudok and Chumarti, and Tibet.

Ladakh played an important role in Kashmir's communication with Central Asia. The Nubra valley is situated on the main caravan route from Leh to Yarkand.

The north-eastern part of the Nubra district consists of the Chang Chenmo valley and the Lingzi Tang plains. Lingzi Tang is also known by the general name of Aksai Chin. It has a ground level of 17,000 ft. These plains form a desolate expanse of earth and rock with no vegetation but small salt lakes here and there.

Dogras under General Zorawar Singh had conquered Ladakh in 1834. Before the Dogra conquest, Alexander Cunningham had calculated the total population of Ladakh to be 168,000 of whom 122,000 were Lamas.

Before the introduction of Buddhism in Ladakh about the Third century B.C., the religion of Ladakh consisted of animistic and totemistic beliefs.

Lamaism is a nauseating perversion of Buddhism. Buddhism was first debased by the mumbo jumbo of Tantriks. Later, the Lamas impregnated it with spirits of former inhabitants making it a hash of superstitions and wild rituals.

Although Dogra Wazir Zorawar Singh conquered Ladakh in 1834, it was formally annexed only in 1842, when the Ladakhi Gyalpo was permanently deposed. Writes C.L. Datta: about earlier history:

"By the end of the 14th century, Muslim rule had established itself over Kashmir. Its kings were anxious to extend their conquests in the north and east. In 1405 AD, King Sikandar of Kashmir (1394-1416 AD) conquered Baltistan and adopted most brutal and ruthless means of converting its Buddhist population into Muslims ... In September, 1532, Ladakh suffered one of its most disastrous invasions from the north....."[16] in the shape of Mongol onslaught from the north. In 1532, Sultan Abu Sayed of Kashgar set out with his army for a holy war against the infidels of Tibet ... One part of his army was placed under the control of his able Commander Mirza Haider, who though a brave warrior, was a narrow-minded and fanatical Muslim. This contingent ... took the old caravan route over the Karakoram and entered Nubra, the northern district of Ladakh."[14]

Zorawar Singh led several Dogra expeditions into Ladakh Baltistan, and also undertook the conquest of Western Tibet. The Dogra conquest of Western Tibet caused a flutter in the dovecotes of the Kathmandu Darbar. The British Government was also perturbed over the prospect of Dogra-Sikh-Nepalese axis which would cause stoppage to the import of the lucrative shawl wool. The British, therefore, pressurised Lahore Darbar to recall Zorawar Singh from Tibet. However, Zorawar Singh was killed on 12th December, 1841 in a battle with the ferocious Tibetan army which captured Gurtok, Rudok, Tholing and other Dogra strongholds. By the end of March 1842, Dogras had been driven out of Tibet and "the high hopes of the Dogras to annex the eastern part of Tibet with in their dominions were shattered to smithereens".[14A] John company had secured lucrative trade of shawl wool and Pashmina for themselves.

Nearly 95 percent of the people in the Kashmir valley were Muslims. Now that the Kashmiri Pandits have been hounded out by Islamic terrorism, the Muslim population in the valley is expected to be more than 99 percent - a remarkable demographic feature which enables the Islamic fundamentalists to strive for an Islamic State on the pattern of Pakistan and Iran - a theocracy in a secular India.

Muslims also predominate in Poonch, Rajouri and Doda districts of Jammu province. Poonchi Muslims have nothing in common with Kashmiri Muslims. Actually they have been closer to the Pathans of Hazara district in North West province of Pakistan.

Poonch became a part of J&K in 1935-38. Poonchi Muslims resented this merger and it burst out in the rebellion of 1947.

The Hindu population is confined to Jammu, Kathua and Udhampur districts of Jammu province.

Sikhs live mostly in Jammu and Poonch. However, they are also to be found in Srinagar and Baramullah. In reality there is hardly a place anywhere in the world where Sikhs are not to be found!

We will discuss the conflict of interests of the three regions later.

Kashmir's Relations With Central Asia

We cannot understand the origin of Kashmiri people unless we study Kashmir's relations with Central Asia.

The term 'Central Asia' is often used vaguely to describe the whole of the vast territory between the Caspian in the west to the Great Wall of China in the East, Siberia in the north and Khorason (Persia), Tibet and Afghanistan in the south. The term 'Central Asia' has been shifting its boundaries with the vicissitudes of political empires. For instance in contemporary usage, Central Asia is taken to mean only the five Soviet Republics - Kazhakistan, Uzbekistan, Tajikistan, Kirghizia and Turkemia. Though these republics cover an area of four million square kilometers, that is almost a sixth of the territory of the Soviet Union, yet they do not form more than a part of Central Asia. In real terms 'Central Asia' covers not only the Soviet and Chinese Central Asia but northern Afghanistan and Tibet also because of the intimate linkage of their culture and commerce from times immemorial.

The area, lying between the rivers Amu-daryu (called Oxus by the Greeks) and Syr-daryu (Jaxartes to the Greeks), falls within Soviet Central Asia and so does the area represented by the mountains between Tienshan, the Alai and the Translai, and the Pamirs, with minor ranges along the upper Zafarshan and south of Samarkand.

Those who would like to know more about Central Asia may address themselves to the book *Between Oxus and Jumna* by Arnold J. Toynbee. He refers to the watershed between the Indus and the Oxus[14]. Further he refers to the mountain range whose crest is under snow during the greater part of the year. Observes he: "Running from south-west to north-east this range keeps on gaining heights. It starts at the Hindukush; it culminates in the Pamirs ... The present name of the range is said to mean `Hindu Killer'. An older name, transliterated in Greek as `Pasopanisos' is said to mean `Higher than the ceiling of an eagle's flight"[15]. He further observed:

"Civilization in the old world seems to have started in Iraq about 5000 years ago and in the meantime it had spread from Iraq both eastwards and westwards."[16]

The British did not want Russian and British empires to be co-terminus. When a Russian officer, Captain Grombehevsky reached Ladakh from Yarkand, the British felt concerned over Russian intentions vis-a-vis Ladakh.[15] Their suspicion of Russian intentions was so intense that they encouraged the Chinese to occupy the territory between Karakoram and Kuen Hun. In his minute dated 28 September, 1889, Lord Lansdowne, the then Viceroy of India, recorded that the Chinese should be activated in Kashgar-Yarkand region to act as an obstacle to Rusian advance. The British felt certain that the Chinese would allow a British Consul in Kashgar as they had allowed Russia to have a Consul there. To avoid co-terminity of borders with Russia the British concluded Pamirs Boundary Agreement with the Chinese in 1895, leaving unclaimed lands in Chinese possession.

Baltistan or Skardu extends on both sides of the river Indus for 150 miles. It is bounded in the north by the Karakoram mountains; on the west by Dardistan; on the east by Ladakh and on the south by Himalayas. The people of Baltistan are of the same stock as Ladakhis but by inter-marriage with the Dards, their features have undergone a considerable change. They are hardy and cheerful.

The valley of the Shyok and the areas of Shigar and Skardu are well populated.

P.N.K. Bamzai writes:

"The political relations of Kashmir with Central Asia led to a continuous influx of people from there to the valley. There were other causes, too, of this immigration, e.g., the low cost and abundance of foodstuffs which induced these northerns to permanently settle downward on account of the barren and unproductive nature of their homeland."[17]

However, this migration from north to the valley was not one-way only.

Long before the advent of Buddhism in Kashmir, Kashmiri settlements existed in Khotan and other important towns of Central Asia. A good proportion of Kashmiris was seen in the bazaars of Yarkand, Kashgar, Lhasa and Khotan, etc. Moorecraft, the British veterinary physician, who travelled in these areas extensively, claims to have seen thousands of Kashmiries in Central Asia. Some consider Kashmir as a part of Central Asia. Lord Birdwood writes of Kashmir as : "A completely artificial area, a geographical monstrosity."

The various dialects spoken by the people of Ladakh, Baltistan, Gilgit and the Kashmir valley are closely allied to the Dardic language. Dr. Grierson's researches have shown that Kashmiri language has a Dardic base. The word Dard occurs frequently in the Puranas written in Sanskrit. The Greek and the Romans included under the name of the Dard country the chain of mountains between the Hindukush and the frontiers of India proper.

Thus the origin of Kashmiri people and their language appears to be Dardistan. We have also to keep in view that the Hindukush ranges of mountains provided the "corridor" for the passage of the Aryans, Greeks, Scythians, Tartars, Turks, Mughals and Afghans to invade India and ultimately settle in the fertile plains of India, forsaking their original inhospitable lands in Central Asia.

A Divided People

The people of Jammu & Kashmir are ethnically heterogenous. Ladakh, with an area of more than 95,8000 sq. km., covers about 70 per cent of the total area of the state. Its population is one lac twenty-five thousand only. It is peopled by mainly Buddhists and Shia Muslims of Mongolian and Dardi origin. Shias are confined to the Kargil sub-division whereas Buddhists are in Leh area and in the Indus valley area. Ladakh is one of the highest land masses in the sub-continent and the day and night temperatures experience extreme variations (25 degrees). Fierce winds sweep the region. Dust storms are common and winters are extreme. The mountain ranges of the Great Himalaya Zanskar Ladakh Muztagh and Kuen Aun fascinate the tourists as does the lamaist Buddhism. Ladakh has come up as a place of tourist attraction and the presence of army units has injected a modicum of prosperity in this backward, freezing desert. But the people have a distinct identity. Ladakh has nothing in common with the Kashmir valley or Jammu.

The economic interests of the three regions, like their religion and culture, are not only disparate but at times antagonistic to one another. Kashmiri Muslims complain that though they constitute eighty per cent of the population yet Kashmiri Pandits and Jammu Dogras had grabbed all the eminent places in the governmental apparatus. Now that the Kashmiri Pandits have been exiled from their own land and their houses, which were generally ramshackle structures, have either been pulled down or are padlocked in a derelict condition, the Kashmirs Muslims can have no cause of complaint. Ladakh has been the worst sufferer so far as their share in government jobs is concerned.

In addition to this adversarial relationship over the distribution of small economic largesse, their religions being different, each accuses the other of fuelling the communal cleavage. During Sheikh Mohd. Abdullah's regime, Jan Sangh in Jammu region was pretty strong and it charged Sheikh Sahib and his National Conference of being communal, being in league with Pakistan, and ignoring the genuine difficulties of Jammu region. Buddhists in Ladakh too have branded National Conference as a Muslim outfit. On the other hand Sheikh Mohd. Abdullah and his colleagues accused Hindus of Jammu as rabid communalists who wanted to destroy Kashmiriat of the valley and justified their drift away from India as an inescapable step to preserve their identity and religion. Kashmir, the land of serenity, has thus turned into an inferno of competitive communalism.

Kashmiri Language and Culture

Kashmiri belongs to the Dardic branch of Indo-Iranian group of languages. It has been nourished by both Sanskrit and Persian literary traditions over the centuries.

The Kashmiri literature blossomed into a new beauty in the Fourteenth century with the works of Lalla Didi, a Saiva woman-saint whose compositions are on the lips of every Kashmiri. Lalla Didi was born in 1335 A.D. during the rule of Udayana Deva - the last Hindu king of Kashmir. Her marriage is said to have been a disaster. She became a *sanyasini,* roaming and singing her poems bathed in mystic perception of Siva, the Supreme. It is said that she had met Shah Hamdani, the first great Sufi saint and Islamic preacher from Iran. The Kashmiri Muslims consider her to have been converted to Islam by this contact with Shah Hamdani, and she is described by them as 'Lalla Arifa' while the Kashmiri Pandits call her 'Lalla Yogsveri'. G.A. Grierson has published four Kashmiri classics by Hindu writers and these include 110 poems of Lalla.

Lalla's poetry was followed by the mystic poetry of Sheikh Nuruddin (1377-1440) - who came to be called 'Nanda Pir' (the sage Nanda) by Kashmiri Hindus and is regarded as a patron-saint by the Kashmiri Muslims.

Art and literature really flourished in the Fifteenth century under the patronage of one of its enlightened rulers Zain-ul Abidin (1420-70). Himself a scholar of Sanskrit and Persian, he encouraged the growth of literature both in Sanskrit and Persian. During his regime Sufistic Islam came to regard Kashmiri Saiva mysticism with respect.

We cannot conclude without mentioning the works of Habba Khatun (1551-1606 AD) also called Zun, that is the moon-light, consort of Sultan Yusuf Shah Chak who was captured by Mughals and imprisoned in Bihar. She has been described as a scholar and musician and a poet par excellence and a paragon of beauty. When Akbar took away her husband, she wailed "O friend when shall fate smile on me; when shall I see the face of my lover?"

Aranimal is the third great poetess of love lyrics, who too led an unhappy married life like Lalla Didi and Habba Khatun. She was deserted by her husband, Munshi Bhavanidasa. Frustration found expression in her beautiful poems. "Her little lyrics with their abandon and profound yearning for her husband, and charming imagery redolent with the beauty and the fragrance of flowers, resemble similar lyrics of Habba Khatun ... and form some of the most exquisite flowers in the garden of Indian poetry".

Mehjoor is the poet of freedom. He wrote: "Mosques, temples, churches, shrines and viharas.

For all these prayer houses, I will make one door.
Muslims are like milk and Hindus like sugar.
I will mix milk and sugar and make nectar."

There have been a number of Sufi mystic poets like Qalandar Shah, Mohiuddin Miskin, Khwaja Akram Rahman Dar and Ramzan—Both who in 1900 composed Alh-Nanda - an old Hindu religious tale about the loving parents of the only son being compelled by a religious vow to put him to death and cook his flesh as an offering to a yogi who had ordained this sacrifice. But afterwards the son was restored to life after this test of his parents' devotion. The tale is narrated in simple and racy Kashmiri.

Kashmiri language has suffered a tremendous handicap in not possessing a viable alphabet. It is written in the Perso-Arabic script which is unsuitable for the genius of language. The old Sarada alphabet is confined to the Kashmiri Brahmins or is restricted to religious and ritualistic purposes only and is again an archaic tradition.

We have written only about poets and poetry, yet the prose forms like the novel and short stories have also been developed by present day Kashmiri writers. Akhtar Mahiuddin has made a mark with his novels *Dod Dag* and *Zuvta Zolna*. His collection of short stories *Sathsagar* (1955) won the Sahitya Akademi award in 1958. Amira Kamil, Gulam Nabi Gauhar, Harikrishna Kaul and Faruk Masudi have also distinguished themselves in the field of fiction.

REFERENCES

1. *The Indo-Pakistan Conflict* by Russel Brines-Pall Mall Press, London 1968, page 64.
2. *Two Nations and Kashmir* by Lord Birdwood, published by Robert Hale Ltd. London 1956, page 25.
3. *Kashmir in Crucible* by P.N. Bazaz, Pamposh Publications F. 38. Hauz Khaz, New Delhi, page 3.
4. *Travels in the Mogul Empire* 1656-1668 by Francois Bernier, page 397.
5. *Ibid.*, page 399.
6. *Ibid.*, page 402.
7. *Ibid.*, page 400.
8. *Ibid.*, page 401.
9. *Kashmir* by Sir Francis Younghusband KCSI KC IE, published by Cassel and Co. Ltd., Soho Square, London W. 1 Pages 98-99.
10. *Ibid.*, page 111.
11. *Ibid.*, page 108.
12. *Ibid.*, page 109.
13. *Ibid.*, page 107.

14& 14A. *Ladakh and Western Himalayas,* 1819-1848 by C.L. Datta.

15. *Between Oxus and Jumna* by Arnold J. Toynbee
16. *Ibid.*, page 1.
17. *Kashmir and Central Asia* by PNK Bamjai T, published by Light and Life Publishers. N. Delhi & Jammu, page 6.

2

A Brief Ramble Through the History of Kashmir: Islamisation of Kashmir

The chief source of Kashmir's ancient history is Kalhan's epic *Rajtarangni* (River of Kings). This book is said to have been written in AD 1148-50. It essays to portray the entire history of ancient Kashmir. However, it is clear from the internal evidence of this renowned work that it is not entirely factual and the *Rajtarangni* not only embellishes facts but luxuriates in poetic hyperbole bordering on the mythological.

Recent excavations at Burzoham, just off the road Naseem Bagh to Shalimar Bagh, on the outskirts of Srinagar, started in 1961, show caves and pit chambers. Burzoham is a prehistoric site dating back to the third millennium B.C. There are 11 megaliths at this neolithic site. Many bone and stone implements have been found here. There is also the evidence of rock painting. Thus Kashmir is an ancient civilization in its own right.

It is said that Kashmir valley was inhabited by such tribes as Nagas, Dars, Bhutas and Khosas. Aryans moved into the valley and the original tribes were Aryanised by compelling them to give up their tribal totems and animism. Aryans enfolded these tribes into their system of worship of nature deities.

They also established their system of governance with king being the real head of the government. It is said that Lord Shiva ruled the Himalayas and Parvati was his consort. Parvati is mythologically represented as the daughter of Himalayas (literally meaning the abode of snow). Parvati, Kali, Durga, Uma are other aspects of Jaganmatri according to the Puranic Hinduism. Shiva in his transcendental aspect is inactive in creation. His Shakti (energy) operates only through his consorts that is Parvati, Kali, Durga, etc.

The course of Kashmir's history later came to be fashioned by captivating women full of tremendous courage. Jayadevi, the mother of Avantivarman, and Didda of Poonch, whose role led to the decay and decline of Hindu rule, are a few prominent examples.

Avantivarman (AD 855-883) was a great builder who founded Avanatipur in the south of Kashmir valley. His two imposing temples, the larger one Siva Avantivarman with massive walls, is in ruins, the second one being Avantivasvam Vishnu is better preserved. The successor of Avantivarman started on a round of foreign expeditions, in the words of a historian, 'to revive the tradition of the conquest of the world'. The practical action has not been much more than the invasion of Hazare, attack on Kangra and the subjugation of what is now Gujarat in Punjab (Pakistan). However, it proves the fact which is interesting that the conquering tendency originated from Kashmir outwards, and not from the Punjab into Kashmir. But this was the last outward effort and from this reign onward, the record of Kashmir is one long succession of events of struggle between the rulers and usurping uncles, cousins, brothers, ministers, nobles and soldiers. As an aside I may describe that during the Indo-Pak war of 1971, the Pakistani bombers everyday bombed Srinagar and Avantipur airfields. Border Security Force companies were deployed for the defence of the two airfields. So, one fine morning, I and my Inspector General, late Shri R.C. Gopal, a brave extrovert, drove to Avantipur to talk to our men to raise their morale. As soon as ourcar left the national highway and took the right turn towards Avantipur, aircraft bombers appeared on the sky, as if from nowhere, and started straffing our car. We ran for cover and lay prostrate on our faces in the scrub on the left side beam of the road. The fire by the four of Pak aircraft was so inaccurate that none of us was injured nor was our car damaged. However, when we reached the Avantipur airfield we found that the runway had been rendered unserviceable by carpet bombing by the Pak aircraft; there were huge craters. The BSF fire from LMGs in their anti-aircraft role had proved ineffective. Why was BSF not equipped with anti-aircraft guns? What a pity!

The next phase in Kashmir's history is one of the purest coincidences. I am referring to the arrival of Ladakhi adventurer Rinchen who was to usher in Islam into the valley. Kashmir's King Sahadeva was the personification of cowardice itself. As soon as he heard that Rinchen had crossed Zozila with a band of his followers, he fled his palace leaving his family and Kashmir to their own fate. Rinchen found Kashmir's throne waiting for him. He married Kota Rani to legitimize his rule. To become more acceptable to Kashmiris, he decided to disinvest himself of Buddhism and convert himself as a Hindu. Thus he entreated Saiva guru Devaswamy to convert him as a Saivate Hindu but the arrogant Kashmiri Pandit declined the request. Frustrated Rinchan then got himself converted to Islam by Bulbul Shah on the advice of his friend and wazir Shah Mir. Bulbul Shah was a sufi from Iran. Rinchan became the first Muslim ruler of Kashmir and lord of Brahmins who had arrogantly and idiotically rejected his entreaty to be converted to Hinduism. He took the Muslim name of Sultan Sadr-ud-Din. He demolished a Buddhist temple and at its site built the first mosque for offering prayers by the Muslims. Rinchan died on November 25, 1323.

The rule of Kashmir reverted to the pusillanimous Udayana Deva who again fled in the face of Mongol invasion, leaving behind his wife. Kota Rani tried to rule but committed suicide when Shah Mir compelled her to marry him. So, Shah Mir proclaimed himself to be the king of Kashmir. He built a number of mosques and tried to spread the gospel of Islam by arranging matrimonial alliances between Kashmiris and Muslims. Here I must explain that when I talk of conversions by force I do not mean that Hindus or Pandits never showed violence. Some of them were as cruel as the Muslim kings of whom the following accounts speak'.

During the reign of Qutub-ud-din (1374-89) Saiyed Ali Hamdani arrived in Kashmir from Herat (Iran) in 1379; he was accompanied by his six hundred followers in the wake of harassment of Sufis of Herat by Timur Lang who by 1370 had established himself as the undisputed ruler of Samarqand and Bukhara and had extended his power in the neighbouring countries with lightening speed. He conquered Khurasan (1369-70) and Herat in 1380. He ruthlessly persecuted the Naqshbandi Sufi order and Saiyeds of Hamdan. Thus this exodus to Kashmir. In Srinagar Saiyid Ali Hamdani selected for his residence the extensive plot of land, situated on the right bank of Jhelum, between the third and fourth bridges, where there was a temple of Goddess Kali. Ever since Saiyid Ali Hamdan rested here, it came to be known as Khanqah-i-Moulla or Khanqah of Shah Hamdan. Only the faithfuls are allowed entry to this Pagoda–like wooden structure. A magnificent mosque was raised at this place by Sultan Sikander (1398-1413). The rule of Sikander is known as a reign of terror who gave the Kashmiri Pandits the option either to embrace Islam or leave the valley. Thus the Sufi movement, initiated by Bulbul Shah and nurtured by Saiyed Ali Hamdani with its ambience of universal brotherhood, degenerated into proselytization through sword. Sikander ordered melting of gold and silver idols of Hindus. Under the guidance of Saiyeds, Islam spread through the patronage and persecution by Muslim rulers. During the "golden age" of Zain-ud-din (1420-1470) not only did arts flourish but the Hindus also were permitted to pursue their religion. He is endearingly called Bud Shah (Great King) and was a benevolent monarch who shines among otherwise dreary procession of kings. However, during the reign of his son Haider Shah (1470-72) who was a drunkard and profligate, Kashmiri Pandits were again subjected to massive persecution.

The State was later attacked by Moghuls in 1587. Their rule lasted for 166 years. Sultan Yusuf Shah Chak is known only because of his consort Habba Khatoon who is described as a paragon of beauty in addition to being a musician and a poet. With the decline of Moghuls, Ahmad Shah Abdali conquered

Kashmir in 1752. It may be mentioned that Kashmiris themselves had invited him in disgust against the rapacious rule of the Moghul Governors. The Afghan Rule of Kashmir lasted from 1753 to 1819. Afghans let loose a reign of cruelty and plunder. To free themselves from the yoke of Durranis people turned to Maharaja Ranjit Singh of Lahore in 1819. However, the three-decade rule of Sikhs (1819-1846) was no less rapacious.

Dogra Rule (1846-1947) and Muslim Backlash

The ascendancy of Dogras, Rajputs of Jammu, was as devious as interesting. Dogras had joined Sikh army in the wake of annexation of Jammu and Kashmir by Maharaja Ranjit Singh of Lahore. Gulab Singh was recognised in 1818 as Raja of Jammu by Ranjit Singh; his brother Dhyan Singh was recognised as Raja of Poonch but was later killed by the Sikhs. In 1834, Raja Gulab Singh took up the conquest of Ladakh - the land of Buddhists - which had been a part of Tibet but had acquired an independent status by the 17th century under its own ruler called Galpo. Though Gulab Singh succeeded in acquiring Ladakh when Dogra troops under Zorawar Singh defeated King Trapal, however, Dogras reinstated him on conditions of furnishing indemnity and annual tribute. Yet Ladakh retained diplomatic relations with the Tibetan authorities in Lahasa. Chinese considered Tibet to be their dependency. This ambivalence in the relationship of Ladakh with the State of Jammu and Kashmir and Tibet simultaneously was to have significant consequences for the independent India. Downstream from Ladakh on the Indus lay Baltistan, ruled by a Sultan with its capital at Skardu. The original population was Buddhist who had later been converted to Islam. Gulab Singh undertook the acquisition of Baltistan and his General Zorawar Singh subjugated Sultan of Skardu, making it a part of Jammu State in 1842. Zorawar Singh grew ambitious and attacked Tibet but he and his army were killed by the "General Winter" on a plateau 15,000 ft. high exposed to wintry chill and winds as Napoleon's army had perished in the environs of Moscow.

Maharaja Ranjit Singh died in 1839. His son Maharaja Kharak Singh too died next year i.e. in 1840. The Sikh kingdom fell prey to a war of succession. The foxy East India Company Bahadur was on the look out to annex territories of Ranjit Singh. The Company Bahadur purchased the loyalties of both the Prime Minister Lal Singh and the Commander-in-Chief of Sikh Army, Tej Singh, and defeated Sikh Army in a fierce battle at Sabraon on 10th February, 1846. Under the "Treaty of Lahore" signed on March 9, 1846, the Sikhs ceded the whole country situated between the river Beas and Indus, including provinces of Hazara, to the British.

The transaction between the British and Raja Gulab Singh of Jammu was finalised in Amritsar on March 16, 1846 by a separate agreement which came to be called Treaty of Amritsar. Article I of this Treaty reads as under:

"The British Government transfers and makes over for ever in independent possession, to Maharaja Gulab Singh and heirs male of his body, all the hilly or mountainous country, with its dependencies situated to the eastward of the river Indus and westward of the river Ravi, including Chamba and excluding Lahore, being part of territories ceded to the British Government by the Lahore State according to provisions of Article IV of the Treaty of Lahore dated March 9, 1846 A.D."

Article 3 reads as under : In consideration of the transfer made to him and his heirs by the provisions of the foregoing article Maharaja Gulab Singh will pay to the British Government the sum of seventy five lakhs of rupees, fifty lakhs to be paid on ratification of the Treaty and twenty five lakhs on or before the 1st October of the current year, A.D. 1846."

Thus the British ceded the Kashmir Valley to Dogras for a sum of Nanakshahi Rupees seventy five lakhs only.

It is necessary to say that the Dogras had expanded in the north to Dardistan which included Chitral, Hunza, along the Indus between Dardistan and the plains to the north of the river which extended to borders of Chinese Turkistan, the Central Asian Khanat (Under Soviet rule) and Afghanistan. All these petty States had Muslim populations under Islamic dynasties.

In 1864, the Kashmir Government was successful in establishing a military post at Shahidilla at lower ridges of the

Korakash river and it persisted in maintaining claims to the territory north of the watershed between Kashmir and the Chinese Turkistan.

In 1870, the Kashmir ruler, Maharaja Ranbir Singh was compelled by the British to appoint Mr. Drew and next year Mr. Johnson, as his Commissioners for the district of Ladakh. In 1865 Johnson had crossed over from Leh to Khotan by a new route through the high Aksai Chin not the usual Koraihoam route which lay across 1800 ft. high pass. This adventure of Johnson led to Sino-Indian conflict of 1962 because it was Johnson who had taken J & K border close to Khotan.

After the setback in the Crimean war and the denial of access to the Mediterranean, Russian troops marched 600 miles eastward, occupying Tashkent (in 1865) Samarqand (in 1868) and Khiva (in 1873). As "the tramps of the Russian soldiers echoed loud and louder", Sir W.W. Hunter is quoted as saying: "During the past third of a century the Russians' march across Central Asia has been as the rush of the tidal wave..." With the Afghan war looming on the horizon and the Russians' boast to put their flag at Kashmir's frontier Maharaja Ranbir Singh was encouraged by the British to reassert his suzerainity over Chitral.

The British came to realise the strategic importance of Kashmir, situated as it was in the north-west corner of the sub-continent. In view of the strategic lay of the state, the British established a British Residency at Srinagar after the death of Maharaja Ranbir Singh in 1865. In 1877, Gilgit Agency was established by the British. In this period Russians had mounted pressure on northern Afghanistan. Accordingly, the British established effective control over the Gilgit Agency. Captain Durand took over Gilgit on 27th July, 1889. Meanwhile communications to Gilgit had been improved and a military road was constructed connecting Gilgit with Srinagar. The tribals of Hunza and Nagar under the instigation of Russians attacked the British positions. The British mounted their offensive and captured Hunza and Nagar in December 1891 and drove away the tribals with punitive losses. Thus, the British reached up to the heights of the Central Asia through Kashmir and they held monopoly on Pashmina shawl industry.

With the opening of a commercial road to Ladakh, appointment of a Political Officer in Gilgit by the British and Lt. Col. Colvin of the political department being appointed as Prime Minister (1932-36), the British took over total control of Kashmir frontiers along Central Asia and Tibet. Only after consolidation of this frontier policy, the British Prime Ministers of Kashmir were allowed by the British to be replaced by the Indians such as Sir N. Gopalaswami Ayyangar in 1936 who continued to hold the post till 1943. He was succeeded by Raja Sir Maharaja Singh, Col. Sir K.N. Haksar and the Jurist Sir B.N. Rau. In 1945 Sir Rau was replaced by Kashmiri Ram Chander Kak who could not deal with the accession issue successfully, though he wanted Kashmir to accede to Pakistan. At the time of accession of the state to India Shri Mehar Chand Mahajan was the Prime Minister of Jammu and Kashmir.

Thus the state of Jammu and Kashmir, as it existed in 1947, as a result of the expansionist policy of the Dogras, particularly, Gulab Singh and Ranbir Singh, formed a vital link between Indian sub-continent and Central Asia.

Area of the state of Jammu and Kashmir has been shown differently according to different censuses; census report in 1861 declared it to be 86023 sq. miles, whereas earlier the State Government had come out that the area was 84,471 sq. miles. The Pakistan Government accepts the area to be 84,471 sq. miles. According to 1941 census, Kashmir valley had 93 percent of Muslim population and the whole state of Jammu and Kashmir had 77.11 per cent Muslim population. Jammu at present is Hindu majority area.

The earliar Muslim majority in Jammu was reduced to a minority when Jammu Province saw ugly communal riots and Muslims migrated to Pakistan and Hindu and Sikh refugees from Pakistan settled in Jammu.

Before 1947, Kashmir and Jammu state, taken as a whole, had a Muslim majority of about 80 per cent. According to the census of 1981, the population of the state was 5,98,16,000 and the rate of growth in the population was 23.04 percent over the previous census of 1971. The state has never been a homogenous unitary region either in terms of religion, culture or language. In the Gilgit region, people are of Dardi language group, in Ladakh major language was Tibetan. Tibetan was also in vogue in Baltistan. The people of the Valley used Kashmiri language called Sarda. In Jammu Dogri which is akin to Punjabi is used.

Till 1947, there were three major roads from the sub-continent to the Kashmir valley. Two major roads converged onto Domel; one beginning from the main G.T. Road from Peshawar to Lahore. The highway from Wah on the G.T. Road was wide and the only all weather road. It ran through Abbotabad, Mansera and Garhi Domel. The second road from Rawalpindi ran through Murree running almost parallel to Jhelum river. From Domel a road goes alongside Jhelum to Chinari, Chakoti and Uri to Baramulla and Srinagar. The third route to Kashmir Valley was also from Punjab and started from the G.T. Road at Wazirabad through Sialkot, Suchetgarh, Jammu, Udhampur, Kud, Ramban and across the Banihal pass. This is the road which India uses now, after building Jawahar Tunnel at an altitude of more than 9000 ft. This road has become the major link between India and the Kashmir valley.

The strategic importance of the state of Jammu and Kashmir has been exaggerated by Sir Olaf Caroe and his colleagues. True Jammu & Kashmir provided a link with Tibet and Chinese Turkistan but the bogey of Afghan and Russian adventures across Pamirs into Kashmir had been highly exaggerated. In the north east Kashmir borders on Sinkiang, the line running south and east for some 400 miles; then for 450 miles it finds itself close to Tibet. It has a fairly long border with Afghanistan. On some maps it joins the erstwhile Soviet Union for about 20 miles while on others it ends at a common point with the borders of both Sinkiang and Russia. It is true that Russians strongly resented when Pakistan allegedly tried to make available air facilities at Gilgit to the USA. To say that a Russian Army in 1920 under M.N. Roy was to invade India after conquering the Khante of Bokhara is a figment of imagination. Roy's adventure had resulted in a disaster even before they could reach Afghanistan.

In his book *Danger in Kashmir* Joseph Korbel has dwelt at a very great length on the Russian designs on India Korbel writes. "In 1722, the founder of Modern Russia, Peter the Great, after he had reached the Gulf of Astrabad on the Caspian Sea, pointed to India and was reported to have declared that from there (Astrabad) to Balkh and Badakshan with pack of camels is only twelve days journey and on that road no one can interfere with us"[1]. Joseph Korbel further writes that in the nineteenth century several Russian Generals drew elaborate plans for penetration of Central Asia as a stepping stone to further advance. Writes Korbel: "In 1878 General Skobalev elaborated a much inspired detailed invasion of India by three columns, one of which would advance in the direction of Chitral and Kashmir. The project was published in 1883"[2].

Korbel quotes from Louis Fischer's *The Soviets in World Affairs* (1951) as quoting the Russian historian A.E. Snesenev saying, "The Czarist Government never looked upon invasion of India as a serious matter and only permitted the military Governors in Turkestan to toy with the idea"[3]. Perhaps that is the crux of the matter. The letter addressed by S. Covet Nesscolrodue, Russian Foreign Minister, to Maharaja Ranjit Singh and the king of Ladakh in 1820 had raised "fresh fears among the British".

So it is a pity that Indian Foreign Department displayed similar obsession when through a telegram it informed the British Government as follows on 25th October, 1947:

"Kashmir's northern Frontiers, as you are aware, run common with all the three countries, Afghanistan, the USSR and China. Security of Kashmir, which must depend on internal tranquillity and existence of stable Government, is vital to the security of India". In an age of satellite surveillance and state-of-art weaponry locations have ceased to be so important.

Even Korbel, who has dwelt upon Russian penetration of the sub-continent at a great length, both ideologically and militarily, had to concede that there were serious doubts regarding plan of a large scale Soviet invasion. Writes he, "The lessons of history caution against hasty conclusions. Indeed they raise serious doubts as to the practical possibility of a large-scale Soviet invasion of the sub-continent. Yet the old Czarist dreams of conquering India indicate at least a traditional desire of the Russian empire to expand in that direction"[4]. Then why such monumental fuss as to devote nearly one-third of his book *Danger in Kashmir* to non-existent danger of Soviet invasion of India through Kashmir?

Surrounded by almost impregnable ramparts of Pir Panjal and Karakoram ranges, it was natural that Kashmiris should acquire an insular focus of evolution. They came to look on every non-Kashmiri culture and mode of governance as exploitative as they came to be ruled by unscrupulous governors on behalf of Moghuls (1587-1752), Durranis ruling from distant Kabul from (1752) and the non-Islamic Rule of Sikhs (1819-1846) and Dogras (1846-1947). Earlier their land had been ravaged by Mongols under Dulacha in the thirteenth century. All these rapacious rulers had lacerated the collective psyche of Kashmir.

Mughal rule lasted for 166 years. It ended in anarchy when people were preyed upon by Mughal governors like vultures. Under Mughal rule Kashmiris had been dispossessed of their lands and all the cultivable lands had come to vest in the Emperor. This most iniquitous appropriation of land by Mughals had turned the vale into a land of misery. The Kashmiri landlords were entered in the revenue registers as tenants of the Emperor. Kashmiris call Akbar the Great, the Mughal King who had conquered Kashmir valley on 5th June, 1587, as Akbar the Great Villain who had for the first time imposed the will of Delhi on them.

Regarding the Pathan rule P.N. Bazaz writes: "The Pathan rule proved the worst of despotisms that the Kashmiris had suffered in their long history. By stealing the last pennies from the poverty stricken people and by inventing diabolical methods to torture them, the Pathan subedars made themselves the most despicable of rulers". So far as Sikh rule is concerned Moore Croft, as quoted by P.N. Bazaz, wrote "The Sikhs seem to look upon Kashmiris a little better than cattle"[5].

The successive foreign conquests and exploitation of Kashmir by alien rulers have left an impression that Kashmiris are a docile people who invited oppression due to their spinelessness. It will be shown that this assessment of Kashmiri ethos is without factual basis. Lord Birdwood calls them "a gentle, friendly people of little stamina who in trouble bark loudly and who seldom really bite"[6]. Josef Korbel quotes Vincent Smith as saying about Kashmir, "Few regions in the world can have had bad luck partly due to the cowardly character of the population which invited oppression"[7]. (*The Oxford History of India,* The Clarendon Press Oxford 1928, page 176), Joseph Korbel refers to a legend (*Danger in Kashmir,* page 11) that Akbar was enraged by the docile character of Kashmiris, "You Kashmiris have stomachs to eat but not to fight". And to show his contempt, he ordered them to change their dress into a skirt-like costume as a symbol of their feminine behaviour. Maud Diver (*Royal India,* Appletion Century Co. New York, 1942 page 7) is quoted as having written. "Men? Faint–hearts, not lion hearts". Sir Walter Lawrence in his classic, *The Valley of Kashmir,* written in 1895, says: "When one reflects on what thou saw one cannot help the thought that many races, had they lived through generations of oppression like the Kashmiris, might have been more cunning and more dishonest. In a country where there was practically no justice the only weapon in the hands of the weak is subterfuge" (page 274). The same Walter Lawrence writes at another place, "As they gained confidence they threw off their indolence, and I saw large tracts of country which had been left waste turned by their skillful toil into fat belts of fertile fields. I saw, also, the growth of self-respect and manliness and am confident that under a just government they will win a good crop".

No people are brave nor coward for ever. To brand Kashmiris as cowards is a travesty of truth. True long periods of oppression had sapped their energy and morale. Yet they had been splendid fighters and even ruthless in their pursuit of power. It was because of their valour that the valley provided 5420 cavalry and 50,530 infantry to the Imperial Mughal Army, according to Abul Fazal in *Ain-i-Akbari.* This lends more credence to the contrary legend described by Josef Korbel that Akbar was fearful of the Kashmiris' fighting spirit and ability so that he ordered them to put on over their trousers a clumsy skirt which would make their movements, and, therefore, their fighting more difficult.

The British Political Resident, Sir Frances Younghusband, described the ruthlessness of Kashmir rulers as follows:

"When I visited Hunza in 1889 the then Chief-now in exile-had murdered his father, poisoned his mother and thrown his brothers over a precipice". Can we cite a more gruesome tale of ruthlessness?

I myself have seen Kashmiri men and women in action for more than seven years (1967-1974) and later too. I have found not only the Kashmiri youth defiant of authority and of death, as youth generally is, but their middle aged men and women also throng the roads and thoroughfares and defy imposition of curfew and consequently suffer casualties. The Kashmiri youth seems to be bursting with rebellion and utter defiance and would never miss an opportunity to pick the gauntlet. Not only youth, their women folk, I found, were never near pusillanimity. Kashmir's history is replete with expeditions by Kashmiri kings when they defeated armies superior in numbers because of their valour and skill at arms; space does not permit detailing accounts of these historical episodes. Was Kota Rani not defiant? Was she not valiant to withstand Tartar invasion? Thus the tales of Kashmiri cowardice are not well founded. True, incessant periods of subjugation had made them circumspect as well as distrustful of all non-Kashmiris. "The Kashmiri is indeed made up of contradictions (who is free from contradictions by the way?), he is timid yet persistent mystical yet adventurous, shrewd and business like" says G.M.D. Sufi.

What sustained Kashmiris to survive centuries of repression, loot, mayhem and pillaging? This question can be answered in one word: "faith" - faith in his religion. Kashmiri Muslim's faith in Islam, say Pan-Islamism, is so deep rooted that a sacrilege of Holy Koran or a mosque in distant Uttar Pradesh or Jerusalem propels masses of them into ruthless violence. Anything to derogate Islam throws them into paroxysms of violence and mass hysteria. I have personally seen United Nations Observers Headquarters at Srinagar being surrounded when Jews had harmed their sacred Masjid Al Aqsa, the site in Jerusalem where the Prophet ascended to heaven in the eleventh year of his mission (Koran 117:2). Similar religious frenzy burst out during the Holy Relic Theft agitation in 1963-64.

G.M.D. Sufi in his *'History of Kashmir'*, not only describes Kashmiris as feared warriors but calls them as `fanatical Muslims'. on the basis of a report called `Remonstrantie' written by Francisco Pelsott who was in the service of Dutch East Indian Company from 1627. Similarly, Sheikh Abdullah spoke to Joseph Korbel of "the fanatical devotion of his followers to Islam"[7]. Masses in Kashmir lionised Sheikh Mohammad Abdullah; it was not because of his being a political leader. They perceived him not only a Kashmiri patriot but as the leader of Islamic resurgence.

REFERENCES

1. *Danger in Kashmir* by Josef Korbel published by Princeton New Jersey, 1966 page 275.
2. Ibid page 277.
3. Ibid page 277
4. Ibid page 274
5. P.N. Bazaz, *Kashmir in Crucible,* page 211.
6. *Two Nations and Kashmir* by Lord Birdwood.
7. *Danger in Kashmir* by Josef Korbel page 11.

3

Accession of Jammu & Kashmir to India

Two months after the victory of the Allies in World War II, there was a General Election in the United Kingdom. Winston Churchill, who had saved his country with his monumental courage and prodigious defiance of the Nazis, was voted out of power in February, 1946. How ironic democracy can be!

Labour Party triumphed at the hustings and their leader Clement Atlee as Prime Minister embarked upon the liquidation of British Empire. His first priority was to pull out of India. Thus he made a statement on February 20, 1947, in the British Parliament that the British were to leave India by June, 1948.

Towards this end the British Government sent Lord Mountbatten to replace Lord Viscount Wavel as the last Viceroy of India. Since Atlee had served in the Simon Commission (1927-1930) for two years in India, he had come to the conclusion that all the Indian politicians were permanently in opposition and unless responsibility was thrust upon them, they would continue squabbling and blaming the British.

When on 20th February, 1947, the British Prime Minister announced that the British would quit India by June, 1948, he was opposed vehemently. During the debate in the House of Lords, Lord Simon, of Simon Commission fame, said that this business was "not going to be the establishment of peace in India, but rather this is going to degrade the British name." Lord Halifax, an ex-Viceroy of India, spoke of his "feelings of failure, frustration and foreboding over the plan."[1]

In the House of Commons, Sir Winston Churchill, participating in the debate on 6th March, 1947, observed that the laying of deadline was the "Operation Scuttle". He said: "India is to be subjected not merely to partition but to fragmentation and to haphazard fragmentation. The time limit, far from bringing the Indian parties to their senses, was calculated to make them step up their demands."[2] According to him the time-limit laid was to lead to "disastrous transaction". Did this "time-limit" not lead to perishing of millions during the partition of India?

The Cabinet Mission had arrived in India on 23rd March, 1946. Sir Stafford Cripps, who had made an abortive attempt of settlement of India's self-government in 1942, and Patrick Lawrence, Secretary of State, and A.V. Alexander, the First Lord of the Admiralty, were its three members. Since Congress and Muslim League had failed to arrive at a mutually acceptable settlement, the decision of the Cabinet Mission was announced on May 16, 1946. Cabinet mission plan had envisaged a Union of States having jurisdiction over Foreign Affairs, Defence and Communications only and eventually ironing out a Constitution by a Constituent Assembly to be elected by an electoral college of Members of Provincial Legislatures.

The proposals of the Cabinet Mission were accepted with some reservations by all parties and the elections to the Constituent Assembly took place in July, 1946. An Interim Government of fourteen members was formed—five each representing the Congress and five representing the Muslim League and one each representing the Sikhs, Anglo-Indians, Parsis and Indian Christians. Muslim League refused to participate in the Constituent Assembly deliberations. The working of the Interim government of fourteen members was hamstrung - Finance being with Mr. Liaqat Ali who vetoed all proposals which would promote what he perceived to be Congress interests.

Lord Mountbatten was sworn-in as the last Viceroy of India on March 24, 1947. This haste without administrative arrangements was to plunge northern and eastern India into bloodbath of unprecedented magnitude and migration of communities of gigantic dimensions - a tragedy which defies description.

Lord Mountbatten was also to complicate the accession of Jammu and Kashmir to India as we will be seen. First let us understand what Paramountcy meant which was to lapse once the Dominions of India and Pakistan were to come into existence. During the British rule the rulers of all the Princely States had ceded to the British their authority in respect of External Affairs, Defence and Communications. This was the essence of the British Paramountcy which meant that the British would control State's foreign relations and the ruler had to acknowledge British supremacy.

Indian Independence Act, 1947, was passed by the British Parliament on 17th June, 1947. Section 7 of this Act bears the heading "Consequences of the setting up of the new Dominions". Sub-Section (1)(b) of this Section which is relevant is reproduced below. It reads:

"The suzerainty of His Majesty over the Indian States lapses and with it, all treaties and agreements in force at the date of the passing of this Act between His Majesty and the rulers of Indian States, all functions exercisable by His Majesty at that date with respect to Indian States, all obligations of His Majesty existing at that date or the rulers thereof and all powers, rights, and authority or jurisdiction exercisable by His Majesty at that date or in relation to Indian States by treaty, grant, usage, sufferance or otherwise."

Thus paramountcy having lapsed, the Rulers of the Princely States were free to accede to either of the two dominions or live as free states.

There were five hundred sixty-five Princely states, some of whom were states in name only, being so puny in size as spread over a few acres of land and the population not exceeding a couple of hundred souls and a revenue of Rupees five hundred only. For instance, there were 222 states and estates (449 units if calculated on the basis of the numbers of shareholders) in Kathiawar which came to be known as Saurashtra later. Of the 565 states, 140 were fairly large and their rulers were described as fully empowered. Of all the states Hyderabad and Kashmir were the largest, each occupying more than 80,000 sq. miles area, that is, more than the area of England and only a little less than the whole of the United Kingdom.

The accession of all the Princely states to the two Dominions of India and Pakistan proceeded smoothly except for Jammu and Kashmir in the north, Hyderabad in the south and Junagarh in Kathiawar in the west. All the three states which gave trouble in respect of their accession had one common feature that is the ruler had each time been of a different community from the overwhelming majority of his subjects.

We will briefly discuss accession of Junagarh and Hyderabad as their accession had a bearing on the accession of Jammu & Kashmir which is our subject of study.

Accession of Junagarh

Junagarh was ruled by Sir Mahabat Khan Rasul Khanji. His Dewan was Sir Nawaz Bhutto. The state was surrounded by small estates on three sides and on the fourth by Arabian Sea and its port was Veraval which was 325 nautical miles away from Karachi. Junagarh's Nawab after emptying state treasury, flew to Karachi, and it was stated that while in Karachi, the Nawab had signed Instrument of Accession of his state to Pakistan.

Campbell Johnson in his diary for 16th September, 1947, writes that this accession "was one of the traps and teasings on Jinnah's part. He (M.A. Jinnah) hopes, by luring India into a militant reaction to secure a verdict on legal points and to create a valuable precedent for any attitude, he may care to adopt towards the far greater Princely objectives of Kashmir and Hyderabad. For Junagarh is, in some respects, Hyderabad—in miniature-a Moslem Prince and oligarchy, ruling over a predominantly Hindu state in the middle of Indian territory."[3]

Before acceding to Pakistan the Nawab of Junagarh had entered into a Standstill Agreement with Pakistan. Mangrol had acceded to India but the Nawab of Junagarh maintained that Mangrol was his vassal state and he sent his troops to Babariawad which too had acceded to India. The entry of Junagarh state troops in Mangrol was an act of grave provocation yet Government of India refrained from taking military action though it moved an Infantry brigade into Kathiawar. On 7th November 1947, the Junagarh Dewan, Sir Nawab Ali Bhutto, requested the Government of India to take over the administration of the state. Accordingly, India took over its administration on November 9, 1947, to maintain peace. India had kept Pakistan's Prime Minister fully apprised of the developments. Out of its idealistic fervour India held a referendum on the issue of accession in Junagarh on February 2, 1948. Only 911 persons voted for accession to Pakistan whereas all the rest voted in favour of accession to India.

Hyderabad

The Nizam who ruled the state of Hyderabad, predominantly inhabited by non-Muslims, was determined to keep Hyderabad as an independent state. He had made his intention known to even Lord Wavell much earlier. On August 15, 1947, he announced that his state would maintain an independent status. Hyderabad had its own currency and postal system. He was, however, ultimately informed by Governor General Lord Mountbatten that his aspiration was not legally feasible under the Indian Independence Act, 1947. On 17 August, 1947, Nawab Chhatari, President of Nizam's Executive Council, asked for negotiations on status of Hyderabad state. After protracted negotiations, a draft was ultimately agreed to by negotiating parties and the Hyderabad delegation left Delhi, leaving an undertaking that they would return to Delhi with the Nizam's signatures as a token of his acceptance. Though this draft was approved by the Nizam's Executive Council after prolonged discussions, the Nizam did not accept the same because Qasim Rizvi, the head of Ithad-ul-Musilmeen, was not ready to accept any relationship with India. Qasim Rizvi was the leader of an organisation of volunteers called Razakars, a quasi-military force, which Nizam thought could stem any military action by India along with his state forces.

In the meanwhile, the state of affairs in Hyderabad went on worsening. Ultimately Indian troops comprising a brigade under Brigadier J.N. Choudhary, who ultimately became the Chief of Army staff after 1962 debacle and fought the 1965 Indo-Pak war, entered Hyderabad state on 13th September, 1948. The state forces laid down their arms within four days after offering hardly more than token resistance. Razakars suffered heavy casualties and their leader Qasim Rizvi was arrested on 19th September, 1948. Nizam accordingly acceded to India.

Kashmir

The next largest state which did not accede either to India or Pakistan was Kashmir. The state had overwhelming Muslim population but was ruled by Dogra Maharaja Sir Hari Singh. The Maharaja entered into Standstill Agreement with Pakistan. India, however, refused to enter into such an Agreement. Pakistan imposed an economic blockade on the state so that the people were starved of foodgrains, salt, kerosene oil and petroleum products and this blockade was a prelude to the ultimate tribal invasion of the state which was to follow. There were two main political parties in the state: Muslim Conference which was founded in 1931 and of which Sheikh Mohd. Abdullah, Bakshi Gulam Mohammad, Khwaja Ghulam Mohd. Sadiq too had been members. However, in June 1939 these leaders, who had secular outlook, had changed the name of Muslim Conference to National Conference and opened its doors to the members of all the communities. They had campaigned against autocratic Dogra rule. In 1946, Sheikh Mohd. Abdullah and his colleagues were arrested and held in prison. Pt. Nehru who was negotiating with the Cabinet Mission left New Delhi at that time to visit the valley. He was intercepted at Korala. Muslim Conference was revived with some vigour, after 1940 Pak resolution, by Ghulam Abbas. This Conference sought state's accession to Pakistan. However, Ghulam Abbas too was imprisoned in 1946, to be accurate. Here it will be appropriate to reproduce in original correspondence exchanged between Kashmir state and Pakistan and the Maharaja's accession offered to India and its acceptance later.

Kashmir-Pak Standstill Agreement

Telegram from Prime Minister, Kashmir State, to Sardar Abdur Rab Nishtar, State Relations Department, Karachi, dated 12th August, 1947:

"Jammu and Kashmir Government would welcome Standstill Agreement with Pakistan, on all matters on which these exist at present moment with outgoing British Indian Government. It is suggested that existing arrangements should continue pending settlement of details and formal execution of fresh agreement."

Government of India had sent V.P. Menon to meet the Maharaja when the Defence Committee of the Indian Cabinet was informed by General Lockhart that a telegram had been received from Headquarters of the Pakistan Army stating that some five thousand tribesmen had attacked and captured Muzaffarabad and Domel and that considerable tribal enforcements were on the way. Menon had reported back to the cabinet that Maharaja had suffered nervous break-down and on his advice ultimately Maharaja had left Srinagar with his wife and son. The Maharaja had handed over to Mr. Menon the Instrument of Accession duly signed by him.

Maharaja's Accession Offer to India

Text of the letter dated October 26, 1947, from Sir Hari Singh, the Maharaja of Jammu & Kashmir, to Lord Mountbatten, the Governor General of India:

"My dear Lord Mountbatten,

"I have to inform your Excellency that a grave emergency has arisen in my State and request immediate assistance of your Government.

"As your Excellency is aware, the State of Jammu & Kashmir has not acceded to the Dominion of India or to Pakistan. Geographically, my State is contiguous to both the Dominions. It has vital economical and cultural links with both of them. Besides my State has a common boundary with the Soviet Republic and China. In their external relations Dominions of India and Pakistan cannot ignore this fact.

"I wanted to take time to decide to which Dominion I should accede, or whether it is not in the best interests of both the dominions and my State to stand Independent. Of course, with friendly and cordial relations with both.

"I accordingly approached the Dominions of India and Pakistan to enter into Standstill Agreement with my state. The Pakistan Government accepted this agreement. The dominion of India desired further discussions with representatives of my Government. I could not arrange to this, in view of the developments indicated below. In fact, the Pakistan Government is operating Post and Telegraph system inside the state.

"Though we have got a standstill agreement with the Pakistan Government it permitted steady and increasing strangulation of supplies like food, salt and petrol to my state.

"Afridis, soldiers in plain clothes, and desperadoes with modern weapons have been allowed to infiltrate into the State at first in Poonch and then Sialkot and finally area adjoining Hazara District on the Ramkot side. The result has been that the limited number of troops at the disposal of the State had to be dispersed and thus had to face the enemy at the several points simultaneously, that it has become difficult to stop the wanton destruction of life and property and looting. The Mahora powerhouse which supplies the electric current to the whole of Srinagar has been burnt. The number of women who have been kidnapped and raped makes my heart bleed. The wild forces thus let loose on the State are marching on with the aim of capturing Srinagar, the summer capital of my Government, as the first step to over–running the whole State.

"With the conditions, obtaining at present in my State and the great emergency of the situation as it exists, I have no option but to ask for help from the Indian Dominion. Naturally they cannot send the help asked for by me without my State acceding to the Dominion of India. I have accordingly decided to do so and I attach the Instrument of Accession for acceptance by your Government. The other alternative is to leave my State and my people to free-booters. On this basis no civilised Government can exist or be maintained. This alternative I will never allow to happen as long as I am the Ruler of the State and I have life to defend my country.

"I may also inform your Excellency's Government that it is my intention to set up immediately an interim Government and ask Sheikh Abdullah to carry out the responsibilities in this emergency as my Prime Minister.

"If my State has to be saved immediate assistance must be available to Srinagar. Mr. Menon is fully aware of the situation and he will explain to you, if further explanation is needed. Whereas the Indian Independence Act, 1947, provides that as from the fifteenth day of August, 1947, there shall be set up an independent Dominion known as INDIA, and that the Government of India Act, 1935, shall, with such omissions, additions, adaptations and modifications as the Governor-General may by order specify, be applicable to the Dominion of India'

"And whereas the Government of India Act, 1935, as so adopted by the Governor-General provides that an Indian State may accede to the Dominion of India by an Instrument of Accession to be executed by the Ruler thereof.

"Now, therefore, I, Shriman Indar Mahendar Rajrajeshwar Maharajadhiraj Shri Hari Singhji, Jammu Naresh Tatha Tibbet adi Deshadhipati, Ruler of Jammu and Kashmir State, in the exercise of my sovereignty in and over my said State, do hereby execute this my Instrument of Accession and;

1. I hereby declare that I accede to the Dominion of India with the intent that the Governor General of India, the Dominion Legislature, the Federal Court and any other Dominion authority established for the purpose of the Dominion shall, by virtue of this my Instrument of Accession but subject always to the terms thereof, and for the purpose only of the Dominion exercise in relation to the State of Jammu and Kashmir (hereinafter referred to as "this State") such functions as may be vested in them by or under the Government of India Act, 1935, as in force in the Dominion of India, on the 15th day of August, 1947 (which Act as so in force is hereafter referred to as "the Act".).

2. I hereby assume the obligation of ensuring that due effect is given to the provisions of the Act within this State so far so they are applicable therein by virtue of this my Instrument of Accession.

3. I accept the matters specified in the Schedule hereto as the matters with respect to which the Dominion Legislature may make laws for this State.

4. I hereby declare that I accede to the Dominion of India on the assurance that if an agreement is made between the Governor–General and the Ruler of this State whereby any function in relation to the administration in this state of any law of the dominion legislature shall be exercised by the ruler of this state, then any such agreement shall be deemed to form part of this Instrument and shall be construed and have effect accordingly.

5. The terms of this Instrument of Accession shall not be varied by any amendment of the Act or of the Indian Independence Act, 1947, unless such amendment is accepted by me by an instrument supplementary to this Instrument.

6. Nothing in this Instrument shall empower the dominion legislature to make any law for this state authorising the compulsory acquisition of land for any purpose, but I hereby undertake that should the dominion for the purposes of a dominion law which applies in the state deem it necessary to acquire any land. I will at their request acquire the land at their expense or if the land belongs to me, transfer it to them on such terms as may be agreed, or, in default of agreement, determined by an arbitrator to be appointed by the Chief Justice of India.

7. Nothing in this Instrument shall be deemed to commit me in any way to acceptance of any future constitution of India or to fetter my discretion to enter into arrangements with the Government of India under any such future Constitution.

8. Nothing in this Instrument affects the continuance of my sovereignty in and over this state or, save as provided by

or under this Instrument, the exercise of any powers, authority and rights now enjoyed by me as ruler of this state or the validity of any law at present in this state.

9. I hereby declare that I execute this Instrument on behalf of this state and that any reference in this Instrument to me or the ruler of the state is to be construed as including a reference to my heirs and successors.

Given under my hand this 26th day of October, nineteen hundred and forty seven.

sd/-

(Hari Singh)

Maharajadhiraj of Jammu & Kashmir state.

SCHEDULE

The matters with respect to which the dominion legislature may make laws for this state.

A. Defence

1. The naval, military and air forces of the dominion and any other armed force raised or maintained by the dominion, any armed forces, including forces raised or maintained by an acceding state, which are attached to, or operating with, any of the armed forces of the dominion.
2. Naval, military and air force works, administration of cantonment areas.
3. Arms, firearms, ammunition.
4. Explosives.

B. External Affairs

1. External affairs; the implementing of treaties and agreements with other countries; extradition, including the surrender of criminals and accused persons to part of His Majesty's dominions outside India.

2. Admission into, and emigration and expulsion from India, including in relation thereto the regulation of the movements in India of persons who are not British subjects, domiciled in India or subjects of any acceding state, pilgrimages to places beyond India.

3. Naturalisation.

C. Communications

1. Post and Telegraph, including telephones, wireless broadcasting and other like forms of communication.

2. Federal railways; the regulation of all railways other than minor railways in respect of safety, maximum and minimum rates and fare, station and service terminal charges, interchange of traffic and the responsibility of railway administration as carriers of goods and passengers; the regulation of minor railways in respect of safety and the responsibility of the administration of such railways as carriers of goods and passengers.

3. Maritime shipping and navigation, including shipping and navigation on tidal waters; admiralty jurisdiction.

4. Port quarantine.

5. Major ports, that is to say, the declaration and delimitation of such ports, and the constitution and powers of port authorities therein.

6. Aircraft and air navigation; the provision of aerodromes; regulation and organisation of air traffic and of aerodromes.

7. Lighthouse, including lightships, beacons and other provisions for the safety of shipping and aircraft.

8. Carriage of passengers and goods by sea or by air.

9. Extension of the powers and jurisdiction of members of the police force belonging to any unit to railway area outside that unit.

D. Ancillary

1. Elections to the Dominion Legislature, subject to the provisions of the Act and of any order made thereunder.
2. Offences against laws with respect of any of the aforesaid matters.
3. Inquiries and statistics for the purposes of any of the aforesaid matters.
4. Jurisdiction and powers of all courts with respect to any of the aforesaid matters but, except with the consent of the Ruler of the acceding State, not so as to confer any jurisdiction or powers upon any courts other than courts ordinarily exercising jurisdiction in or in relation to that State."

Before proceeding further, we have to examine the contents of the Instrument of Accession itself. It should be understood that this Instrument of Accession was drafted as part of the Government of India Act, 1935, which was enacted in pursuance to the discussion during the Round Table Conferences and with intent to set up a federal polity with a central government and provinces driving their jurisdiction by direct devolution from the Crown. The federation envisaged by the 1935 Act was to come into existence after the rulers of the princely states had signified their consent to accede to the Federation. It was Lord Linlithgow, the Viceroy, who had conducted negotiations with the rulers of princely states over the drafting of a standard Instrument of Accession. The almighty princes foresaw unacceptable attenuation of their powers in the proposed federal structure. Thus negotiations went on lingering. The outbreak of World War Two in 1939 saw the abandonment of these negotiations. In 1947 and later the princes of the states signed one and the same Instrument of Accession which forms Appendix VIII to the White Paper issued by the then Ministry of States published in 1950. Every state which acceded to India or Pakistan acceded on the subjects only as given in Schedule enclosed with Appendix VII. The contents of the Schedule are of vital importance and have been produced above. Attention needs to be paid to paras 5 and 6 of the Instrument of Accession which not only limits decision to the subjects outlined above but also forbids the Dominion Legislature to legislate beyond these without the consent of the ruler.

Every princely state had acceded to only Defence, External Affairs, Communications and Ancillary subjects as elections, etc., as detailed above. These are the subjects on which federal structure of India was to be built as per the recommendations of the Cabinet Mission's Plan of May, 1946, which both Congress and Muslim League had accepted but which Congress under the Presidentship of Pt. Jawahar Lal Nehru had later wriggled out from.

The fact remains that the state of Jammu & Kashmir had acceded to India only with regard to External Affairs, Defence and Communications as the accession of other states was also restricted to the same subjects. It is interesting to note what Sardar Patel said to the princes and how he violated his own solemn pledge over the same.

Sardar Patel, while addressing rulers on 5th July, 1947, said : "There appears a great deal of misunderstanding about the attitude of the Congress towards the states. I should like to make it clear that it is not the desire of the Congress to interfere in any manner whatever with the domestic affairs of the states." That is how the princes were lured (had they any other option?), and then gobbled up. The obsession of the Government of India to invest itself with all the powers has ultimately unleashed many disruptive forces.

Reply of 27th October, 1947, from Lord Mountbatten to Maharaja Sir Hari Singh :

"My dear Maharajah Sahib,

"Your Highness' letter, dated the 26th October, has been delivered to me by Mr. V.P. Menon.

"In the special circumstances mentioned by Your Highness, my Government has decided to accept the accession of Kashmir state to the dominion of India.

"Consistently with their policy that in the case of any state where the issue of accession has been the subject of dispute, the question of accession should be decided in accordance with the wishes of the people of the state, it is my government's wish that, as soon as law and order have been restored in Kashmir and her soil cleared of the invader, the question of the state's accession should be settled by a reference to the people. Meanwhile, in response to Your Highness' appeal for military aid, action has been taken today to send troops to defend your territory and to protect the lives, property and honour of your people.

"My government and I note with satisfaction that Your Highness has decided to invite Sheikh Abdullah to form an Interim Government to work with your Prime Minister.

Yours sincerely,

Sd/-

Mountbatten of Burma."

Documents have been reproduced above so that the readers may see that legally and constitutionally the accession of the state of Jammu and Kashmir was valid and binding. There is no provision to show that this accession was temporary. Lord Mountbatten in his reply of 27th October, 1947, to the Maharaja had stated that the state's accession should be settled by a reference to the people. This proviso introduced by Lord Mountbatten was extra constitutional and has no binding foundation in terms of any Statute on the subject. At the same time, it has left India with a legal accession internationalised and a dispute when there was no scope for doubt regarding the constitutionality of accession.

There is the famous ruling of U.S. Supreme Court on Federalism in the matter of Texas Vs. White (74 U.S.) 700, 19 L. Ed. 227 (1869) where the court speaking through the Chief Justice (Chase) spoke as follows :

"when, therefore, Texas become one of the United States, she entered into an indissoluble relation. All the obligations of perpetual union and all the guarantees of republican government in the Union, attached at once to the State. The act which consummated her admission into the Union was something more than a compact; it was the incorporation of a new member into the politic body. And it was final. The union between Texas and other states was as complete, as perpetual, and as indissoluble as the Union between the original states. There was no place for reconsideration, or revocation, except through revolution, or through the consent of the states"

Thus to treat Kashmir's accession to India as provisional has been violative of law itself. The grounds on which the U.S. and U.K. have reservation on the legality of Instruments of Accession are dealt in chapter 12.

Internationalising Kashmir's Accession to India

Responsible delegates to the U.N. Security Council have debated Kashmir dispute almost without end and volumes of their speeches fill the U.N. archives. There is no point in discussing these as the subject has been so exhausted that neither India nor any other country wants it to be discussed at international forum. Though Pakistan has written letters to President, Security Council in 1990 and its delegates to keep the issue alive by referring to it at various fora, however, the following points deserve recalling because India, particularly Pt. Nehru indulged in righteous indignation against the US in not branding Pakistan as an aggressor. We are no apologist for Pakistan but it is time that Indians know where and how they had mishandled their reference to the UN. We reproduce below the part of the first paragraph of India's complaint made to the President of Security Council on Ist January, 1948, per letter S/628 from the Representative of India :-

"The Government of India have instructed me to transmit to you the following telegraphic communication :

"Under Article 35 of the charter of the United Nations any member may bring any situation whose continuance is likely to endanger maintenance of international peace and security to the attention of the Security Council. Such a situation now exists between India and Pakistan due to the aid which invaders, containing of nationals of Pakistan and of tribesmen from the territory immediately adjoining Pakistan on the north-west are coming from Pakistan for operations against Jammu & Kashmir, a state which has acceded to the Dominion of India and is part of India"

"Now Article 35 of UN Charter reads as under

"Any member of the United Nations may bring any *dispute* or any situation of the nature referred to in Article 34, to the attention of the Security Council or of the General Assembly".

Thus by referring to the Kashimiri situation under Article 35 India had accepted that it was a "dispute or situation". Thus fulminations by India's representatives or Krishna Menon by making marathon speeches against Western conspiracies are meaningless. The anger of Nehru against Security Council for not having branded Pakistan as aggressor is without legal justification. He as Minister for External Affairs had committed a monumental blunder by making reference under Article 35 whereas the Article under which action is required in case of aggression is Article 39 under Chapter VII entitled ACTION WITH RESPECT TO THREATS TO THE PEACE, BREACHES OF THE PEACE, AND ACTS OF AGGRESSION Article 39 reads as under:-

"The Security Council shall examine the existence of any threat to the peace or act of aggression..." Thus by invoking Article 35 instead of Article 39 India had forfeited the right to ask Security Council to look into Pakistan's aggression in Kashmir. It was right that the Security Council treated it as dispute in terms of Art. 35, which India had herself invoked, and which Pakistan's shrewd Foreign Minister Zafarullah Khan, exploited fully in favour of his country. Instead of punishing the mandarins of South Block, Mr. Nehru and Krishna Menon went on fuming against conspiracies of Western Bloc. By the way what was the attitude of their dear friend, the USSR? Till 1952 the USSR had not voted in favour of India in the Security Council; it had consistently abstained. Why? Because it regarded Indian government as a bourgeois government and had heaped choicest vituperation upon Mahatma Gandhi and not even spared Mr. Nehru. It started favouring India in 1952 because India, notwithstanding Russian abuses, had taken a stand in favour of peace in Asia and had overlooked Russian depredations in East Europe.

Again does a matter become right only because your delegate can speak for hours or days without refreshments as

V.K. Menon did or because your delegates like Gopalaswamy Aiyangar could spew prosaic legal phrases?

Philip Zeiglar, the biographer of Lord Mountbatten, writes: "The inept presentation of the Indian case as opposed to the skilled professionalism, both, legal and oratorical, of the Pakistani representative, Zafarullah Khan, was a factor in India's lack of success.[4]

·India has to start looking within and be realistic.

Again when Pakistan's Foreign Minister Sir Zafarullah Khan told the UNCIP that three Pakistani brigades had been in Kashmir territory, since May 1948, the UN mediator did brand Pakistan as follows:-

"When the frontier of the state of Jammu & Kashmir was crossed in October 1947 by `hostile elements', it was contrary to international law and that when in May 1948 as I believe units of regular Pakistan moved into the territory of the state that was not in consonance with international law." What more could be said. But India's sophistory was endless - we need not traverse the ground which has been covered again and again by several writers.

The Security Council sessions in 1957, 1962 and 1964 were called at the requests of Pakistan and her allies. The Security Council seemed to have exhausted itself over the issue finding no response nor settlement acceptable to both India and Pakistan finally realising the fact that the matter could be settled only by bilateral negotiations and not through her efforts any more.

This conclusion is also proved from the decline in the number of meetings of Security Council held after 1948. Council had held 19 meetings beginning from 12 February, 1948. There were only two meetings in 1949, five in 1950, seven in 1951, fifteen in 1957. Though the Kashmir question still remains on the United Nations agenda, India and Pakistan had bound themselves to find a solution through bilateral discussions only by ratifying Simla Agreement of July 1972.

Pakistan's Foreign Minister Sahabzada Yaqub Khan in his letter of May 16, 1990, to Clause Tornude, President of the

Security council, said India had stepped up its policy of collective punishment against a popular uprising and demanded that the world body might ask India to 'exercise restraint'. Pak Foreign Minister further claimed that the Pakistani Occupied Kashmir was "beginning to receive an influx of refugees who have brought gruesome stories of Indian atrocities."

The above mentioned letter was circulated to the members of the Security Council. It appears that Pakistan said good bye to Simla Agreement of July 1972. After a five–day debate Pakistan National Assembly had ratified Simla accord on 15th July, 1972. Z.A. Bhutto had said that he would do everything to "restore the balance of power". And then Pak will struggle to free Kashmir. Bhutto told National Assembly, "There was only one way to free Kashmir' from the `Indian yoke' that was, that the people of Kashmir should start `their struggle for power'. Bhutto said he would like to give a `solemn' pledge. If Kashmir ever launched their freedom struggle the people of Pakistan would go `all out in support and assistance'. They would not hesitate to `shed their blood' for the people of Kashmir.

Now that his daughter and Nawaz Sharif consider that the balance of power has been restored in Pakistan's favour, Pakistan has started redeeming Bhutto's pledge by solemnly arming and aiding terrorists and insurgents but has taken a low-key accusatory stand in her complaint to the United Nations Security Council. The President of the Security Council, Mr. Tornuda, has pointed out that in principle Security Council resolutions remain valid as long as the problem remains but added : "But they must be seen in the light of changing circumstances."

Realising the implications of Simla Agreement, Pakistan has been crying hoarse over the oppression of Kashmiri people and violation of their human rights. This strategy only partly succeeded because there is, a fervent wave sweeping the corridors of power in the USA and European countries in favour of securing human rights.

REFERENCES

1. Mission With Mountbatten by Alan Campbell-Johnson, Jaico Publishing House, Bombay (1951), page 20.

2. Ibid, page 22.

3. Ibid, page 162-163.

4. Mountbatten - the official Biography by Philip Zaiglar: Collins 1985, page 450.

4

Consequences of Indo-Pak Wars on Kashmir

India and Pakistan have fought two wars over Kashmir. The first started in October 1947, continued to rage throughout 1948 and a ceasefire came into existence on 1 January, 1949. During 1948 war, India as well as Pakistan had British Commanders-in-Chief. Sir Robert Lockhart was C-in-C in India till December 31, 1947, when he was replaced by Sir F.R.R. Bucher. Some commentators held, that Bucher's advice to the Indian Prime Minister to accept ceasefire effective in January 1949 was frought with serious implications for India's strategic position in J&K. In his memoirs, *Untold Story*, Lt. General B.M. Kaul holds British officers of the Indian army responsible for not tendering correct advice to the Indian Government. The fact is that since May 1948 Indian army was fighting regular Pak army and no more the Azad Kashmir tribals. Pakistan had gained the strategic Gilgit Agency as early as 3 November, 1947, when Major W. Brown, commander of Gilgit garrison had declared that Gilgit had joined Pakistan. Again, Pakistan army had captured Skardu in Baltistan in August 1948. Azad Kashmir had held almost one-third area of Kashmir state. Then, by the end of 1948 situation was not bad for Pakistan. It is Pakistan's contention that Pakistan Army could not intervene in Kashmir in October 1947, as Field Marshal Auchinleck had told General Sir Frank Messervy, the first Pakistan C-in-C, that the former would withdraw all the five hundred British officers from Pakistan Army if the latter intervened in Kashmir. At that time Pakistan Army was in the process of organization when this threat was held out to it. Thus Pakistan could not intervene in Kashmir at that juncture and this enabled Indian Army to throw out the irregular tribals and occupy the major part of Kashmir. Pakistani army unit entered Kashmir in May 1948 when their C-in-C General Douglas Gracy advised such intervention and they could halt the advance of the Indian army in an effective manner. They also pooh-pooh the claims of victory and glory put forth by the Indian army against the irregular infiltrators. They also claim that once their 12th Division had intervened, the Indian army's progress was reduced to a snail's pace and that too because they were supported by the Indian Air Force whereas Pakistan Air Force had not intervened.

The military representatives of India and Pakistan met together in Karachi from 18th to 27th July, 1949, as truce Sub-Committee of the United Nations Commission for India and Pakistan (UNCIP). The Indian delegates were: Lt. Gen. S.M. Shrinagesh, Maj. Gen. K.S. Thimayya, Brig. S.H.F.J. Manekshaw and Messrs. H.M. Patel and V. Sahay were observers.

Pakistan was represented by Maj. Gen. W.J. Cawthon, Maj. Gen. Nazir Ahmed, Brig. M. Sher Khan and Messers M. Ayub and A.A. Khan.

As a result of the deliberations of the two delegations under U.N. auspices, ceasefire line was evolved in two parts of J&K. However, the wars of 1965 and 1971 changed this ceasefire line which came later to be called Line of Actual Control (LAC) after the war of 1971.

Consequences of the ceasefire in 1949 and the wars of 1965 and 1971 merit consideration.

Territorial and Other Consequences of Ceasefire

"Azad" Kashmir

On October 2, 1947, some hard-liners of the Muslim Conference assembled in Paris Hotel Rawalpindi and declared to form a free Government of Kashmir. One of the prominent

Pakistanis in the meeting Ghulam Nabi Gilkar assumed the fictitious name of Anwar and proclaimed himself as the first head of Azad Kashmir Government.

They issued a declaration deposing Maharaja Hari Singh with effect from October 4, 1947. They had planned to arrest the Maharaja at Srinagar with the help of tribal marauders.

On October 24, 1947, i.e. before the accession of the state to India, the rebels in Poonch and their allies set up what was to be known as the Azad Kashmir Government. The Azad Kashmir Government changed its capital several times in the span of a few months. It had its headquarters first in Rawalpindi then it shifted to Poonch where it took into possession the deserted houses left behind by the Hindu fugitives. The so called Azad Kashmir Government then moved to Palandari. Finally, it moved to Muzzaffrabad as its fourth permanent capital which is situated at the junction of Jhelum and Kishan-ganga rivers.

On October 24, 1947, the Azad Government issued the following declaration: "the new Government will establish cordial and friendly relations with both Pakistan and India and safeguard the state's geographical integrity and political identity. The question of state's accession to Pakistan or India shall be resolved through plebiscite". Its first President was Sardar Mohammad Ibrahim Khan, an obscure advocate who had been the Assistant District Advocate in the Maharaja's Government. In June 1949, the Azad Government entered into an Agreement with the Government of Pakistan ceding to it almost all the powers of the Government. The Agreement which was signed by Nawab Mushtaq Ahmed Gurmani, Pakistan's Minister for Kashmir Affairs, on one side and by Sardar Mohammad Ibrahim Khan, the President of the so-called Azad Kashmir, ceded the following to the Pakistan Government:

(a) Defence

(b) Foreign Policy of POK

(c) Tackling of the UN Commission for India and Pakistan;

(d) Publicity to be done abroad;

(e) Rehabilitation of the refugees;

(f) Publicity for propagating for holding the plebiscite; and

(g) Direct control over the northern areas of Gilgit and Baltistan.

Azad Kashmir state which has not been recognized by any country has no vestige of sovereignty or autonomy.

The crux of the Agreement between the so called Azad Kashmir Government and Pakistan was the ceding of Northern Areas of Gilgit and Baltistan to Pakistan. Since Azad Kashmir government was not lawfully established, it had no authority to cede any territory. Thus Pakistan's occupation of Gilgit and Baltistan is unlawful. The strategic areas of Gilgit and Baltistan went to Pakistan not through plebiscite upon which Pakistan harps ceaselessly but by intimidation of an unlawful government in POK.

President Mohammad Sardar Ibrahim Khan was succeeded by Chowdhary Ghulam Abbas who was closer to Pakistan's Prime Minister Liaquat Ali Khan and was the senior-most leader of Jammu and Kashmir Muslim conference. He was in prison in August 1947, and was released by Sheikh Mohd. Abdullah to migrate to "Azad Kashmir". He reigned over the state from 1948 to 1951. His government was paralysed by supporters of Sardar Ibrahim Khan.

"Azad Kashmir" is so subservient to Pakistan that it is called the 5th province of Pakistan, the other four being Punjab, Sind, Baluchistan and North West Frontier.

In the election of May 21, 1990, Pakistan People's Party of Ms. Benazir Bhutto got only 14 seats whereas Muslim Conference had won 19 seats in the "Azad Kashmir" Assembly. Yet it was Pakistan People's Party which was invited to form a government with the help of independents. Ms. L.A. Raja Mumtaz Rathore was nominated Prime Minister of POK. Sardar Abdul Qayyuam Khan became President on the advice of Inter Services Intelligence (ISI). He is considered a benign despot. He believes in the inevitability of war between Pakistan and India because POK could not allow the alleged repression of their Kashmiri brethren in the valley by Indian security forces.

On March 30, 1991, President Sardar Abdul Qayyum Khan dissolved the POK Assembly since the Prime Minister, Raja Mumtaz Hasan Rathore, had allegedly lost confidence of the legislature though the real reason was Pak Prime Minister's allergy to Pakistan People's Party running government even in this scrubby and undeveloped part of the country.

After the dissolution of the Assembly fresh elections were held on June 29, 1991. In the elections Pakistan People's Party was soundly trounced and Muslim Conference of the President Abdul Qayyum Khan emerged victorious winning 31 seats. But PPP Prime Minister Raja Mumtaz Rathore refused to quit by declaring the elections, which had been conducted by his own government, to be fraudulent! Such a thing can happen only in POK! Now the turn of the drama.

On July 5, 1991, the Secretary of Ministry of Interior of Islamabad accompanied by a Brigadier from the army met the "Prime Minister Rathore" and apprised him that the Chief of the Pakistan Army, General Aslam Beg, had sent them to fetch the 'Prime Minister' for an important meeting with the latter. Raja Sahib was told that he would be meeting the General in an army mess. After inveigling him out of his house, the 'Prime Minister' was arrested, thrust into a helicopter and flown to Islamabad; there he was told that his government had been sacked by Pakistan government.

The acting Chief Justice of POK's Supreme Court was Sardar Mohammad Ashraf. It was he who had organised the elections as the POK Chief Election Commission.

Sardar Mohammad Ashraf, the acting Chief Justice of Supreme Court cum Chief Election Commissioner, was sworn in as the Prime Minister of POK on 6th July, 1991. Since Muslim Conference had emerged victorious in the 'polls', whose records were described by various groups as fabricated and manipulated, and its leader Sardar Abdul Qayyum Khan, the President of Azad Kashmir (i.e. POK) announced his intention to step down from the office of Presidentship and assume the reins of the government as Prime Minister replacing Sardar Mohammed Ashraf.

The election system in POK in itself is a fraud. There are 40 directly elected seats in an Assembly of 48 members. Of these, the five districts of POK—Muzaffarabad, Bagh, Rawalkot, Kotli and Mirpur—elect only 28 members. Twelve seats are for Kashmiris settled in Pakistan. Once these 40 seats are filled by direct elections, Assembly members elect the remaining eight. The Ulemma, technocrats, and overseas Kashmiris get a seat each. In 1974 Azad Jammu & Kashmir Interim Constitution was amended to provide for this arrangement.

In the elections held on June 29, 1991, Muslim Conference had won 31 seats. The Muslim Conference has the support of Islamic Jamhoori Itehad (I.J.I.) of Mian Nawaz Sharif. P.P.P. had got only three seats. Sardar Abdul Qayyum Khan became the Prime Minister. He may last longer because he is closer to Pak Inter Services Intelligence. Prime Ministers are changed and arrested and Presidents replaced according to partisan interests of rulers in Islamabad. However, one thing never changes in the so-called Azad Kashmir. It is religious frenzy and India-baiting. The puppet regimes in Pak Occupied Kashmir thrive on war rhetoric and gigantic verbosity. War-mongering cries of Jehad always rend the POK air.

Sheikh Aqeel-ur-Rehman of the POK Jamiat-e-Tulba told *India Today* correspondent Kanwar Sandhu in August 1991, "We will spill every drop of our blood in the Jehad for which we are preparing people." Kanwar Sandhu further writes:

"In POK, the sabre has never rattled louder. Posters screaming `Na guerrilla Jang, na quami Jang al Jehad" (It is neither a guerrila nor a national war. It is a holy war adorn all available space on bazar walls.)

As a result of ceasefire of 1st January, 1949, India had the three districts of Baramulla, Srinagar and Anantnag in the Kashmir Valley, Ladakh, and in Jammu province districts of Jammu, Kathua, Poonch and Udhampur. At present Indian state of Jammu and Kashmir has the following 14 districts after administrative re-organisation. As already stated, according to 1981 census Jammu and Kashmir had a population of 5,981,609. No census could be held in 1991 due to disturbed conditions in the State.

Jammu	Kashmir		Ladakh	
1.Doda	1.	Anantnag	1.	Ladakh
2.Jammu	2.	Srinagar	2.	Kargil
3.Kathua	3.	Badgam		
4.Poonch	4.	Pulwama		
5.Rajouri	5.	Baramulla		
6.Udhampur	6.	Kupwara		

It is estimated that Pakistan had come to occupy 39 percent area of the state in 1947-48 by the demarcated ceasefire line. At present POK has a population of 2.5 million.

However, there was another consequence of the failure of the Pakistani adventure in Kashmir which resulted in the arrest of Major General Akbar Khan, who had self-styled himself as General Tariq who had led Muslims' invasion of Spain 1,000 years ago. In what has come to be known as Rawalpindi Conspiracy case, for the failure of his military adventure against India, this megalomaniac general blamed the working of Pak Government. He thus thought of toppling the Pak Government through a military coup d'etat. Lt. General B.M. Kaul writes that he had heard from a reliable authority that Maj. General Akbar Khan was convinced that the only way to solve the mounting problems of Pakistan was to have a military dictatorship. About how he approached officers for military coup, B.M. Kaul writes:

"Among his informal discussions with Service Officers he used to pose to them various solutions to the deteriorating state of affairs of Pakistan. When some agreed with him and voiced their resentment with feeling.... he would take them to a sacred chamber in his own house for enlistment. The atmosphere in the room was inspiring and solemn. On the wall hung an enlargement of Jinnah, the Father of Pakistan. Just below lay Quran. The candidate had to take an oath of allegiance by kissing the holy book.... They then signed a register with their own blood...."

Sino-Pak Border Agreement of 1963

On March 2, 1963, Pakistan and China signed a Provisional

Border Agreement settling the claims of the two countries to the territories in Kashmir. Pakistan had laid claim to more than 12,000 sq. miles in the occupation of Chinese. In the Agreement concluded it had to content itself on acquiring the grazing rights over an area of 750 sq. miles only and some salt mines. China got a big chunk of 2500 sq. miles of Hunza, north of Mintaka Pass and pointing towards Gilgit controlling all the Northern Passes in Karakoram range. Thus it has acquired strategic area whence it can threaten Indian as well as Pakistani forces in Northern Areas. All commentators hold the view that Zulfikar Ali Bhutto, in his anxiety to spite India and curry Chinese help in case of Indo-Pak conflict, bartered away strategic areas to China without requisite compensation. Russel Brines comments, "the Pakistanis had made a deal of doubtful value to themselves and of a considerable potential danger". He quotes another commentator as saying: "Foregoing a claim to 12050 sq. miles in order to clinch a deal may have been realistic, but such concession did not represent a first rate achievement."[1] Russel Brines rightly points that when entry passes were ceded to Beijing, retention of exit passes in the southern Karakoram by Pakistan was of little value.

Karakoram Road linking China and Pakistan across Mintaka pass running along river Indus can be ultimately dangerous to Pakistan as China's military might is stupendous and friends of today can be enemies of tomorrow. In defence of Pakistan ceding these areas to China, it has been said that Hunza was never a part of Jammu & Kashmir and therefore re-alignment of Sinkiang border in the region of Khunjerab and Shimnhal parts was merely a rectification. The pre-eminence of China in these strategic areas cannot be gainsaid.

After 1965 war, Pakistan decided to rely more on China since the USA had not come to the aid of Pakistan in Indo-Pak war of 1965. It had already entered into a secret agreement with China to extend the road from Gilgit over the Karakoram to Sinkiang. By 1968 the road had been completely surfaced and become a highway. It was formally opened to traffic in 1969. A second highway connecting China with Pakistan was built via Khunjerab Pass, 15,800 feet above sea level. This road was formally opened by General Zia-ul-Haq and Vice Premier

Kesg Piao of China in June 1978. It is a forlorn, metalled road fit for heavy traffic. It is a major communication link between Indus basin in Pakistan and Chinese Central Asia.

A copy of the Sino-Pakistan Frontier Agreement (1963) is at Appendix A

1971 War and Kashmir

On 3rd December, 1971, Pakistan launched its offensive on the western front with aerial strikes on Srinagar, Adampur, Jodhpur and other airfields. Simultaneously, it launched a number of offensives to capture Suleman-ki headworks as well Hussainiwala in Ferozepur district in Punjab and a number of enclaves in Gurdaspur.

We will discuss only the Indo-Pak operation of December 1971 in J&K.

The 12th Division of Pakistan launched a major offensive to capture Poonch. It was assisted by 2 AK Brigades and 26 Infantry brigade. However, their advance was held up by the Indian forces who had dug defences well in advance. The Pakistanis could advance only two to three miles in Poonch, and suffered heavy casualties in the north-east.

In Chhamb sector, Pakistan's 23 Division under Major General Iftikar Khan had the objective of driving upto the river Tawi. It had the support of armed regiments and additional Divisional Artillery but Divisional Commander Iftikhar Khan planned to capture Jaurian by a drive from north to south, an unfavourable terrain for tank warfare. He got the support of additional Brigades 66 and 111. His offensive was met by swift Indian response through heavy artillery barrage and straffing from air. He then struck Indian positions between Chhamb and Munawar and reached the bank of river Tawi on the morning of 8th December, 1971. Major General Fazl-e-Muqueem Khan in his book *Pakistan's Crisis in Leadership* acknowledges that the attack on Poonch had not succeeded as planned. He calls the Pak drive upto the bank of river Tawi as a great success. Major General Iftikhar Khan, ordered his troops to cross the river Tawi on 9th December, 1971. He was killed in a so-called accident of his helicopter. Nonetheless, 111 Brigade, 4 Punjab and 10 Baluch did cross Tawi. The Indian forces had well dug defences and two companies of the Pakistan's troops were decimated. Pakistan claimed it had been successful in establishing a bridge head in this area to Poonch but they withdrew under the order of new Divisional Commander. Maj. General Fazl–e–Muqeem Khan acknowledges, "The overall impact was not favourable for this Pakistani offensive".

From the foregoing it is clear that Pakistan had made only limited gain by capturing Chhamb.

However, the Indians struck in strength and registered notable successes in northern areas of Kashmir. The Indian troops operated through snowy and difficult mountainous terrains and captured 225 sq. miles of area. Pakistan had 366 posts dominating Srinagar and Leh highway which passes through Dras and Kargil. (India captured all these Pak posts). The important Indian gains were capture of Chaunka and Turtok, the two important places along the river Shyok. Thus the Indian lines of communication to Ladakh were completely secured in these battles.

In terms of Simla Agreement of July 1972, concluded between Smt. Indira Gandhi, Prime Minister of India, and Z.A. Bhutto, Prime Minister of Pakistan, the ceasefire line which had come into existence in 1949, had ceased to exist and was replaced by the Actual Line of Control and the areas captured by India and Pakistan in J & K were not restored but remained with the two countries respectively.

A copy of the Simla Agreement is given under Appendix B.

Confrontation on Siachin

Siachin is said to be the largest glacier in Asia being 76 kms. long. According to B.L. Kak, it overlooks Pakistan, India, Tibet, China, Afghanistan and Russia. Siachin glacier is located in Karakoram in the strategic valley of Nubra in Ladakh. It is at the height of 26,000 ft.

In 1983 a Pakistani patrol in the high altitude of this glacier ran into an Indian patrol. The G.O.C. Northern Command, Kashmir concluded that Pakistan wanted to make a back door entry into Leh via Siachin to threaten Indian defences in the whole of Ladakh. They argued that Gilgit being in possession of Pakistan and commanding all passes over Hindukush and 537 mile Karakoram highway connecting Chinese Sinkiang with Indus Valley in Pakistan, the next move of Pakistan would be to attempt a take–over of Ladakh. On the other hand, Pakistan alleged that India had occupied Siachin to penetrate Baltistan and take over Skardu. Pakistan further alleged that Indian action in Siachin is in violation of Shimla Agreement which forbids use of force and urges peaceful solution of all problems through bilateral talks.

Thus began the most expensive confrontation for India and Pakistan. Though President Zia-ul-Haq is said to have stated that the glacier had no strategic significance for Pakistan or India, yet both were locked in bloody battle causing loss of human lives due to weather alone.

India was the first to locate posts in the area by airlifting men with the help of French Pama helicopters, capable of going upto 20,000 ft. India has positioned two battalians and Brigade Hq. here. The operation is just baffling because maintaining troops at such heights involves staggering costs. Similarly, Pakistan is using U.S. Ch-47 Chinook helicopters which are capable of lifting three ton payload upto 20,000 ft.

Ambitious generals of India and Pakistan have saddled the people of the two countries with the most expensive confrontation straining their scarce resources further though 690–km long border in J & K is seldom free from random firing.

Appendix A

Sino-Pakistan Frontier Agreement of 1963

The Government of the People's Republic of China and the Government of Pakistan;

Having agreed, with a view to ensuring the prevailing peace and tranquillity on the border, to formally delimit and demarcate the boundary between China's Sinkiang and the contiguous areas the defence of which is under the actual control of Pakistan, in a spirit of fairness, reasonableness, mutual understanding and mutual accommodation, and on the basis of the ten principles as enunciated in the Bandung conference;

Being convinced that this would not only give full expression to the desire of the people of China and Pakistan for the development of good, neighbourly and friendly relations, but also help safeguard Asian and world peace;

Have resolved for this purpose to conclude the present agreement and have appointed as their respective plenipotentiaries the following

For the Government of the People's Republic of China; Chen Yi, Minister of Foreign Affairs.

For the Government of the Pakistan Zulfikar Bhutto, Minister of External Affairs.

Who, having mutually examined their full powers and found them to be in good and due form, have agreed upon the following:-

Article I

In view of the fact that the boundary between China's Sinkiang and the contiguous areas the defence of which is under the actual control of Pakistan has never been formally delimited, two parties agree to delimit it on the basis of the traditional customary boundary line including features and in a spirit of equality, mutual benefit and friendly cooperation.

Article 2

In accordance with the principle expounded in Article 1 of the present agreement, the two parties have fixed as follows the alignment of the entire boundary line between China's Sinkiang and the contiguous areas the defence of which is under the actual control of Pakistan.

(1) Commencing from its north western extermity at the height 5,630 meters (the reference coordinates of which are approximately longitude 74 degrees 34 minutes east and latitude 37 degrees 03 minutes north), the boundary line runs generally eastward and then south-eastward

strictly along the main watershed between the tributaries of the Tashkurgan river of the Tarim river system on the one hand and the tributaries of the Hunza river of the Indus river system on the other hand, passing through the Kilik Daban (Dawan), the Mintake Daban (pass), ·the Kharchanai Daban (named on the Chinese map only), the Mutsigla Daban (named on the Chinese map only) and the Parpik Pass (named on the Pakistan map only), and reaches the Khunjerab (Yutr Daban (pass)).

(2) After passing through the Kunjerab (Yutr) Daban (pass) the boundary line runs generally southward along the above mentioned main watershed upto a mountain-top south of the Daban (pass), where it leaves the main watershed to follow the crest of a spur lying generally in a south-easterly direction, which is the watershed between the Akjilga river (a nameless corresponding river on the Pakistan map) on the one hand, and the Taghumbash (Oprang) river and the Koliman Su (Orang Jilga) on the other hand.

According to the map of the Chinese side, the boundary line, after leaving the south-eastern extremity of the spur, runs along a small section of the middle line of the bed of the Koliman Su to reach its confluence with the Elechin river. According to the map of the Pakistan side, the boundary line, after leaving the south–eastern extermity of this spur, reaches the sharp bend of the Shaksgam of Muztagh river.

(3) From the aforesaid point, the boundary line runs up the Kelechin river (Shaksgam or Muztagh river) along the middle line of its bed to its confluence (reference coordinates approximately longitude 76 degrees 02 minutes east and latitude 36 degrees 26 minutes north) with the Shorbulak Daria (Shimshal river or Braldu river).

(4) From the confluence of the aforesaid two rivers, the boundary line, according to the map of the Chinese side, ascends the crest of a spur and runs along it to join the Karakoram range main watershed at a mountain-top (reference coordinates approximately longitude 75 degrees 54 minutes east and latitude 36 degrees 15

minutes north) which on this map is shown as belonging to the Shorgulak mountain. According to the map of the Pakistan side, the boundary line from the confluence of the above mentioned two rivers ascends the crest of a corresponding spur and runs along it, passing through height 6,520 meters (21,390 feet) till it joins the Karakoram range main watershed at a peak (reference coordinates approximately longitude 75 degrees 57 minutes east and latitude 36 degrees 03 minutes north).

(5) Thence, the boundary line, running generally southward and then eastward strictly follows the Karakoram range main watershed which separates the Tarim river drainage system from the Indus river drainage system, passing through the east Mustagh pass (Muztagh pass), the top of the Chogri peak (K-2) the top of the broad peak, the top of the Gasherbrum mountain (8,068), the Indirakoli pass (names of the Chinese maps only) and the top of the Teramn Kankri peak, and reaches its south-eastern extermity at the Karakoram pass.

(Two) Then alignment of the entire boundary line as described in section one of this article, has been drawn on the one million scale map of the Pakistan side in English which are signed and attached to the present agreement.

(Three) in view of the fact that the maps of the two sides are not fully identical in their representation of topographical features the two parties have agreed that the actual features on the ground shall prevail, so far as the location and alignment of the boundary described in Section one is concerned, and that they will be determined as far as possible by print survey on the ground.

Article 3

The two parties have agreed that:

(1) Wherever the boundary follows a river, the middle line of the river bed shall be the boundary line; and that

Wherever the boundary passes through a deban (pass) the water-parting line thereof shall be the boundary line.

Article 4

One: the two parties have agreed to set up, as soon as possible, a joint boundary demarcation commission. Each side will appoint a chairman, one or more members and a certain number of advisers and technical staff. The joint boundary demarcation commission is charged with the responsibility in accordance with the provisions of the present agreement, to hold concrete discussions on and carry out the following tasks jointly.

(1) To conduct necessary surveys of the boundary area on the ground, as stated in Article 2 of the present agreement so as to set up boundary markers at places considered to be appropriate by the two parties and to delineate the boundary line of the jointly prepared accurate maps.

To draft a protocol setting forth in detail the alignment of the entire boundary line and the location of all the boundary markers and prepare and get printed detailed maps, to be attached to the protocol, with the boundary line and the location of the boundary markers shown on them.

(2) The aforesaid protocol, upon being signed by representatives of the Governments of the two countries, shall become an annex to the present agreement, and the detailed maps shall replace the maps attached to the present agreement.

(3) Upon the conclusion of the above mentioned protocol, the tasks of the joint boundary demarcation commission shall be terminated.

Article 5

The two parties have agreed that any dispute concerning the boundary which may arise after the delimitation of boundary line actually existing between the two countries shall be settled peacefully by the two parties through friendly consultations.

Article 6

The two parties have agreed that after the settlement of the Kashmir dispute between Pakistan and India, the sovereign authority concerned will reopen negotiations with the Government of the People's Republic of China on the boundary as described in Article Two of the present agreement, so as to sign a formal boundary treaty to replace the present agreement, provided that in the event of the sovereign authority being Pakistan, the provisions of the present agreement and of the aforesaid protocol shall be maintained in the formal boundary treaty to be signed between the People's Republic of China and Pakistan.

Article 7

The present agreement shall come into force on the date of its signature.

Done in duplicate in Peking on the second day of March 1963, in the Chinese and English languages, both side being equally authentic.

Appendix B

Text of India-Pakistan Agreement on Promotion of a Friendly Relationship (Simla Pact)

(Signed in Simla on July 2, 1972)

(The agreement popularly known as Simla Pact, arose out of the 1971 war between the two countries over developments in the eastern wing of Pakistan. The agreement sought to lay down the principles that should govern their future relations. It also envisaged steps to be taken for future normalisation of bilateral relations. Most importantly, it bound the two countries "to settle their differences by peaceful means through bilateral negotiations".)

1. The Government of India and the Government of Pakistan are resolved that the two countries put an end to the conflict and confrontation that have hitherto marred their relations and work for the promotion of a friendly and harmonious relationship and the establishment of durable peace in the subcontinent, so that both countries may henceforth devote their resources and energies to the pressing task of advancing the welfare of their peoples.

In order to achieve this objective, the Government of India and Government of Pakistan have agreed as follows:

(i) That the principles and purposes of the Charter of the United Nations shall govern the relations between the two countries;

(ii) That the two countries are resolved to settle their differences by peaceful means through bilateral negotiations or by any other peaceful means mutually agreed upon between them. Pending the final settlement of any of the problems between the two countries, neither side shall unilaterally alter the situation and both shall prevent the organisation, assistance or encouragement of any acts detrimental to the maintenance of peaceful and harmonious relations;

(iii) That the pre-requisite for reconciliation, good neighbourliness and durable peace between them is a commitment by both the countries to peaceful co-existence, respect for each other's internal affairs, on the basis of equality and mutual benefit;

(iv) That the basic issues and causes of conflict which have bedevilled the relations between the two countries for the last 25 years shall be resolved by peaceful means;

(v) That they shall always respect each other's national unity, territorial integrity, political independence and sovereign equality;

(vi) That in accordance with the Charter of the United Nations, they will refrain from the threat or use of force against the territorial integrity or political independence of each other.

2. Both governments will take all steps within their power to prevent hostile propaganda directed against each other. Both countries will encourage the dissemination of such information as would promote the development of friendly relations between them.

3. In order, progressively, to restore and normalise relations between the two countries step by step, it was agreed that:

(i) Steps shall be taken to resume communications, postal, telegraphic, sea, land including border posts and air links including over flights.

(ii) Appropriate steps shall be taken to promote travel facilities for the nationals of the other country.

(iii) Trade and cooperation in economic and allied fields will be resumed as far as possible.

(iv) Exchange in the fields of science and culture will be promoted. In this connection, delegations from the two countries will meet from time to time to work out the necessary details.

4. In order to initiate the process of the establishment of durable peace both the Governments agreed that:

Indian and Pakistani forces shall be withdrawn to their side of the international border.

(ii) In Jammu and Kashmir the Line of Control resulting from the cease-fire of December 17, 1971, shall be respected by both sides without prejudice to the recognised position of either side. Neither side shall seek to alter it unilaterally irrespective of mutual differences and legal interpretations. Both sides further undertake to refrain from the threat or the use of force in violation of this line.

(iii) The withdrawals shall commence upon entry into force of this Agreement and shall be completed within a period of 30 days thereafter.

5. This agreement will be subject to ratification by both countries in accordance with their respective constitutional procedures and will come into force with effect from the date on which the Instruments of Ratification are exchanged.

6. Both Governments agree that their respective Heads will meet again at a mutually convenient time in future and that, in the meanwhile, the representatives of the two sides will meet to discuss further the modalities and arrangements for the establishment of durable peace and

normalisation of relations, including the questions of repatriation of prisoners of war and civilian internees, a final settlement of Jammu and Kashmir and the resumption of diplomatic relations.

Sd/-	Sd/-
(Indira Gandhi)	(Zulfiqar Ali Bhutto)
Prime Minister	President
Republic of India	Islamic Republic of Pakistan

Shimla, the 2nd July, 1972.

REFERENCE

1. Russel Brine, The Indo-Pakistan Conflict, Pall Mall Press, London, page 203.

5

Pakistan's Successful Clandestine Aggression

After losing two open wars in 1948 and 1965 over Kashmir, Pakistan has relentlessly pursued clandestine aggression to destablise and annex Kashmir. I call it a successful aggression as it has dangerously destabilized the valley. Let us begin at the beginning.

After the war of 1948 Pakistan concentrated on sabotage so that the Kashmir problem continued to occupy centre-stage and to keep the state seething with discontent. In 1948 Pakistanis hired one Jehangir Khan of Srinagar for sabotage purposes. He, with his collaborator Gulam Nabi, brought into Kashmir a large quantity of arms and ammunition and cached them in different parts of the valley. However, police was successful in recovering 643 bombs, 666 hand grenades, and 83 tons of explosives at the instance of the accused persons. The conspiracy, when unearthed, revealed the involvement of 35 persons of whom 22 were apprehended; however, 13 including Jehangir Khan absconded to their haven in Pakistan. On trial, the accused were sentenced to various terms of imprisonment.

In August 1951, Abbas Ali Shah, S.P., CID, Rawalpindi, Major Ashgar Ali Shah (POK) and Taj Din, an Inspector of Police (POK), succeeded in forming a gang of saboteurs consisting of 32 persons with the objective of disrupting elections to Jammu and Kashmir Constituent Assembly. The gang was found responsible for arson at :

(i) Singpora Bridge on Srinagar-Baramulla Road;

(ii) Sugipore Bridge on Srinagar-Kupwara Road;

(iii) Kangan Bridge on Srinagar--Kargil Road;

(iv) Disconnection of Army Telephone line, Gulmarg;

(v) Forest Hut at Negerag Handwara and Govt. Rest House at Akkar on Pehalgaon Road were put to torch.

Several of the conspirators were convicted and sentenced to various terms of imprisonment, whereas others succeeded in slipping back into Pakistan.

Pakistan Field Intelligence Units exploited affairs of heart for sabotage of various vital installations in Kashmir. One Abdul Aziz Parwana crossed cease-fire line in his bid to marry a girl. Pakistan Field Intelligence Unit recruited him for sabotage purposes. He was successful in importing large quantity of explosives from Pakistan and enlist help of 45 conspirators. However, the whole affair proved a damp squib except for two explosions, one near Palladium Cinema in Srinagar and the second blowing of Alacha Bagh Bridge.

In 1957 Jehangir Khan was again reactivated. The same Sajawal Khan, who had recruited Abdul Aziz Parwana, recruited one Mohib Ullah Beg. This gang planted booby traps in a mosque in Maisuma Bazar, Srinagar, causing the death of two boys and injury to two others. On 13th August, 1957, they also blew culverts at Ramy and Cheriri Pora in Tehsils Pulwama and Badgam respectively.

Kashmir National Liberation Front

In 1960s Kashmir National Liberation Front spearheaded dacoities and murders in Kashmir valley.

This front was organised by Mohammad Maqbool Bhat who was born in Tregham, Tehsil Handwara, District Baramulla in 1938. He was a student of Government High School, Tregham, and graduated from St. Joseph College in Baramulla in 1958. He was a member of Jamait-e-Islami. The same year (1958) he crossed over into Pakistan and settled in Karimpura locality of Peshawar. He joined Peshawar University for Post-graduation course in Urdu.

Later, he adopted journalism as his career and worked for *Injan* and *Imroz* newspapers. In 1960 he married Raja Begum, a divorcee from Baramulla. He was imbued with dreams of liberating his motherland Kashmir.

K.H. Khurshid, who had been President of Pak Occupied Kashmir, formed Plebiscite Front when he had to quit office Maqbool Bhat joined Plebiscite Front of POK. However, he felt disgusted with the lackadaisical approach and work of the Front. When Sheikh Mohammad Abdullah and Mirza Afzal Beg visited Rawalpindi in 1964, he met Beg and the latter advised Bhat to strengthen Plebiscite Front in POK. The same year Bhat met Major Aman Ullah Khan who, alongwith his brother, was running a furniture shop at Peshawar.

In mid August 1965, Major Aman Ullah Khan, Mohd. Maqbool Bhat and Aman Ullah editor of *The Voice of Kashmir*, Karachi, formed Kashmir National Liberation Front to wage a politico-military campaign on Algerian pattern for liberation of Kashmir. Funds started flowing to the Front which enabled it to purchase rifles, revolvers and sten guns etc. The group was joined by Aurangzeb-e-Tahir of Gilgit but residing at Peshawar and Kale Khan, ex-subedar of Pak Army, who had served under Major Aman Ullah Khan.

In June 1966, the Front infiltrated into Kashmir dividing themselves into two groups for security reasons. The first group was headed by Kale Khan and the second by Major Aman Ullah Khan and Mohammad Maqbool Bhat. The latter was joined by Mir Ahmed alias Ana Alias Ghulam Qadir alias Mohd. Yazsir who had worked in military depots as a labourer. It appears Major Aman Ullah Khan never crossed the Cease-fire line., on the pretext that he, with his 200 followers, would engage Indian army posts in a diversionary army attack.

The first objective of the group was to raid banks at Srinagar and loot the treasury at Sopore. The group led by Maqbool Bhat committed two dacoities. On 12th September, 1966 they removed cash and jewellery from the house of Jai Lal, a rich fruit merchant of village Bomai in Baramulla district. On the midnight of 12th and 13th September, 1966, they raided Nadihar, abducted CID Havldar Amar Chand and later murdered him by stabbing him over 20 time

J&K Police and Border Security Force mounted operations in the affected areas. Kale Khan and Ghulam Mohammad Dar were arrested on 14th September, 1966, after offering token armed resistance. However, a major encounter took place between the infiltrators and police at village Kunyal wherein Aurangzeb was shot dead and Maqbool Bhat and Mir Ahmed-e-Usasin were arrested and a number of arms and looted property were recovered from them.

Prosecutions were launched against all the three arrested accused in the court of Special Judge, Srinagar. Mohammad Maqbool Bhat and Mir Ahmed Yasin Ana, both of Baramulla district, were awarded death sentence and Kale Khan of Muzzafrabad of POK was awarded life imprisonment on 17th August, 1968. The three accused filed a Revision petition in J&K High Court against enforcement of their sentence. While the petition was pending, Maqbool Bhat and Yasin escaped from Central Jail Srinagar on the morning of 9th September, 1968. The escape was effected by making holes in two walls of the cell and the main outer wall.

The Special Judge, Mr. Nilkanth Ganjoo, who had awarded death sentence to Maqbool Bhat, was gunned down by militants in Hari Singh street on November 4, 1989, as a measure of reprisal.

Hijacking of Fokker F-27

Hijacking of I.A. flight from Srinagar to Jammu on the afternoon (1305 Hours) of 30th January, 1971, added a new dimension to the on-going tension between India and Pakistan. Congress daily of Srinagar, the *Khidmat* had carried a news item a week earlier that Al-Fatah was planning to hijack a Kashmir flight. We have to go into details to show how the diabolical plan was implemented. Border Security Force was a fledgling organisation when it came in touch with a youngster named Hashim Qureshi. He had matriculated in 1968 from Islamia High School in Srinagar as a private candidate.

During his studies he worked as booking clerk in Regal Cinema, Srinagar for one year. After leaving his job he spent four months in Pakistan in 1969-70. He had his uncles and other relations at Karachi and Peshawar whom he had visited earlier too. There he came in contact with Aman Ullah or someone close to him. They invited him to work for Kashmir Liberation Front and help hijack a flight whose pilot should be the then Prime Minister's son Rajiv Gandhi. On his return to Srinagar from Pakistan he sought to get in touch with B.S.F. officials assigned for collection of subversive intelligence. He told them that he had visited Pakistan on several occasions and could procure them good information provided he was given a regular post in B.S.F. The operative information was quietly but directly passed on to the late Prime Minister, Smt. Indira Gandhi, and Rajiv Gandhi was taken off the Srinagar route discreetly. On the pretext of remaining on the look out of suspected hijackers, Hashim Qureshi visited Srinagar airport several times to study how the security check was made and how he could dupe the staff. Ultimately on 30th January, 1971, at 1305 hrs. he boarded IA Flight (Fokker Friendship) VT-DMM named Ganga bound from Srinagar to Delhi via Jammu, under the assumed name of Mohammad Hussein. He was accompanied by his co–hijacker Mohammad Ashraf, again a relation of his, living in his neighbourhood in Nowhatta in Srinagar. When the plane reached Jammu, Hashim Qureshi with a pistol entered the cockpit and Ashraf with a grenade in hand stood against the cockpit door to bar any entry. This was the first hijacking of an Indian aircraft and the staff had no training or experience as to how to handle such an emergency. As directed by Hashim Qureshi, Captain G.S. Oberoi and K.K. Kachru, commander, took the aircraft to Lahore. Passengers were allowed to disembark at Lahore airport and they were treated well by Pak authorities and later were sent to India by road through Hussainiwala in Ferozpur district.

However, the Fokker Friendship F-27 plane was allowed to remain in possession of the hijackers. The plane was blown up on the tarmac of Lahore airport at 8.35 P.M. on 2nd Feb., 1971. Both the hijackers were granted asylum by Pakistan government, contrary to the international law and the advice of International Civil Aviation Organisation. It is said that the two hijackers were acting on the directions of Z.A. Bhutto who had hailed the hijackers as "two brave men" that they had demonstrated that no power on earth could suppress Kashmir's struggle for independence.

Kashmir National Liberation Front, headed by Maqbool Bhat, claimed the responsibility for the hijacking and destruction of the aircraft. It was alleged that the Liberation Front had been receiving instructions from London for early hijack of aircraft and that the Bureau in London was headed, at that point of time, by a relation of Sheikh Mohammad Abdullah. Sheikh Mohammad Abdullah called the charge against his son as 'fabricated'. The government held a high-level enquiry into the whole episode as G.M. Sadiq, the then Chief Minister, without naming BSF had charged it with ineptness and non-cooperation with State Police and other Central Intelligence Agencies.

During the inquiry, we in the BSF had harrowing experience because the Kashmir Police, though polite on surface, was hostile to BSF and wanted to give up its role of collecting intelligence. They knew that BSF was not collecting intelligence regarding border matters only but also the information about the political happenings in the state. Our stand was that because the whole of J&K had been declared a border area, we were performing a legitimate task in collecting intelligence in the state. The Inquiry Committee was headed by the Cabinet Secretary.

To prepare our defence, we had to know what evidence J&K Police had against us. Accordingly, the Police file was got removed and its contents noted. The missing of the file for a couple of hours was never noticed by the state officers.

Now that we had noted the concoctions the state Police had made against us our evidence before the committee was flawless and it gave a clean chit to BSF. But J&K Government and some of its Police Officers never forgave BSF.

Other Activities of KLF

Encouraged by Pakistan, Maqbool Bhat made another foray into Kashmir for the second time. This time he concentrated on dacoities. He was arrested on 7th July, 1976, at Langet near Handwara after a bank dacoity in Tregham. Commission of this dacoity was to end his life, as we will presently see.

Kashmir National Liberation Front later came to be called Jammu & Kashmir Liberation Front (J K L F). It proclaimed its aim to achieve independence for Jammu & Kashmir. It moved its headquarters from Rawalpindi to London. Its operatives kidnapped Ravindra Hareshwar Mahatre, 48 years old India's Assistant Commissioner in Birmingham Consulate on Friday, February 4, 1984. JKLF made two demands on India if it wanted the release of the diplomat who had served earlier in Dhaka and Tehran. The first condition was payment of one million dollars as ransom and the second, release of Maqbool Bhat from Tihar jail in New Delhi, as well as release of its six other activists. India rightly refused to comply and JKLF carried out its threat of executing Mahatre. His dead body was found on 6th February, 1984, by Joyee Jakis, a farmer's wife, 30 kms. south west of Birmingham. Indian response was swift. Maqbool Bhat whose death sentence had been confirmed was hanged on February 11, 1984. This response of Mrs. Indira Gandhi was in utter contrast to that of V.P. Singh who released hard-core terrorists to secure the release of his Home Minister's daughter, Dr. Rubaiya Sayeed. Terrorists were again released though their arrest might have cost the security forces a few lives, in a swap for the release of the daughter of National Conference M.P. Saifuddin Soz, who had been abducted earlier by the terrorists. New Delhi showed similar pusillanimity in getting an ONGC executive released from the captivity of Kashmir terrorists.

Jamaat-e-Islami

Jamait-e-Islami was founded on 25th August, 1941, with a membership of only 75 persons. Syed Abdul Maududi who hailed from Hyderabad was the moving spirit behind the organisation. A great Islamic scholar, Maududi believed in purity of Islamic teachings by means of indoctrination at the school level itself. The organisation has, therefore, concentrated on teaching of Quran and Sunna in the exclusive Muslim schools. The leader of a religious organisation in Islam is addressed as Ameer. None can offer himself as a candidate for the office of Ameer. Nor is Ameer elected. He has to be chosen by consensus. After preliminary meeting on 25th August, 1941, a panel of seven heads and scholars was appointed to select and nominate the Ameer. The panel consisted of scholars from Bareilly, Da-ul-Islam Moradabad,

Arcot (Madras), Imam Jama Masjid of Kapurthala and Sultanpur Lodhi, Layalpur, Allahabad and Lucknow. This panel recommended the name of Syed Abu Ala Maududi to be the Ameer. He was accordingly chosen as Ameer unanimously.

The following departments were created :

(1) Education

(2) Department of Publication and Publicity

(3) Department of Organisational Development

(4) Department of Finance

(5) Department of Proselytisation

The budget for the year 1941 was Rs. 4774 only. A meeting of the Majlis-i-Shoora was convened from 26th to 28th February, 1942. The headquarters of the Jamait was located in Jamalpur near Pathankot on 15th June, 1942. In one year the budget had gone up to Rs. 13963.

President Zia-Ul-Haq had consolidated his position in Pakistan by 1979 after suppressing all repercussions against Zulfikar Ali Bhutto's 'Judicial Murder'. He activated Inter Services Intelligence of Pak Army not only to provide training and arms to Afghan Mujahideen but to implement a remarkable plan to destabilise India in Kashmir. The plan can be summed up thus: fundamentalise Kashmiri Muslims particularly the youth and infiltrate the local government in the valley. Fundamentalist as he was, Zia had risen to power with the doctrinaire help of Jamait-e-Islami in Pakistan. He thought of using the same fundamentalist organisation for destabilisation and later grabbing Kashmir valley. He knew that this had to proceed gradually and with circumspection not to arouse Indian suspicions or reaction. So far as Indian Prime Minister Morarji Desai was concerned, Pakistan President Zia-Ul-Haq took him for granted because of his pacifist posture but reaction of Mrs. Indira Gandhi could be unpredictable. Zia treated Rajiv Gandhi with condensation as the latter had back tracked over Indian exercise 'Brasstacks' organised by India's Chief of Army Staff General K. Sunderji.

Jamait-e-Islami in Pakistan, therefore, was selected as the conduit for the supply of finance (on one paper submitted by me to the Prime Minister Mrs. Gandhi had asked as why was smuggling of Indian currency into Pakistan on the increase ?) This explains her query to Jamait-e-Islami Kashmir, which was founded by Peer Sabudin in 1945 and had failed to take off the ground. It was only in 1979 that all the fundamentalist organisations in Kashmir started strengthening themselves. They had good reasons for doing so. New Delhi was ineffective because of Sheikh Abdullah's ability to resist pressures. Secondly, the Sheikh had started showing signs of age. He himself was growing more religious with age.

Jamait-e-Islami, led by Syed Shah Geelani, had started flexing its muscles since 1979. It concentrated on enriching its treasury. It not only raised money in the valley from the Government servants and the merchant class but received generous aid from the Gulf countries. It encouraged Kashmiri youth to seek employment in the Gulf and on return contribute to Jamait generously. It won its first success when it successfully agitated against the introduction of NCERT syllabus in educational institutions in the state. Dr. Farooq Abdullah proscribed the book for class sixth on the plea that it allegedly contained derogatory reference to Islam. The banning of the book made Jamait-i-Islami and Tableegal Islam as the crusading protectors of Islamic values in the valley. It is worth noting that as early as 1975, Islamic fundamentalists had prevailed upon Sheikh Abdullah to remove several books from syllabus for Kashmir which were allegedly repugnant to Islamic tenets, such as Darwin's *Theory of Evolution, A Short History of the World* by H.G. Wells and *Monument of Civilisation* from public libraries. During the tenure of Sheikh Mohd. Abdullah as Chief Minister Jamait-e-Islami built hundreds of mosques. Sheikh Sahib had told the concerned people in Delhi that he would not permit interference in the propagation of Islamic tenets and culture. His son-in-law, G.M. Shah, during his tenure as Chief Minister had allowed construction of mosques within the premises of government offices and establishments.

It is estimated that Jamait had been running 300 schools in the valley imparting Islamic education. To overcome the paucity of teachers, it imported rabidly communal teachers from Uttar Pradesh. Its network of schools runs throughout the length and breadth of the valley.

The erstwhile governor of J&K, Jagmohan, said on 30th May, 1990: "All Jamait schools planted subversion in innocent minds" and he had to ban them. The Jamait also raised buildings for new mosques and ensured that each mosque was equipped with public address system so that the Khutba of the Imams reached even those who did not visit the mosque. Politically Jamait-e-Islami called, as could be expected, for the state's accession to Pakistan.

Jamait-e-Islami vainly tried to extend its influence to students' organisations. Both Islamic Study Circle, founded by it in 1968 and Students Islamic Organisation in 1974, failed to woo the students and these organisations were ultimately wound up. However, Islamic Jamait-e-Tulba was founded in September, 1977 when Janata Government was in saddle in Delhi. The name Islamic Jamait-e-Tulba was borrowed from Pakistan where Jamait-e-Islam's student wing also works under the same name.

The person who made Islamic Jamait-e-Tulba a force to reckon with was Sheikh Tajmu-Ul-Islam. Impelled by religious frenzy, he organised the Jamait with the zeal of a missionary. Having been elected 'Nizam-e-Aila' (Chief Organiser) in the three-day convention of Islami Jamait-e-Tulba at Chandura on 24th February, 1979, he entrusted organisational work to Javid Nowshahri in Srinagar, Hamid Naseem of Sopore in Baramulla and Faya Hamidullah in Anantnag District.

On 1st March, 1979, its workers with support from Peoples Conference and Mohaz-e-Azadi launched a student's agitation for compulsory Islamic education in the government schools, and that admission to various courses in Kashmir be on the basis of population rather than merit.

In June 1979, an International Islamic Conference was held in London where its delegates prevailed upon the Conference to call upon the United Nations for deciding the future of J&K in accordance with the wishes of people as expressed through plebiscite.

The Islami Jamait-e-Tulba held a convention in Srinagar from 31st August to 3rd September, 1979, which was attended by representatives of other Muslim countries. It was accorded recognition by the "World Assembly of Muslim Youth" of Saudi Arabia and International Federation of Islamic Students Organisation in 1979.

The Jamait-E-Islami and Islamic Jamait-e-Tulba organised a secret conference in May 1980, which is stated to have been attended by the Imam of Kaaba too.

The same year in August, Sheikh Tajmul Islam (Nizam-e-Aila) held a press conference at Jahangir Hotel Srinagar where he made the following points :

(1) The Jamait does not accept the Constitution of India nor of Jammu and Kashmir.

(2) They would work for implementation of the United Nations resolution on holding plebiscite in Kashmir.

(3) The organisation would prepare people of Kashmir for establishment of Islamic government on the pattern of Iranian Islamic Republic.

Thereafter the Jamait announced holding of an International conference at Srinagar from 22nd to 25th August, 1980. The conference was to discuss the role of Islamic Movement in Kashmir. Invitation cards were got printed in Arabic in Saudi Arabia for ten thousand delegates. However, the Government refused permission for convening of the conference.

The Jamait had divided the valley in 150 *halquas* or areas. Its hard core membership exceeds 6000. It has been successful in sending 200 of its ardent supporters to Middle East to collect funds. Sheikh Tajmul Islam visited Saudi Arabia in 1979 to raise funds for the party. Dr. Ayub Khan, who used to look after education and foreign affairs in the party, worked in Shah Faisal University is Saudi Arabia and helped to raise funds. Though at times differences were reported between Jamait-e-Islami and Tajmul Hussain regarding apportionment of funds collected, Jamait-e-Tulba remained the Youth Student wing and Jamait-e-Islam exercised great influence over it.

Probably Jamait-e-Islami and Jamait-e-Tulba would have remained shorn of political ambitions for some time more but for the emergence of Dr. Qassi Nisar Ahmed, Imam of Jami-e-Masjid of Anantnag on the centre stage of fundamentalist movement in Kashmir. Till 1985, Srinagar had been the stronghold of anti-Indian elements and the nerve centre of Kashmir politics in the sense it is even now, but the communal riots which broke out in Anantnag district in February 1986, shifted the centre of activities from Srinagar to Anantnag. Anantnag has had a fair population of Kashmiri Pandits not only in the town but also in villages. Very unfortunate communal riots engulfed Anantnag district in October 1986. These riots catapulted Dr. Qazi Nisar Ahmed to the centre-stage. As Imam of Jami-Masjid he appealed to the Muslim business establishments to close business on Friday in place of Sunday. He vigorously campaigned for the release of all those who belonged to Jamait-e-Islami and People's Conference, headed by A.G. Lone who had once been an Education Minister in Congress Ministry but had turned extremist due to his differences with the party.

After the imposition of Governor's rule on 7th March, 1986, Dr. Ahmed called all the like-minded fundamentalist organisations to come at one platform. This meeting took place in May 1986, with Ghulam Mohammad Bhat, Ameer Jamait-e-Islami, in chair, and the following organisations participated :

1. Muslim Employees Front of J&K (Governor Jagmohan had launched a campaign to rid the administration of ineffective and corrupt officers and this Front was launched to frustrate this drive, and it came to play a crucial role in 1989-90 insurgency.)
2. Islamic Study Circle of J&K.
3. Jamait-e-Islami
4. Husseni Medical Front
5. Islami Jamait-e-Tulba
6. Ummat-e-Islamia (founded by Dr. Qazi Nisar Ahmed)
7. Majlis-e-Tuhafoz-Ul-Islam of J&K

8. Shia Rabita Committee of J&K.
9. Muslim Education Trust

In the meeting a Majlis-e-Shoore, that is a consultative committee, was formed to which each participating party was to send two members. It was decided to form a Muslim United Front (MUF), and a committee of five members, with Maulvi Mohammad Abbas Ansari as convener and Ghulam Qadir Wani as Secretary, was founded. A constitution was adopted on 13th July (Martyrs day since 1931), 1986, whose main points are briefly summed up as under :

(1) Quran and Sunna will be the final authority for Muslim United Front.

(2) Muslim United Front will fight for the Muslim cause.

(3) Muslim United Front will not take part in un-Islamic politics.

(4) Leaders of the Muslim United Front will not criticise leaders and workers of constituent units.

(5) Majlis-e-Shoora (here meaning the council of constituent parties/units) will meet as frequently as necessary.

Thus fundamentalisation under Dr. Qazi Nisar Ahmed got equipped with a formal structure. Some people call him the Ayotullah Khomeini of Kashmir. This individual provided the ideologically fertile ground from which armed militancy was to sprout. We may clarify here what we mean by fundamentalisation. Fundamentalisation of a religion is not only religious revival but such deification of it that the followers must be ready to lay their lives for it and if necessary, kill others on a call of their religious leaders.

Some people think that only recently Pakistani money has started flowing into Kashmir. The fact is that from its very inception Pakistan had tried to suborn loyalty through money. Families of prominent leaders (barring a couple of exceptions) benefited from Pakistani largesse. Then Pakistan started pumping money into front organisations. The most successful use of Pakistan money was to fundamentalise and forge unity among Muslim organisations. Once ideological foundation had been laid, the other sinews of insurrection would follow. There is a lot of talk of smuggling of narcotics through Kashmir. One journal has called the present situation as arising out of narco-terrorism. The money which flowed into Kashmir from the Gulf countries was by way of over-invoicing of exports and was essentially Pakistan's money. The organisation and financing of various terrorist outfits in the valley had been overseen by Pak Inter Services Intelligence (ISI) during the time of Lt. General Gul Hamid. The organisation showed ingenuity and expertise of uncommon order. Gul Hamid himself was as big a fundamentalist as President Zia-Ul-Haq.

After imbuing the youth with fundamentalist ideology, training them and equipping them with arms was no difficult task. Within Kashmir, the highest paid were motivators who toured urban localities and rural areas, advising youth to cross over to Pakistan Occupied Kashmir (POK) for armed training. Sometimes they coerced the youth too. Intelligence agencies have been able to identify a large number of them and the wealth earned by them is amazing. Next come the guides who lead the motivated youth to gallies and passes avoiding security pickets. Generally guides are trusted carriers of the revolt. Next to guides come activists whose task is to mobilise public opinion in favour of the militants. They act as spokesmen, as messengers and as contacts. It is their duty to keep the political parties informed and make them agitate for release of the militant operatives and mobilise public opinion against the action by the security personnel. Each outfit has been assigned a separate group of financiers so that in case one outfit is busted the others remain secure. Only JKLF stands for Independence whereas all other outfits like Hizbul Mujahideen, Hizbe Islamia, Allah Tigers, Al Umar, Dukhtraine-e-Millat propagate for Kashmir's accession to Pakistan. In addition to these major outfits, there are dozens minor outfits who commit sundry terrorist acts for petty gains.

The success of the clandestine operation started in 1979 by President Zia has come late; it took eight years to take off. But its extent is unmistaken. President Zia succeeded in reaching the rural areas through the network of madrassas and the women folk, who in Kashmir were always in the forefront; they were aroused with fundamentalist fervor to frentic pitch. In mass defiance of curfews the women are the most vocal partners.

India's rulers cannot be exonerated of the charge of creating conditions where insidious fundamentalist insurgency would thrive. Though tourism and handicrafts flourished and the general level of economic life improved considerably, the state government, whether autonomous under Sheikh Abdullah or puppet under his son-in-law, failed to gauge the extent of unemployment and its ultimate consequences. Capped on this unemployment factor was the concentration of wealth in the hands of a limited number of families, whether through trade or corruption. Indeed, corruption has corroded the fabric of Kashmiri society as without greasing palms nothing could be moved. The Kashmiri perception was that this massive corruption was a concomitant of Indian economic aid. Hence anti-Indianism came to be equated not only with colonial practice of installing puppet regimes of defectors and others but also the all pervasive corruption which stifled the rise of the under–privileged. Thus the passive central governments allowed the quality of life in the valley to be dominated by unbridled corruption and nepotism so long as the Kashmir ruling echelons were with Delhi. The efforts of Islamic organisations in the valley to infiltrate services, particularly police, were connived at by the Kashmiri ruling class as a measure to cover their own acts of malfeasance. The fundamentalist organisations had succeeded in infiltrating the Kashmiri administrative apparatus through intimidation of the corrupt and ethnic affinity of those who thought the government had not succeeded in slicing the Indian largesse to their, or their families' enrichment. New Delhi neglected the health of Kashmiri bureaucracy and ruling elite thus enabling the fundamentalist outfits not only to create insurgency–like conditions but to infiltrate every instrument of governance whose duty it was to report on the new fundamentalist virus and suggest remedies. In his book *Crisis in Kashmir* (1947-1966) Alstair Lamb maintains that India by keeping Kashmir in her fold has been trying to contest two-nation theory and prove that religion should not determine the political complexion of a polity. However, the basic tenet of Jamait-e-

Islami is that state and religion cannot be separated and there can be no compartmentalization of state and religion. It propagates that sovereignty belongs to Allah and not to people. Only such laws are to be obeyed which are not repugnant to Quran and Sunna. Thus, while Zia-Ul-Haq was Islamising Pakistan polity, Jamait-e-Islami in Kashmir was fundamentalising the Kashmiri Muslims. President Zia was busy steering Pakistan towards Nafaz-e-Nizam-e-Islam his front organisations in Kashmir, Jamait-e-Islami and Islamic Jamait-e-Tulba moved in tandem to fundamentalise Kashmiri Muslims. These organisations also drew inspiration from Ayotollah's experiments in Iran. Jamait-e-Islami derives inspiration from the sayings of the Divines.

In Iran and Pakistan religious cleric came to wield the ultimate political powers and not organisations like Parliament. In Pakistan Shariat Act made Pak Parliament subservient to the Shariat Court, a judicial body of Mullahs. Ms. Benazir Bhutto resisted its enactment and had to pay heavy price in the General Elections of October 24, 1990.

What surprises people is that a Kashmiri should turn out into a terrorist. Their surprise is compounded when they see this beautiful valley turned into an insurrectionary inferno of bomb blasts and ruthless killings. This surprise shows their naivete. They have not studied Kashmir's history. I have shown from history that Kashmiris would show ghoulish ruthlessness in wars of succession—their rulers killed their own fathers, brothers and mothers when it came to the question of seizure of power.

Kashmiris are exquisite craftsmen but this does not detract from their sub-culture of violence. Stories of their docility are without foundation. They suffered Moghul, Afghan, Sikh and Dogra subjugation for centuries which did not wipe out the traits of ruthlessness from their collective psyche, and the mark of docility which they seem to wear was a time serving ruse. For terrorism to create a sub-culture of violence, particularly when it has the sanction of religion which fundamentalism bestows upon it, provides fertile ground. A deep sense of injury or neglect and perceived injustices helped the cult of bomb and gun to take birth. The fuse of fundamental insurgency was waiting to be lighted since mid 1980s; could they not see what was happening in Punjab, orchestrated by the Inter Service Intelligence of Pakistan? The temptation was too much to be shunned either by Kashmiris or Pakistanis. The stark reality of non-governance in Jammu & Kashmir was well known to Pakistan as well as the collusive character of the administrative machinery. Kashmiris had been apprising Indians of their impatience and their hate yet India tried to gloss over the ghostly reality weaving myths of justice of their electoral process when actually nothing of this sort existed on ground. What appears crime in a conventional social milieu becomes exemplary behaviour when the same is sanctioned by 'cause' - the cause being religious or a fight against imposition. The insurgents are not after territorial gains. Their aim is to spread fear and dramatise their cause and the Kashmiri terrorists have succeeded in all this.

The exodus of Kashmiri minority is complete. The Government has been pulled down and the two Governors, General K.V. Rao and Jagmohan have 'resigned' (or say were given marching orders; General Rao was re-inducted as Governor by P.V. Narasimha Rao). The administration is at sea knowing not how to deal with subversives in the services. The whole governmental process has been disrupted though the ritualistic governance continues. Maulvi Farooq's assassination and its aftermath exemplifies the potential for havoc. Kashmir is under siege—a formidable seize indeed—as terrorism plus public sympathy for them paved the way for long drawn out, unconventional warfare. 'The rebel' wrote Camus, 'proceeds to put self respect above everything else and proclaims that it is preferable to life itself.' However, a wise strategy is not to allow bands of rebels coalesec. When terrorist groups amalgamate en masse insurrection rises. Whereas terrorism has nowhere succeeded, whether in Palestine, Ireland or Punjab but insurrections during the World War II helped the Allies to succeed. Shall India learn from history or merely allow it to be repeated?

6

Dramatis Personae of Kashmir Tragedy

Kashmir valley has gone through a tragic trauma. The youth has taken to the cult of the gun and the ruling machinery has been in shambles. The valley, which used to pulsate and throb with beauty and ineffable charm, was reduced to a ghost of its former self. Where peace and serenity presided earlier, now the bursts of automatic weapons pierce the ghostly and eerie stillness; padlocked houses of Kashmiri Pandits, who have migrated are wrapped in spectral muteness. Who are the architects of this gruesome tragedy and human misery?

Historically, the valley was always ravaged by the invading hordes from the north as well as the south. The honourable East Indian Company had ceded the state to the Judas of Sikh Empire in Punjab, Raja Gulab Singh and his male heirs in perpetuity for the sum of Rs. 7,50,000. With the attainment of Independence by India in 1947, it was hoped that the valley will be able to lead a life of its own and with self-respect. The hope was soon belied when Maharaja–Adhiraja Sir Hari Singh prevaricated for more than two months on state's accession; he had been hoping that he could remain independent. When Lord Mountbatten, Viceroy of India, visited Kashmir on 14th June, 1947, and tried to talk to the Maharaja on the subject of accession, the latter had resorted to evasion putting off Mountabatten on the plea that he was unwell, a very convenient alibi by the sub-continental rulers. Writes

Campbell Johnson in his diary 23rd June, 1947, "When he (Mountbatten) got there he found the Maharaja particularly very elusive and the only conversations that took place were during their various car drives together. Mountbatten, on these occasions, urged him and his Prime Minister, Pandit Kak, not to make any declaration of Independence but to find out in one way or another the will of the people of Kashmir as soon as possible and to announce their intention by 14th August ... He told them that the newly created States Department was prepared to give an assurance that if Kashmir went to Pakistan, this would not be regarded as an unfriendly act by Government of India."[1] In the opening minuet of this tragedy it was the Maharaja–Adhiraj who fled Srinagar when the tribal invaders were to go on a spree of murder and rape in the northern town of Baramulla. This Maharaja had spurned the counsel of Mountbatten to take an early decision on accession by consulting his people, but lost no time in fleeing, leaving the hapless citizens to the Emergency Administration, headed by Sheikh Mohd. Abdullah. Writes Philip Ziegler, "The Maharaja had deluded himself that independence for Kashmir might still be achieved; possibly he was holding out for more favourable terms. When Ismay tried to bring pressure upon him during a visit to Srinagar, all he would talk was polo at Chettenham in 1935 and the prospects of his colt in the Indian Derby. He suffered the usual fate of those who hesitate too long."[2] Over–cleverness is the surest way to perdition.

Jawaharlal Nehru

The Indian Prime Minister Nehru's talk of high ideals, commitment to go by the wishes of Kashmiri people sounded pathetically hollow when he tried to extricate himself from the commitment to hold a UN supervised plebiscite in Kashmir. Once he had pledged his word, he should have fulfilled the same. In fact so far as Kashmir is concerned, he suffered from an adolescent infatuation for the beauty and charms of the valley. Nehru wrote to Edwina Mountabatten as follows on 27th June, 1948, "Kashmir affects me in a peculiar way. It is a kind of mild intoxication - like music something or the company of a beloved person. For years and years I could not visit Kashmir because of prison etc., and the desire to come here became a passion and an obsession. It is not just the beauty of the scene, though I love beauty and beautiful things, but even more the very air of Kashmir which has something mysterious and compelling about it."[3]

Philip Zeiglar says : 'Indian foreign policy over the next decade was to be distorted and to some extent bedevilled by Nehru's devotion to his ancestral land. He continued to pay lip service to the idea of a plebiscite".[4] When infatuation replaces rationality in the rulers of a land, the disasters are not far off.

Sheikh Mohd. Abdullah

The third person to contribute to Kashmir's tragedy was Sheikh Abdullah. "We will send you in chains of gold." Thus spake Jawahar Lal Nehru to Sheikh Abdullah during a discussion which eventually led to the "Delhi Agreement" and to the formulation of Article 370 of the Constitution of India, which was to govern the special relationship of the state of Jammu and Kashmir with the Republic of India. How did those chains of gold come to be replaced by iron shackles on the wrists of the Sher-e-Kashmir not so long afterwards? Again to speak of "gold" rather than speak of chains of affection and mutual respect reveals a warped mind. After his release on January 2, 1968 (he had been detained on 8th May, 1965), and after his pilgrimage to Mecca and after his meeting with Chou En-Lai, at a press conference on 3rd January, 1968, in Algeria where a reporter asked him, "Are you an Indian citizen?" Sheikh Abdullah shot back:

"It is a meaningless question whether I am an Indian citizen or a strange creature from the sky is an irrelevant question."

Sheikh Abdullah was a consummate master of ambiguity. Yet he was a true Kashmiri patriot. He wanted the best possible outcome of his relationship with India for Kashmir. His sway over Kashmiris' feelings was so total that none questioned his methods. To some, he appeared an enigma sometimes upholding secularism of India and the next moment denouncing India as highly communalised. We will try to unravel this riddle by examining his policies in some detail.

Lord Birdwood writes "The lion in him (Sheikh Abdullah) has much subtlety in his make-up. He conveys an impression of some conceit and opportunism; he has an acute sense of the technique and value of propaganda and lustily but shrewdly blows his own trumpet. Through the screen of his exaggerated oratory there is yet perceptible the spark of an ideal"[5]. Sheikh never exactly forsook the ideal of independence for Kashmir and if accession could not be shaken off, it had to be limited to the three subjects of Defence, External Affairs and Communications. He had told Michael Davidson of the *London Observer* of his aspiration for independence as early as 1947 provided it was guaranteed by super powers and the United Nations. Sheikh Sahib was intolerant of opposition, according to P.N. Bazaz and averse to even factual and constructive advice even from friends. This fortifies the assessment of Phillips Edmonds who was Principal of the C.M.S. School in Srinagar and had got in touch with Sheikh Abdullah as his political friends took their education in his school. Lord Birdwood says that Edmonds doubted Abdullah's judgement either of a situation or an individual. He disliked intensely his refusal to accept criticism. He acknowledged the erratic nature of his leadership and yet he ended by admitting that in his view "his human qualities outweighed his obvious limitations."[6]

We have already referred to oratorical prowess of Sheikh Abdullah in Kashmiri and Arabic. Lord Birdwood, too, comments on the same by writing, "Here I would refer to one feature of his technique, which was-his power to move the masses by his oratory in a way that no other Kashmiri can in any way hope to exercise. When Abdullah was to speak, the peasantry would be there in their thousands to drink in his words ..., (his power) led him to dangle the attractions of Independence before his people."[7]

Sheikh Mohammad Abdullah, after resigning the post of the teacher, formed the Jammu & Kashmir Muslim Conference in 1932. He converted the same into Jammu and Kashmir National Conference in June 1939.

He was jailed by the Maharaja in 1946 but released in September 1947; and was made head of the Emergency Administration of Jammu and Kashmir to deal with the menace of tribal invasion. Ultimately he was appointed as the Prime Minister of the state of Jammu and Kashmir on 5th March, 1948. He initiated a number of reforms particularly agrarian. He restored "land to the tiller" by dispossessing the feudal land-lords who had acquired possession through the patronage of the Dogras. The exploitation of peasantry had been callous, inhuman and brutal. On 26th March, 1952, the Constituent Assembly of Jammu and Kashmir legislated empowering Government to acquire land without payment of compensation. According to a release by his government 1,88, 775 acres of land were transferred to 1,53,399 tillers.

His Government also established a number of collective farms such as at Shaltang, Harwan and Gopalpur.

Sheikh Abdullah also took a number of steps to increase the irrigated area, and a number of old irrigation canals were repaired. New ones were taken under construction such as Avantipur canal.

His Government, therefore, freed the Kashmiri peasant from the exploitation of the feudal land-lords as well as tried to improve his economic lot by introduction of new techniques of agriculture and horticulture.

The peasant had groaned under the interminable debts of landlords. Debt Conciliation Boards were established and the debts were scaled down by these boards by 80 per cent. The State Government also gave an impetus to the development of silk industries and for this purpose silk-worm eggs were imported and distributed among the reares.

The Government was a votary of co-operative movement. It encouraged formation of co-operative societies at various levels and in various forms.

His government also initiated the policy of subsidising the essential commodities of life for the common man. Thus rice, sugar, kerosene oil, etc. were heavily subsidised with funds provided by the Government of India for public distribution purposes.

Josef Korbel in his book *Danger in Kashmir* has tried to show that Sheikh Abdullah and his colleagues like Ghulam Mohd. Sadiq were communists. Korbel has misread the Kashmiri movement completely and raised the bogey of communism. The Kashmiri Muslim can never be a communist because he has inveterate faith in Islam and for Islamic shrines. Abdullah kept his hold on Kashmiri Muslims by conforming not only to Islamic tenets but by encouraging the same. A product of Islamia College, Lahore, and Aligarh Muslim, University, he was steeped in Islamic fervour and acquired the posture of a champion of oppressed Indian Muslims in the face of Hindu revivalism encouraged by Jan Sangh. Condemning Hindu communalism was his favourite hobby to prove his secular credentials.

On the issue of Accession to India or Pakistan or Independence for Kashmiri he pondered rather at length. In his address to the Jammu and Kashmir State Constituent Assembly, he observed: "Looking at the matter too from a more modern political angle, religious affinities alone do not and should not normally determine the political alliance of states. We do not find a Christian bloc, a Buddhist bloc, or even Muslim bloc, about which there is so much talk now-a-days in Pakistan. These days economic interests and a community of political ideals more appropriately influence the policies of states." He was an implacable crusader for autonomy for the J&K people. In the same address to the Constituent Assembly, he observed as follows with regard to the independence of the State, after listing disadvantages of accession to India as well as to Pakistan: "The third course open to us has still to be discussed. We have to consider the alternative of making ourselves an Eastern Switzerland, of keeping aloof from both states but having friendly relations with them. This might seem attractive in that it would appear to pave the way out of the present deadlock. To us as a tourist country it could also have certain obvious advantages, but in considering independence we must not ignore practical considerations. Firstly, it is not easy to protect sovereignty and Independence in a small country which has not sufficient strength to defend itself on our long and difficult frontiers bordering so many countries. Secondly, we must have the goodwill of all our neighbours. Can we find powerful guarantors among them to pull together always in assuring us freedom from aggression? I would like to remind you that from August 14 to October 22, 1947, our State was independent and the result was that our weakness was exploited by the neighbour with invasion. What is the guarantee that in future too we may not be victims of a similar aggression?"

He was also aware of Pakistan's proximity and its effect on Kashmir's economy. In the course of the same address he listed disadvantages of accession to India as follows :

"To begin with, although the land frontiers of India and Kashmir are contiguous, an all weather road link as dependable as the one we have with Pakistan does not exist. This must necessarily hamper trade and commerce to some extent, particularly during the snowy winter months ... Similarly, the use of the State rivers as a means of timber transport is impossible if we turn to India except in Jammu where the river Chenab still carries logs to the plains.

"Still another factor has to be taken into consideration. Certain tendencies have been asserting themselves in India which may in future convert it into a religious State wherein the interests of Muslims will be jeopardized. This would happen if a communal organisation had a dominant hand in the government and the Congress ideals of the equality of all communities were made to give way to religious intolerance. The continued accession of Kashmir to India should, however, help in defeating this tendency. From my experience of the last four years, it is my considered judgement that the presence of Kashmir in the Union of India has been the major factor in stabilizing relations between Hindus and Muslims of India. Gandhiji was not wrong when he uttered words before his death which paraphrase, "I lift up my eyes into the hills, whence light comes to my help."

In the same address the Sheikh called Pakistan a feudal State in which a clique was trying to maintain itself in power.

His address to the J&K Constituent Assembly should be considered as the foundation of his political views so far as Kashmir is concerned. Left to himself he would have kept

Kashmir as independent if her independence could be guaranteed by all her neighbours. When the U.S. Ambassador to India, Loy Henderson, visited Kashmir in September 1950, Sheikh Abdullah told him that he would like Kashmir to be independent. A gist of what Sheikh told Loy Henderson is now a part of U.S. Governemnt papers on Foreign Relations. I reproduce below the telegram sent by Henderson to Secretary of State and published on pages 1433-1435 of U.S. Foreign Relations, Vol.V.

"New Delhi. Sep. 29, 1950 - 400 799. While in Kashmir I had two secret discussions with Sheikh Abdulllah, Prime Minister at his request ...

"He denied, with considerable emphasis, stories to the effect that he was pro-Communist, pro-Soviet, anti-West or anti-US.

"In discussing future Kashmir, Abdullah was vigorous in restating that in his opinion it should be independent, that overwhelming majority of population desired this independence."

Sheikh Abdullah resented Kashmir's accession to India at times and called it as "temporary" and yet to be ratified. When he was attacked by communal elements in India or when he was stripped of power, he considered himself the sole leader of Kashmiris. At no stage he advocated the accession of Kashmir to Pakistan. His calls for "plebiscite" and "self-determination" were more of political weapons than an advocacy for accession to Pakistan. Though he had come to the conclusion that Indo-Pak amity was a pre-requisite for progress of Kashmir, nowhere do we find him publicly advocating accession of the State to Pakistan.

However, throughout he maintained that Kashmir's accession to India was only in respect of three subjects that is Defence, External Affairs and Communications. He considered himself in the role of guardian of Kashmir's autonomy. So he got incorporated in Indian Constitution Article 370 and steered the constitutional development in his state towards that end. He prevailed upon the Prime Minister of India to preserve the autonomy through what has come to be called 24th July, 1952, declaration.

We can summarize this Agreement as follows :

1. Citizenship : A common citizenship was recognized but Indians could not be Kashmiri citizen.
2. The Head of the State to be recognized by the Indian President on the recommendations of the State Legislature.
3. The President of India would exercise his emergency powers under Article 352 of the Indian Constitution only in case of invasion. But in the case of internal disturbance, he would exercise his Emergency power only on the recommendation of the State Legislature.
4. The Supreme Court of India was to have only original jurisdiction under Article 131.
5. Fundamental Rights, as enshrined in the Indian Constitution, would apply to the whole of Kashmir except where compensation had not been awarded to the landlords whose lands had been distributed among tillers.
6. For historical and sentimental reasons the State of Jammu and Kashmir was to have its own flag but not as a rival to Indian National Flag which will have the same status in Kashmir as in other states of the Union.

In due course, the autonomy for Kashmir as provided in this Declaration was scuttled by various measures.

Later during his Prime Ministership, the valley came to experience food shortage which resulted in resentment against the Government.

In Ladakh Kushak Bakula, the Head Lama, declared that they would like the domain of Kashmir Government to end and would welcome to be an autonomous constituent unit.

Since early 1952 Praja Parishad in Jammu had launched a violent campaign against the government of Sheikh Abdullah. During elections to the Jammu and Kashmir Constituent Assembly in October 1951, nomination papers of their candidates were rejected without substantial reasons. They then boycotted elections to the Constituent Assembly.

Praja Parishad then launched a movement against totalitarian methods of governance by Sheikh Abdullah. Hindu students raided the Jammu Secretariat, burnt some records and smashed furniture in February 1952. Curfew was imposed for 72 hours. Army aid to quell disturbances had to be invoked. In Jammu the agitation was led by Prem Nath Dogra. He had the support of Jan Sangh and Akalis led by Master Tara Singh.

In June 1952 things came to a head. There were demonstrations at Delhi against Jammu & Kashmir having its own flag and the abolition of hereditary rule by Jammu & Kashmir Constituent Assembly when the Constitution was itself under consideration. In the Lok Sabha N.C. Chatterji argued that there could not be a Republic within the Republic. Praja Parishad continued its agitation for full merger of the state in India throughout 1952.

Dr. S.P. Mukherji entered the state of Jammu and Kashmir without "permit" on 11th May, 1953. He was placed under arrest. Riots broke out all over Jammu, Punjab and Uttar Pradesh where effigies of Sheikh Abdullah were burnt in public. Mukherji, while confined near Nishat Bagh, died in Hari Singh Hospital on 23rd June. Causes of his death were described as heart failure and pleurisy. More demonstrations took place which embittered Abdullah who concluded that India was no more secular and it had been taken over by communal powers. In his book *My Years With Nehru,* B.N. Mullick writes: "It was only from the latter part of 1952 that Sheikh Mohd. Abdullah started having second thoughts. The Praja Parishad and Jan Sangh agitations in January 1953 in Jammu and India respectively gave him the excuse that he required and thereafter he started equating Pakistan with India when earlier he had condemned Pakistan as an aggressor".

Stunned by the Praja Parishad agitation Sheikh Abdullah made a speech at Ranbir Singh Pura or 10th April, 1952, wherein he had observed : "Kashmir's accession to India will have to be of a restricted nature so long as communalism has a footing on the soil of India." He went on to say, "Kashmiris are apprehensive as to what will happen to them if for instance something happens to Pt. Nehru". He warned against applying Indian Constitution to Kashmir in all respects. *The London Times* wrote on May 8, 1952, in its Weekly Edition: "Sheikh has made it clear that he is as much opposed to dominion by India as to subjugation by Pakistan. He claims sovereign authority for the Kashmir Constituent Assembly."

Those who hold Sheikh Abdullah guilty of perfidy should understand that he anguished over the dilemma of Kashmir as early as 1948. Josef Korbel writes :

"One evening Sheikh Abdullah gave a reception for the Commission in the Shalimar Gardens ... After the party I went for a walk with Sheikh Abdullah. He spoke at length about the origin of his movement, his fight against the Maharaja and the problem of accession. Here was a Muslim leader who believed, as did India, in a non-communal, secular state but who was aware of the fanatical devotion of his followers to Islam. (emphasis added.) What then, should he do ? Pakistan was a reactionary country, he said, and he was convinced that union of Kashmir with Pakistan would finally work against the interests of his people. They would be better with India but what could he do if the sentiments of his people pushed them in a direction against his better judgement? Sheikh Abdullah did not conceal his helplessness." After dilating on the impossibility of independence unless guaranteed by India, Pakistan, China and the Soviet Union, Sheikh Abdullah told Korbel :

"There is in my opinion, therefore, only one solution open. That is the division of the country. If it is not achieved, the fighting will continue ... and our people's suffering will go on."[8] Was Sheikh not being prophetic?

With the constant snipping of his governance Sheikh Abdullah came to presume that India was communal and not secular and as such the best course for Kashmir would be to become an independent State. In a despatch in *New York Times* of July 5, 1953 Robert Trumboull reporting from New Delhi said:

"Sheikh Mohd. Abdullah is said to lean towards independent status as this would solve many of his problems, both political and financial and thereby strengthen his personal support which now appears to be falling off."

Early in May 1953, Adlai Stevenson visited Kashmir. He met Sheikh Abdullah in Srinagar from May 1st to 3rd. Indian newspapers carried the news that Kashmir was seeking independence to be guaranteed by both countries and the rest of the State would be partitioned between India and Pakistan roughly along the ceasefire line. The US Ambassador, George V. Allan, and Adlai Stevenson himself denied any interference in Kashmir affairs.

Kashmir Government consisted of only five Ministers—three Muslims and two Hindus. In the prevailing welter of rumours and confusion the split in National Conference Ministers and ranks came out in the open. Sheikh Abdullah warned that the communal happenings of the previous year had shaken the foundation of "Indo-Kashmir Relationship" and at the beginning of August he made the statement that Kashmir's accession to India was forced on her because of India's refusal to give assistance against tribal invasion unless that state acceded to her - the much touted theory of Alistair Lamb. The background of the split in the J&K Cabinet was as follows.

It is stated that the Sheikh had prepared a speech in Urdu which was intercepted and the speech had pointed out that the accession of Kashmir to India was conditional and temporary and that Kashmir's prosperity depended upon relations with both India and Pakistan since rivers and roads in Kashmir lead to Pakistan and the nearest railway station was Rawalpindi. He had criticized the Praja Parishad agitation which had transformed his perspective on India very largely. Josef Korbel has given an English translation of this speech as it appeared in the *Civil and Military Gazette* (Lahore) on 3rd February, 1954. It was the same Sheikh who in May 1949 addressing himself to Nehru had said:

"I want you to believe that Kashmir is yours. No power in the world can separate us. Every Kashmiri feels that he is an

Indian and this India is his homeland." He remained a votary of valley's freedom though aware of dangers surrounding the valley.

The defecting Ministers in his Cabinet charged Sheikh with flouting collective responsibility of the cabinet. Sheikh Abdullah not only ignored this letter of his three cabinet colleagues but also the request by Sadar-I-Riyasat to hold cabinet meeting to iron out differences. Accordingly the Sadar-I-Riyasat dismissed the Abdullah Ministry and invited Bakshi Ghulam Mohd. to form a new Ministry. It was not a sudden development. Sheikh Abdullah had been drifting away from India and Jawahar Lal Nehru right from the beginning of 1953. Nehru had invited Sheikh Abdullah to join him at the annual session of All India Congress Committee. Ajit Parsad Jain, a Minister in Government of India, quotes Nehru requesting Abdullah as follows on phone since he was present when the talk had taken place : Nehru - "Sheikh Sahib, aapki intazaar main hamari aankhey to pathra ja rahin hain; aap kab ainygai ?" (My eyes are turning to stone waiting for you. When are you coming?) Abdullah curtly replied that he was too busy and could not come.

The Hindustan Times of Delhi in its issue of July 8, 1953, has reported Indian Prime Minister Nehru as saying "I invited Sheikh Mohd. Abdullah to come to Delhi. In fact, even when I was in Europe, I had sent word that he should be invited. On returning, I invited him. He did not come, then he said he would come later, and later again. This invitation was repeated by telephone. Ultimately he did not come. In fact before I had come back Sheikh Abdullah and some others had taken to speaking in a vein which seemed strange to me and distressed us greatly."

Bakshi Ghulam Mohd. formed a new cabinet on 8th August, 1953, and it consisted of the following :

1. Bakshi Ghulam Mohd., Prime Minister,

2. G.M. Sadiq

3. G.L. Dogra

4. S.L. Saraf

In the meanwhile Sheikh Mohd. Abdullah alongwith his Revenue Minister Mirza Afzal Beg and Principal Information Officer were arrested at Gulmarg in the early hours of 9th August, 1953. It may be mentioned here that Sheikh Abdullah Cabinet had comprised only five Ministers, and in the split one Muslim and two Hindus had disagreed with the Sheikh and Mirza Afzal Beg. Abdullah had such faith in himself that he had failed to notice signs of dissension and remained confident of his own position. With his arrest widespread violence erupted throughout the valley. Police had to open fire at Amira Kadal in Srinagar at Anantnag, Qazigund, Tral, Kulgam and Pattan, killing 30 people. The valley observed a continuous hartal which was joined by boatmen as well as tonga-wallas. Regarding the arrest of Sheikh Abdullah, Pt. Nehru told Lok Sabha on 10th August, 1953, that two weeks earlier Bakshi Ghulam Mohd. and Mirza Afzal Beg had visited Delhi and held prolonged discussions which indicated a serious rift within the Kashmir Cabinet. Ministers had started publicly advocating rival policies. Writes Lord Birdwood, "Quite suddenly in August, Abdullah threw ambiguity before his arrest. He spoke openly of repudiating the accession to India."

What was Nehru's reaction to the arrest of his friend and colleague Sheikh Abdullah? A.P. Jain writes : "As per General Kaul's story stating that the Sheikh had been arrested on the authority of a junta made up of him and some Kashmiri ministers on their own is no more than unfounded bragging. Nehru certainly wanted the responsibility for the action against the Sheikh to rest with Kashmiri leaders but he would not resist any action including Sheikh's arrest, which they considered necessary." General Kaul had observed that "on August 9, when Nehru rang up Yuvraj Karan Singh and blew him up for allowing Abdullah to be arrested, the latter, after hearing only a part of the outburst and shaken by Nehru's blasting, handed over the telephone to A.P. Jain ... Jain not being able to take in the tirade all by himself passed it to D.P. Dhar".

On the arrest of Sheikh Abdullah and riots, Lord Birdwood makes this pithy observation : "Abdullah had gradually come first to pursue a nebulous independence, with the same fatal attraction which had previously lured Maharaja Hari Singh to his destruction ..."

Sheikh Abdullah was first confined at Udhampur and later moved to Kud Sub Jail on the Jammu–Srinagar highway. In March 1955, a petition for Habeas Corpus on his behalf was moved. Abdullah promptly indicated that he did not want the petition to be pursued. Some commentators of the contemporary scene maintain that Government of India was anxious for his release but the same was blocked by the moves of Bakshi Ghulam Mohd. Anyway Sheikh Abdullah remained in detention at Kud without trial for five years.

Later, Sheikh Abdullah gave his version of the cataclysmic events of August 1953. According to him he had received a letter, written by G.M. Bakshi, Girdhari Lal Dogra and Shyam Lal Saraf only after his arrest. He further revealed that in May 1953 the working committee of National Conference had constituted a sub-committee of himself, Maulvi Mohd. Sayeed Masoodi, M.A. Beg, Bakshi Ghulam Mohd., Khwaja G.M. Sadiq, Sardar Budh Singh, Pt. Shyam Lal Saraf and Girdhari Lal Dogra to suggest ways to terminate the state of prevailing uncertainty and future steps. In their report of 9th June, 1953, the committee had recommended independence for the state for the period of plebiscite and alternatively it had endorsed Dixon Plan that these areas be given independence for the time being where plebiscite was to be held.

The Sheikh was suddenly released on 8 January, 1958. It is so guessed that this release was at the intervention of Prime Minister Jawahar Lal Nehru. On his release Sheikh Abdullah suggested mutual consultations between India and Pakistan on the Kashmir issue but continued questioning the authority of India over Kashmir. He further went on to say that the accession to India was temporary and it had terminated with his arrest. He also alleged that the Kashmir Constituent Assembly had accepted the Constitution under duress and the future of the state could not be decided by the Constituent Assembly. Abdullah was again arrested on 30th April, 1958, after the murder of Mohi-Ud-Din Bandey and injuries to several others at Hazratbal by Sheikh Abdullah's Razakars. Government property was also put to arson. He was charged with an attempt to overthrow the legally constituted Government. Sheikh Abdullah filed a written statement on 8th

August, 1959, and made oral statements in the court of Special Magistrate. In his statements Sheikh stated that he was in continued detention for the period during which the conspiracy was alleged to have taken place except from 8th January to 29th April, 1958. His government was arbitrarily dismissed on 8th August, 1953, on the charge that he had entered into a conspiracy with the United States to establish an independent state of Jammu and Kashmir. His replies were charged with emotion. He said, "I invite the prosecution to produce a single sentence or a word (uttered by me) favouring Kashmir's accession to Pakistan." This assertion is factually true. Sheikh said that while Pakistan's sentimental attraction to Kashmiris cannot be dismissed ... sentimentally they were subject to two divergent pulls. Appeal of Kashmir nationalism has been found to be as powerful as that of Islam. It is the community of Kashmiri Pandits led by P.N. Bazaz who had sought Kashmir's accession to Pakistan. Said Abdullah : "To millions in the sub-continent and all over the world I had become a pariah as to how yesterday's dear friend of Nehru and the idol of India could turn arch communalist and a traitor to the country." He was released on April 8, 1964, following his acquittal of the charges of conspiracy. On his release he again called for the right of self determination for the people of Kashmir. He contended that Kashmir had acceded to India only in three subjects and the residual sovereignty continued to vest in the Kashmiris. He again advocated friendship between India and Pakistan for the settlement of Kashmir problem. He came to envision Kashmir as a bridge between India and Pakistan. Unfortunately he was inherently one party leader. Though Awami Action Committee, led by Mir Waiz Maulvi Farooq, refused to comply, violent clashes took place between followers of Sheikh (Sher) and Maulana (Bakra) reviving memories of conflict from the days of Mir Waiz Yusuf Shah. He held prolonged discussions with the Indian Prime Minister Jawahar Lal Nehru, and some people speculated that he favoured the idea of a condominium of India and Pakistan over Kashmir. Abdullah then went to Pakistan. He publicly stated that Kashmir's accession to India was not irrevocable but called for friendship between India and Pakistan. He met President Ayub Khan and stated that there was intense desire on both sides to settle the question of Kashmir through negotiations and mutual discussions.

In the meanwhile, Pt. Nehru passed away on 27 May, 1964, and the hopes that a meeting between him and President Ayub Khan would lead to the solution of Kashmir problem were dashed.

At the beginning of 1965, Sheikh Abdullah, accompanied by Begum Abdullah and M.A. Beg went abroad for Haj as well as pleading his people's case before other sympathetic nations. In this connection he visited England and Algiers. It was alleged that he wanted the Kashmir issue to be considered by the Afro-Asian Conference in Algiers in March 1965. He met the Chinese Premier Chou-En-lai in Algiers and declared that the Chinese Premier had invited him to visit the Peoples Republic of China since China had always supported Kashmir people's right of self-determination.

It is clear that Sheikh Abdullah had met Chou-En-lai through the good offices of the then ebullient Pak Foreign Minister Zulfikar Ali Bhutto. He claimed that if India denied him passport, he would get the same from Pakistan. When Sheikh Abdullah landed at Palam on May 8, 1965, he was re-arrested and detained in Ooty. In 1967 he was transferred to All India Institute of Medical Sciences, New Delhi, for treatment. He was released on 2nd January, 1968, on the occasion of Id-Ul-Fitar.

On release he again pleaded for negotiated settlement of Kashmir issue. He said that he should be allowed to love Pakistan as much as he loved India, though he had said earlier that Pakistan had not waited for solution but had come for Kashmir "sword in one hand and the Quran in the other."

Demands were made for action against Sheikh Abdullah in connection with Meerut riots. However, the clamour subsided in due course and Sheikh Abdullah arrived in Srinagar on 4th March, 1968, and received a tumultuous welcome. In 1965 Mirza Afzal Beg had founded Plebiscite Front and Sheikh Sahib identified himself with the ideals and objectives of the Front completely. He was accorded a formal reception at Mujahid Manzil, headquarters of Plebiscite Front in Srinagar. A crowd of 25,000 had gathered to accord him welcome. They were addressed by Maulana Masoodi, Maulana Farooq of the Awami Action Committee, Grand Mufti Bashir-Ud-Din and Pt. Raghunath Vaishnavi of the India-Pakistan Conciliation Group. Almost every speaker called for solution of Kashmir problem through plebiscite. The Sheikh in his address spoke of the urgent need for a solution "by plebiscite or other suitable ways". He called for Indo-Pak amity. Speaking at a reception given to him by Kashmir Swatantra Forum on 26th March, 1968, Sheikh Abdullah said India was committed to hold a plebiscite. Pakistan was a party to the dispute as it was in possession of one-third of the State having a population of 1.6 million. Earlier at a reception at Press Club Srinagar on 6th March he had said that it was "wishful thinking" to write off Pakistan as a party to the dispute, following the 1965 conflict. Peace between India and Pakistan was essential for the "very survival of Kashmir". While in New Delhi on May 7, 1968, he said that the militant Kashmir youth were ridiculing his peaceful efforts. "They are inspired by the freedom struggle in Algeria and other places. It is very difficult to control them." He voiced his resistance to any Indo-Pak pact on Kashmir which bye-passed Kashmiris.

In October 1968, Sheikh Abdullah called a week-long convention on Kashmir. Papers were read by several intellectuals. Inaugurating the convention on 10th October, Jaya Prakash Narain called for special status for Kashmir state within the Indian Union. He further said that all those who loudly proclaimed that Kashmir was an unalienable part of India, should understand the persistent discontent in Kashmir valley. Addressing the Convention on 11th October, Sheikh Mohd Abdullah said that "Plebiscite is a fundamental right. If this is not possible nobody insists that it should be held. The only other way is that India, Pakistan and Kashmir should sit together and find the way out."

Anyone who has studied the career of Sheikh Abdullah will be struck by his fervour and passion for Kashmir's autonomy and independence. He was consistent throughout in his advocacy for maintaining Kashmir's distinct identity.

However he equated Kashmir's freedom with his being in power. His oratorial powers gave him the ability to hypnotize his people which lent a touch of megalomania to his life and work.

The worst feature of his life was condonation of nepotism. For instance, it was established that Mohd. Raza, an official of Pakistan High Commission at Delhi, had been in touch with his family when he was under detention in early 1960s. The greatest disservice which he did to Kashmir was to remove his life long colleague Mirza Afzal Beg from his last Cabinet to ensure that reins of Government passed to his son Dr. Farooq Abdullah after he himself took leave of the mother planet earth. Subsequent events prove that by his this one act, Sheikh Abdullah left a dire legacy for his beloved people who now face hardships. His ambivalence and lust for office contributed to Kashmir's tragedy despite his idealism.

REFERENCES

1. *Mission with Mountbatten* by Allan Campbell Johnson, published by Jaico Publishing House Bombay 1951, p. 101.
2. *Mountbatten, the Official Biography* by Philip Zieglar published by Collins London; 1985; page 445.
3. *Ibid*; Uncatalogued letter in Broadland Archives.
4. *Ibid*; p. 445
5. *Two Nations and Kashmir* by Lord Birdwood, p. 3.
6. *Ibid*; p. 4.
7. *Ibid*; p. 151.
8. Josef Korbel - *Danger in Kashmir*, p. 146-147.

7

India's Complacency-Neglect to Rhetoric of War

Every government entertains the self-defeating belief that it can do no wrong. Another name for this attitude is self-complacency.

After the defeat of Pakistan Army in 1971 and creation of Bangladesh, the Indian Government perceived itself not only as creating history, but also the geography. The late Kashmiri writer Shamim Ahmed Shamim had hailed Smt. Indira Gandhi as a creator of geography too. It was also felt that the religion-based two-nation theory which had led to the partition of the sub-continent in 1947 had lost ground completely. India in the eighties behaved not only as the dominant power in South Asia but also its mentor and policeman. It preened itself as an important power in the comity of nations as it had one of the largest standing armies which had been equipped with a formidable arsenal of modern weaponry. By successfully exploding a nuclear device at Pokharan in Rajasthan as early as May 1974, India had shown that it was capable of having nuclear arms. While enjoying its pipe dreams of greatness, it had forgotten its empty coffers. Since arrogance breeds ignorance, it forgot that Pakistan was an implacable foe and would arm itself and nuclearise its defence even if 'Pakistan had to live on grass' as Z.A. Bhutto had proclaimed. India also deluded itself that it had won the hearts of Kashmiris through Rajiv-Abdullah accord of 1986.

It knew Pakistan was smarting under the ignominy of defeat. It knew that Pakistan had started re-arming herself as soon as General Yahya Khan had stepped down handing over the reigns of Pakistan Government to Zulfikar Ali Bhutto since his party had emerged as the single largest party in West Pakistan in 1970 general elections. Bhutto became the first civilian Martial Law Administrator and continued to govern the country under Martial Law till August 1972. The first act of Bhutto was to embark upon a programme of rearmament. Bhutto had undertaken not only the programme of the rearmament but also the reorganisation of armed forces called 'Higher Defence Organisation' so that in future they showed greater cohesion. Again, the same Bhutto, who had signed Simla agreement to get hack 90,000 prisoners of war, gave a 'solemn assurance' to the people of Kashmir, while speaking in Pak National assembly on 15th July, 1972, that as and when they launched their struggle for self-determination, Pakistan would go all out in support and assistance to them. From 1979 to 1989, President Zia-ul-Haq tried to Islamise Kashmir thus preparing a Kashmiri mind-set to throw away the Delhi mantle. In 1990, Bhutto's daughter picked up the gauntlet which her father had reluctantly left to rust. Speaking on Bhutto's death anniversary on 4th April, 1990, on his grave, she resurrected Bhutto's call for 1000 year war with India over Kashmir issue. She has, indeed, been a true daughter of her father and has gone much farther in resurrecting the 40 year old demand for plebiscite in Kashmir.

Exactly a week later, India's Prime Minister V.P. Singh, while speaking in the Indian Parliament (Lok Sabha) on April 10, 1990, asked the Indian people to prepare themselves 'psychogically' for a war which might be forced upon the country. While warning the country against the possibility of a pre-emptive strike by Pakistan, he ridiculed the latter's talk of a 1,000 year war over Kashmir and taunted Pakistan as not to be in a position to sustain a war even for 1000 hours. He told Lok Sabha that Pakistan had doubled its army strength; the strength of Pak air force had gone up by two and a half times and that of navy three times since 1971. Singh was accused of creating war psychosis. His critics forgot that the first call for 1000 year war over Kashmir had been given by Benazir Bhutto though later she accused Indian Prime Minister of threatening Pakistan. Anyway, both the countries teetered over the brink of the war with the armed forces confronting each other. If the war balloon had not gone up, it was due to aversion of the masses of the two countries who are growing more and more aware of nuclear threat to their existence, and the restraint urged by the only super power, the U.S.A.

Indian Prime Minister apprised Indians from each available platform of Pakistan's likely adventurism on Kashmir issue. On 26th April, 1990, he told a Press Conference that Pakistan had become an 'international training ground of terrorists'. In the same breath he added that Pakistan had been single-minded in modernising her forces by inducting high technology weapons for the last 18 years.

How come that the people of the sub-continent did find themselves suddenly face to face with such total annihilation?

The answer is by sheer neglect. First India went on denying that Kashmir was any problem. Even if we accept the position that legally Kashmir had become an integral part of India once the ruler signed the Instrument of Accession, it was fatal to close one's eyes to the fact that it is the 'dispute' in India's own words, and it's on the United Nations agenda, and more than anything else, there were people in Kashmir who felt cheated and disenchanted, besides an ideological war had been thrust by Pakistan on devout Kashmiri Muslims. In today's world there is no status quo. If we insist on status quo in the face of avalanche of change, unleashed by revolution of ideas and the revolution in technology, we succumb to the 'tyranny of status quo' in the words of Milton Freedom. Modern science and modern political processes have unleashed forces which found the USSR disintegrating, and the East Europe has burst out of cocoon built by coercive force. Only such societies can survive which stay ahead of tomorrow. Indian decision makers took Kashmir not only for granted but felt it to be frozen once Sheikh Mohammad Abdullah had accepted the reigns of

Kashmir government in February 1975 accepting Kashmir to be a 'Constituent unit' of the Indian Union. Indians allowed themselves to wrap in blinkers once they dumped money in Kashmir; some rulers had come to believe that all problems are solved if you throw away money on them; they forgot loyalty to a cause or country cannot always be bought. Loyalty can be cultivated if expectations are fulfilled in a just manner and people are assured of dignity and self respect. India has gone on arming itself thinking as if numerical superiority in guns, aircraft and sub marines or missiles is the only insurance against fissiparous tendencies. India's defence budget went on swelling, and being squandered too, it gave the country a false sense of security.

In India every party decided to ride the communal tiger to seize power or maintain itself on the top. Did they expect Kashmiris to be blind to this erosion of secular values in the country? Probably this explains India's lack of response to Pakistani thrust to fundamentalise Kashmir. Or a Fundamentalist India could not object to Pakistan exporting fundamentalism to Kashmir?

By swamping Kashmir rulers with money, which was squandered on non-productive projects rather than alleviating the human misery in the ghettoes in the downtown Srinagar, India thought it had done its duty towards Kashmir whereas India should have acted as a trustee of Kashmiri culture and Kashmir's welfare. Since India prides itself as a democracy, it should have removed all obstacles to the flowering of genuine democracy in Kashmir.

Political opportunism and lack of long term strategy for development and secularisation of the state have proved fatal. This is not to say that there has been no development at all; tourism flourished into industry, enriching the valley by Rs.500 crores every year. Horticulture flourished netting export of apple and other fruit thus earning another Rs. 500 crores. Yet with population rising, inflation increases and corruption and nepotism flourishing, the common Kashmiri was disillusioned. He did not see evil in Kashmiri bureaucrat or elected legislator but by a strange quirk of logic he held Delhi responsible for all that was wrong.

Again, the developmental activity did not lessen the disparity in incomes. While the Boulevard and Residency Road in Srinagar had a number of glitterring new establishments and tourist resorts, the Barzulla area around the new airport had new commercial complexes and a new ambience of 'nouveau rich', the old town went on decaying. The downtown Srinagar has come to provide hideouts and sanctuaries to the terrorists. In *Encounters with the Future*, a forecast of Life into the 21st Century, Mervin and Thomas O'Toole write, "Every survey of national stability uses per capita income as its guideline; of more importance is the income gap between the top and bottom tenths of a country's population. Again, just as important a vital sign for any country is its unemployment rate. Not just unemployment throughout the entire working population but the unemployment of the males between the age of 16 and 18 who face lots of troubles when they are 'penniless and restless'. If everybody gets a fair share of even little wealth, it is all right." They further add: " If everybody's poor no one minds being poor."

Lack of positive vital signs in a community's life are called instability syndromes. All this applies to the Kashmiri society. However, the gravity of the economic malaise cannot be gauged correctly because either statistics were not compiled or they were juggled.

Add to these factors the political instability where everyone was more for himself than for community weal. After passing away of the legendary Sheikh Abdullah, the reins of government went into the hands of Dr. Farooq Abdullah who not only lacked his father's charisma but also his political stature and experience. Congress thought it was the right time to re-assert itself and undo the self-liquidation which Syed Mir Qasim had imposed upon Congress. Congress fought 1983 elections with vigor. Dr. Abdullah's victory provided new boost to Kashmiri sense of self respect. They exulted that they had humbled the mighty Congress which was perceived to be the intruder. However, Sheikh Abdullah's family was divided. G.M. Shah faction of National Conference broke away from the Abdullah National Conference. New Delhi committed the blunder of imposing Defectors Government on Kashmir in July

1984. If Governor's Rule was imposed, it would have been less galling to the Kashmiris or the best course would have been to give a fresh chance to the Kashmiris to elect a new government.

But the manipulative strategy evolved in Delhi foisted an illegitimate government under whom corruption and misrule acquired frightening momentum. The erstwhile Governor Jagmohan in his lengthy statement of 30th May, 1990, said: "Subversion and corruption are interlinked." Anyway, unrest broke all over. It is during this period of instability that fundamentalist organisations started coalescing to forge a new unity under the guidance of Dr Qazi Nissar Ahmed. During Governor's rule, officers, who were indulging in subversive and corrupt practices were removed in a summary fashion. Not that they had not merited action but action has to be proportionate to the gravity of misconduct. Professor Ghulam Rasool Bucha and Professor Mohammed Ashraf of Degree College Sopore, who were so removed from service, formed a `Muslim Employees Front' and appealed to all government servants to join the Front as members and in return it would safeguard their interests. Thus government employees banded together to continue their inefficient and corrupt rule with impunity. In days to come, `Muslim Employees Front' became not only an important constituent of Muslim United Front but also an instrument to instigate government employees and misguide them on communal lines. They helped infiltrate police and other government agencies with militant youth and in return got prior knowledge of all governmental decisions. The extent of infiltration of the government machinery can be gauged by two facts. As many as 800 policemen of 4 Armed Bns. absented from duty. Some 137 senior officers of the state appealed to the U.N.O. against alleged Indian repression in the state in flagrant violation of their Service Conduct Rules. Yet no action. Thus, the administrative apparatus, though weak as it always was, then got further subverted. To quote Marvin and Thomas O'Toole again, a vital sign of a community's stability is the level of administrative competence; without being derogatory to anyone, it has to be said that Kashmir had never had a sturdy administrative apparatus. In normal times, it just functioned on day to day basis. It looked for direction and guidance to the political leadership, say, to Dr Abdullah who had further concentrated power in his hands and yet seldom was he available in urgent crisis–ridden situations. Corruption and inefficiency completely eroded the credibility of the state administrative machinery. The administrative machine had manipulated electoral victory for National Conference and its ally Congress and thus found no impediment in merrily going on its course of non-performance. Why bother to work when promotion and power lie in political alignments? Thus administrative machinery came to work haphazardly and spasmodically. Its collusive inefficiency was eloquently proved by the escape of 12 subversives, including two top JKLF activists, that is, Captain Rashid and Chalkoo, from Srinagar Central Jail.

In the complex world of today nothing can be taken for granted and status quoism in particular is the unmistakable route to self-defeating actions. Kashmiri docility was made into as much as self-deluding fetish as the non-existent secularism (by secularism I mean non-pre-eminence of religion in regulating political and social affairs). Thus whereas Kashmiri society was being fundamentalised, New Delhi rulers not only failed to evolve counter strategy but kept their eyes shut to the new realities and contented themselves with manipulating the ruling elite. Politics cannot be frozen into moulds and stereotypes. In the dynamic age of today, fossilized policies cannot meet the challenge of ever new realities. This happened in Punjab. This has been repeated in Kashmir. In Punjab, it had been happening over decades for fundamentalist terrorism to sprout; one of the reasons for short-gestation for Kashmiri terrorism is the ten year old on-going insurgency in the neighboring Afghanistan. It got a new fillip when the USSR under Gorbachev decided to withdraw from Afghanistan. If the mighty USSR could be forced to withdraw from Afghanistan, could Indian forces be not made to pack up and quit Kashmir? In this state of disarray and confusion, the militant youth, who had been disillusioned with the electoral process, struck methodically leaving administration a mute and helpless spectator rather than the controller of the situation. Right from the beginning of 1988, militants started calling shots in the valley, not the occasional insults to Indian national flag or

Indian teams which had started much earlier but a systematic campaign because the governmental machinery was not equal to the situation and also because the administration, to avoid adverse publicity, started down-playing the outrageous acts of the militants. The Government at New Delhi had done a grave dis-service to the nation when they ignored the warnings of the gathering storm, transmitted by Governor Jagmohan. In April 1989, he had written to the Prime Minister as follows:

"The situation is just deteriorating. It has almost reached a point of no return. For the last five days, there have been large-scale violence, arson, firing, hartals, casualties and what not. Things have truly fallen apart. Talking of the Irish crisis Disraeli had said, 'It is potatoes one day and the Pope next.' This is the position in Kashmir. Yesterday it was Maqbool Butt; today it is Satanic Verses; tomorrow it will be "repression day"; and day after, it will be something else. The Chief Minister stands isolated. He has already fallen—politically and administratively; only constitutional rites remain to be performed. The situation calls for effective intervention. Today may be timely; tomorrow may be too late".[1]

In May 1989, the Governor again wrote to the Prime Minister of India :

"From May 8 to 13, there have been 14 bomb blasts and six cases of firing and cross firing. No worthwhile activity has been visible at the political front to counter the move of the subversionists. What is still more worrying is that every 'victory' of subversionists is swelling their ranks, and the animosity is being diverted against the Central Authorities. I have indicated my anxiety to the Chief Minister."[2]

Rulers at Delhi remained deaf and indifferent to the pleadings of their own Governor.

Later, the same Governor said in December 1989, "Due to total inaction, unbelievable incompetence, widespread corruption and passive connivance, Farooq Government had led the state to disaster".[3] Jagmohan had to resign from governorship for his candid remarks.

REFERENCES

1. *Times of India*: June 17, 1990

2. *India Today* : April 30, 1990

3. *My Years with Indira Gandhi* by Dr. P.C. Alexander published by Vision Books New Delhi; page 146.

8

Transition from Ballot to Bullet

Salman Rushdie says democracy has failed in Kashmir. Writing in the *Independent* (London), he is quoted as saying : "It is the failure of Indian secularist policies in Kashmir that has driven a large number of Kashmiris towards the kind of Islamic fundamentalism from which they shied away earlier. ... In the modern world the demand for self-determination is primarily a failure of democracy." He further writes: "When people are asked to choose between tanks and mosques they do not usually choose tanks". Poor Literateur does not know that democracy was never allowed to nurture in the fertile land of Kashmir. There has been a systematic denial of democratic rights to Kashmiris.

The first elections in the state took place for the Jammu and Kashmir Constituent Assembly in September 1951. These elections were on the basis of universal adult franchise and secret ballot. Each electoral district (constituency) covered forty thousand persons of the population. The elections were so manipulated that all the 73 of 75 Constituent Assembly seats went to National Conference candidates and that too, unopposed.

Some 25 seats are reserved for Pak Ocupied Kashmir. So elctions take place every five years only for 75 seats of which 42 constituencies are in Kashmir valley.

In the 1957 general elections, Ghulam Mohammed Bakshi secured 68 seats out of 75, for National Conference, of which 38 victories were declared unopposed. Praja Parishad had secured five seats in Jammu and Two had gone to Independents.

In 1962, National Conference under G.M. Bakshi contested 41 seats in Kashmir valley, 34 National Conference candidates were returned unopposed.

In 1967, under the so-called communist and liberal G.M. Sadiq, Congress, which had started functioning, won 22 seats in the valley, out of 42, unopposed and for the remaining there was nominal contest only. Congress secured 69 out of 75 seats.

For the sixth Lok Sabha elections in 1971, Sheikh Mohammad Abdullah, Mirza Afzal Beg G.M. Shah were externed from Jammu and Kashmir, and hundreds of Plebiscite Front workers were arrested. Thus Sheikh and Plebiscite Front were prevented from contesting elections. Congress bagged five of the six seats losing only the Srinagar seat.

In 1972 elections, when Syed Mir Qasim was the Chief Minister, out of 42 seats in Kashmir valley, 28 were won by Congress, five by Jamait-i-Islami and nine by independents. There were six assembly seats in Srinagar city. Congress lost all the five but won one, that is Amira Kadal constituency. Here Zainab Begum, the sister of G.M. Sadiq, was declared successful by a margin of 72 votes only. Sheikh Abdullah's party had not been allowed to contest.

In 1977 Sheikh Abdullah was the Chief Minister. His National Conference won 42 seats and Congress won only 11. In public opinion these elections were not rigged. But Sheikh Abdullah, had roused fears among the Muslims and threatened secession of the state from India, if the National Conference was denied power, during the campaigning for elections.

1983 Elections

1983 general elections in Jammu and Kashmir were important from the point of view that for the first time Congress made a determined bid to attain power on its own. Prime Minister Indira Gandhi campaigned for Congress candidates in person.

She addressed a number of public meetings in the Kashmir valley.

I had received a number of reports that the state police had been indifferent to her security. B.S.F. had, therefore, to supplement her security during night halts, though it was not absolutely regular for B.S.F. to do so.

Union Home Secretary T.N. Chaturvedi, and I went to Srinagar on 31st May, 1983, and stayed there upto 2nd June, 1983. He had to transact some business with the Governor whereas I wanted to coordinate deployment of B.S.F. during elections since J. & K. Government had asked for a large contingent to be at their disposal. I found the state officers in rather a defiant mood. There was lack of usual courtesy in receiving the Union Home Secretary. I could not pinpoint the reason. However I felt uneasy.

On the same day that is 2nd June, 1983, the Prime Minister was to address a public meeting in the Sher-e-Kashmir Park near Tagore Theatre in Srinagar. That was the last public meeting she was to address and with it the electioneering was to conclude. We returned to New Delhi in the afternoon thinking that her tour had gone without any major unpleasant event. Thus we left prior to her own departure.

When it was 10:30 p.m. that when suddenly, received a call from her asking why we had left Srinagar before her departure. Her voice sounded to me somewhat choked. She asked me to see her early next morning. When I presented myself at her residence I was informed that the meeting was not necessary and I could go to my work.

Here I may point out that I had had rather unusual relations with her since July 1959. I had incurred the wrath of the mighty Sardar Pratap Singh Kairon in a case which had come to be called Mangati Kand case which had rocked Punjab in 1957. At that time I was working as Superintendent of Police, Kapurthala. The Chief Minister, Sardar Kairon, had assumed without any evidence that I had not arrested the Magistrate of Phagwara speedily. My contention was that a Magistrate should not be arrested on unsubstantiated statement of a call girl. Anyway, to satisfy his whims, he sent me on a punitive deputation to the cold hills of Himachal Pradesh. In July 1959, I was working as the Superintendent of Police Mahasu district -a district which started from Solan and went up to Shipkila on Tibetan border across Hindustan-Tibet road. I had gone to the police station, Chopal for its annual inspection. At midnight I got a wireless message from my Inspector General asking me to return to Shimla immediately. The wireless message did not spell out why I should return without completing my job. I could not start back for Shimla at midnight as I had to walk on foot for six or seven miles and the forest was said to be full of wild bears. So I started at 4.00 a.m. On reaching Kotkhai, I drove back in my jeep to police station at Theog where I was told that the Prime Minister Pt. Jawaharlal Nehru with his family, was coming to the "Retreat" at Mashobra. I was required to drive there directly. So in my ramshackle jeep, I reached the "Retreat." I found the place bristling with uniformed policemen and found Mrs. Indira Gandhi very indignant. She was telling my Inspector General that they had come for a holiday and not to a police camp. To the alarm of everyone, particularly A. Dutt, the Inspector General who worked as personal security officer to the Prime Minister of India, I removed all the uniformed policemen. After removing their uniforms, the same policemen in plain clothes as gardeners and foresters were assigned security duties round the clock in the thick forest surrounding the Retreat'. This pacified her ire. Next day, Rajiv and Sanjay suddenly slithered down fire escape ropes which gave way and the two teenagers hurtled down. I and the Himachal Pradesh Lt. Governor, Sh. Bir Bahadur Singh of Bhadri, were sitting on chairs in the raised terrace and Mrs. Gandhi was away in the lawn browsing through some book. So seeing Rajiv and Sanjay hurtling towards fatal injuries, we rushed towards them. I held Sanjay in my arms and so did Raja Bir Bahadur Singh hold Rajiv in his arms. We had averted a tragedy. By then Mrs. Gandhi had come towards us and mumbled some words. We could not make out whether she spoke some words of thanks to us or she reprimanded Sanjay and Rajiv. Then the question of horse riding cropped up. Pt. Nehru never left his room but Mrs. Gandhi never stayed in. She not only went for long walks (a security nightmare for me), but she also went riding every morning and evening even if the morning was foggy. I had given her a docile pony and I myself rode as her escort on a rather headstrong horse named `Rustum'. She then insisted on riding `Rustum'. I told her that `Rustum' was unmanageable. She did not reply but the next moment she brought a tin of biscuits and fed him. Thus pampered, the unmanageable `Rustum' became putty in her hands. The second incident, showing her unusual character, occurred in May 1967 in Srinagar. She had come to stay in the forest sanctuary `Dachigam'. The Kashmir Government had made the security arrangements for her stay with the Border Security Force and I was incharge of all the arrangements at `Dachigam'. Due to the folly of one man from Bihar Military Police, the forest was set on fire. The Chief Minister, Khwaja G.M. Sadiq, and the Inspector General, Sh. E.S. Modak, were deeply annoyed with the Border Security Force and me because of this fire. We had tried to control the fire but did not succeed. So when Mrs. Indira Gandhi alighted from her car, she addressed the Chief Minister, and recognising me, she said that she had never seen such a beautiful sight in her life and that she was thrilled with the marvellous spectacle. The Chief Minister and his officers, who had been berating me, felt relieved. I used to accompany her on brief walks in the afternoon throughout her stay at `Dachigam'.

After these incidents, Mrs. Gandhi had come to trust me somewhat and she spoke to me even on phone in case of such a need.

When I reached my office, I learnt that the meeting in Sher-e-Kashmir Park, being addressed by her, was not only disrupted but the lumpen elements of the National Conference made obscene gestures against the lady Prime Minister of India by disrobing themselves in the open.

This filled me with utter shame and explained to me why the Prime Minister had rung up and why she had cancelled morning meeting in an abrupt manner.

I got in touch with the Director General of Police, Kashmir, and requested him to register a criminal case against the National Conference leadership. He maintained that the meeting had been disrupted but there was no disrobing as reported. Evidently he was trying to show that Kashmir was not India and Kashmiris had the right to display their independence even in revolting manners and such infraction of law could be resorted to with impunity by the Kashmiris. I gave a bit of my mind to him that this incident was going to recoil upon them. He maintained that National Conference was going to win and they had been functioning within the four walls of the law.

The elections of 1983 in Kashmir proved, if a proof was required, that our electoral laws were seriously flawed and the results depended on the sympathies of the presiding officers and their staff. It was clear that if there was a collusion between a presiding officer and any political party the former could sway the results in favour of that party.

This is what happened on 5th June, 1983, the day of actual poll. We received a number of complaints of intimidation of minority community voters and their being denied access to the polling booths. Thus junior staff had been fully suborned by the state machinery.

The Jamait-e-Islami's official organ, *Azzan*, said, "Even one percent of the genuine voters were not allowed to cast their votes." The election machinery in the state functioned as a subordinate department of the National Conference. Even the senior officers of the state government brazenly flaunted their contribution to the return of the National Conference to power and bragged having discomfited the Prime Minister of India.

The state government had asked for a very large number of companies of Central Forces. None was deployed on election duty. However to camouflage the matter, they were kept in reserve. According to one report, five battalions were sent to Leh where not even one was required.

Very early on the morning of 5th June, 1983, PM's office rang me up to say that the Prime Minister had been receiving complaints from Srinagar that the voters of the minority community were not being allowed to cast their votes on any polling booth. I told them that B.S.F. could not intervene, the law being what it was. Five minutes later, the Prime Minister rang me up and told me that she knew law more than anyone else but there was always a way to be more effective in an emergency. She inquired why there was no effectiveness that day? She then banged the telephone.

I felt that we had to somehow meet the situation without violating the law. I, therefore, rang up the B.S.F. headquarters at Srinagar to withdraw the B.S.F. from State Police Control Room and that they should be sent in platoon strength in areas where the minority community lived. I added that they could tell the state authorities that it was being done on the orders of the D.G., and if they made any inquiry about it, I would own responsibility for the same.

Thus, B.S.F. platoons went marching into Rainawari, Amirakadal, Jawahar Nagar, Karan Nagar etc. They did not do anything except showing their presence. This a lone was enough to raise the morale of the minority community and deter the polling booth officers from being brazen and openly denying access to the minority community voters to their booths. After about one hour, I got a call from PM's office telling me that the Prime Minister wanted the B.S.F. patrols to continue in the vicinity of the polling booths in the minority community area as was being done. I felt somewhat relieved that I had been of some use in making the polling booths accessible to the minority community voters. We continued monitoring the situation every hour throughout the day.

However, the election machinery in the valley had been so thoroughly suborned that even when the Election Commission had directed the Doda Returning Officer to stop counting votes, he went ahead and declared the results. What a defiance and what a loyalty to the ruling party!

In 1983 elections Congress won 26 seats. Six of them were Muslims. Three of them were from the valley and three from Jammu. In Pulwama and Anantnag district Congress won 45 per cent votes falsifying the premise that Kashmir valley Muslims voted only for the National Conference. The myth of communal divide was further exploded by the fact that in Jammu, National Conference had secured 29 per cent of the non-Muslim votes.

It is not a question of seats or percentage of votes. The main question is of rigging, of fraud and of manipulation. Our Election Commission used to be a helpless spectator where lower echelons of the election machinery were determined to vitiate the electoral process and perpetrate a fraud upon the electorate. It is now only that T.N. Seshan had given teeth to the Commission. For this he had to muster boundless courage and strategic harnessing of laws of the land.

The remoteness of Jammu and Kashmir had allowed the sentinels of Government to murder democracy with impunity over decades. Whereas the death of one candidate in Meham constituency of Haryana attracted the moral indignation of the nation and state Chief Minister Om Parkash Chautala had to resign, yet in the valley of Kashmir we had allowed several polling stations to count more votes than the number of voters on the rolls! This indifference to election malpractices on a gigantic scale over decades has given birth to gruesome terrorism in post-1987 election era. Shutting our eyes to such grotesque mutilation and travesty of elections and massive corruption at all levels provoked the kashmiris to say : "They were bad leaders who sold us to Delhi and in return Delhi leased out Kashmir to them."

1987 Elections

After having humbled Mrs. Indira Gandhi in 1983, National Conference and its collusive administration thought of worsting Muslim United Front (MUF) with the same brazen methods of rigging. However, Muslim United Front represented a fundamentalist upsurge and its voters could not be denied access to the polling booths. As they had also infiltrated the administrative machinery. They kept a tag on the so-called verbal directions. MUF had openly declared that Qoran and Sunna were the final authority to guide the organization. MUF had been founded as a repercussion to the communal riots which had taken place in Anantnag. Dr. Qazi Nissar Ahmed had decided to bring different Muslim groups with fundamentalist bias at one platform. In May 1986, he succeeded in bringing 14 such outfits to weld together to form Muslim United Front. Some of the more important constituents were Husseni Medical Trust, Muslims Employees Front Islami

Jamait-e-Tulba (which had the blessings of President Zia of Pakistan), Muslim Education Trust, Majlis-e-Tuhaffoz-ul-Islam Sopore, Bandipur and Baramulla and Anjuman-e-Tahafoz Muslims and Ummat-Islamia. This composition shows that MUF took into its fold the whole spectrum of activists, that is, Muslim students, Muslim employees and financial institutions and organisations embodying Islamic precepts. MUF never minced words. Its only purpose was to bring about Islamic rule and not allow Islamic energies to be frittered away in competition or internecine conflicts. It gave a clarion call for the establishment of a fundamentalist polity where religion controls political dispensation. Jamat-e-Tulba, with its umbilical connections with international organisations under its leader Sheikh Tajmul Islam, had denounced Indian policy on Afghanistan and called upon Russia to leave that country.

Thus MUF was a combine of fundamentalist forces in the valley embracing students and youth cadres and had enough financial resources. It was confident of its victory at the hustings. For the poll of March 1987, it had fielded candidates for 55 seats out of the total of 75. They had not reckoned with the rigging, the pliant presiding officers would do on the behest of National Conference which was declared victorious and presenting Muslim United Front the crumbs of success in four constituencies. The polling agents of MUF were mostly young students, and when they saw the brazen rigging during counting, they lost faith in the electoral system itself. They came to believe that the Sheikh Abdullah and his family, who had treated Kashmir as their pocketborough, were the fountain-head of electoral corruption and sell-out of Kashmiris to Delhi. What they saw was nothing but the murder and non-functioning of the electoral process whose sanctity India had been proclaiming from various fora. Thus these young men joined Jammu Kashmir Liberation Front and Hizab-ul-Mujahadin in strength; of eighteen of these polling agents, five joined JKLF, twelve Hizb-ul-Mujahideen and one Islamic Students Federation. Yasin Malik, who was JKLF Area Commander for Srinagar was reported to have been a polling agent of the MUF and Shaukat Ahmed Bakshi, who was injured in an encounter with security forces on April 8, 1991. Abdul Hamid Sheikh, another polling agent, was injured in an encounter in October 1989. People surrounded him and did not allow police to arrest him. They took him first to a private nursing home which refused admission. Then he was taken to the Government Hospital where he was arrested. He had to be released in exchange of Dr. Rubbaiya Mufti, daughter of Sayeed Mufti, the then Union Home Minister. The swap took place on December 13, 1989. He had gone across into Pakistan for organising infiltration of trained militants into Kashmir valley. Another polling agent was Nabi Khan of Pulwama. He was indoctrinated by Jamait-e-Islami. Working as a polling agent on behalf of Muslim United Front, he lost faith in the peaceful transfer of power. He then joined Hizb-ul-Mujahideen. He was arrested by the security forces. Similar is the case of Mohammad Ahmed Sogar, resident of Batmaloo, Srinagar, who worked as polling agent, and after the rigged defeat of Muslim United Front, joined Hizb-ul-Mujahideen. He was arrested in the wake of an encounter. Similar is the case of Sheikh Ahmed Bakshi of Batmaloo who, seeing how the elections were manipulated, left Jamait-e-Islami. He was later arrested by the security forces.

Muzzafar Ahmed of Bandipur and Farooq Ruhmani of Kaloora Bandipur, who were polling agents and belonged to Peoples Conference, joined Hizb-ul-Mujahadeen and went to Pakistan-Occupied Kashmir, for taking care of the training camps for the Kashmiri youth.

Thus the electoral victory which National Conference and Congress claimed for themselves in the elections of March 1987, was nothing but an usurpation of power. This electoral 'victory' proved to be pyrrhic which plunged the sub-continent into a turmoil with both India and Pakistan teetering on the brink of another meaningless war. The rulers had forgotten the fate of Bhutto who by rigging polls in 1977, had invited his own doom through usurption of power by his nominee General Zia-ul-Haq.

9

The Insurrection

It is pertinent to ask as to when the insurrection against India started in the Kashmir valley. If one is not to go by manifestation of physical violence, the answer is simple. The mental separation of Kashmir from India started as early as 1950. It is a pity that India's rulers failed to see the writing on the wall and deluded themselves that they would steer Kashmir into Indian mainstream. On the contrary, with the erosion of Article 370 of Indian Constitution and emergence of Jan Sangh as a political force on Indian horizon (though Jan Sangh had only two members in Lok Sabha at that time), Kashmiris' fertile imagination conjured up the emergence of India as a Hindu Rashtra using Jammu's Hinduism to denigrate Sheikh Mohammed Abdullah's government and wipe out Kashmir's ethnic and religious identity i.e. what is now called Kashmiriat. As a Kashmiri Muslim friend told me bluntly, though not truly, that the Jan Sangh wanted to Hinduise the Kashmir valley. Ever since this type of Kashmir mind-set has led to the physical insurrection and horrendous crimes and loss of countless innocent lives. Kashmir's transformation from a secular to theoretic polity deserves to be examined more closely.

It is fashionable these days to decry vociferously Muslim and Sikh fundamentalism as tearing the fabric of Indian polity. Yet is it not a fact that these minorities had followed and not preceded Hindu renaissance and resurgence in Bengal and fundamentalism in Maharashtra? Were the Hindu Congress leaders themselves not behind this Hindu revivalism or was Congress not the product of Hindu revivalism which went on growing strident and belligerent and aroused fundamentalist urges, which were not buried deep, among Sikh and Muslim minorities to protect their interests and start their own revivalist movements.

Historically, the Hindu revivalist movement, the Rashtriya Swayam Sevak Sangh (RSS), had emerged as a weak militant movement during a wave of Hindu-Muslim riots in the early 1920's after the breakdown of the Lucknow Pact of 1916 between the Indian National Congress and Muslim League. Hindu revivalists were particularly incensed by the widespread communal carnage which occurred on the Malabar coast of south western India during August 1921. "Muslim resentment against the British rule in Malabar area was coupled with anti-Hindu sentiment, and the rioting rose to such proportions that the civil administration was unable to contain the violence in many places. This uprising was accompanied by forced conversion of Hindus—a result of the intensification of Hindu–Muslim tensions between 1921-23. The dormant Hindu Mahasabha, formed in 1915 as a forum for protection of a variety of Hindu interests (e.g. cow protection, Hindi in the Devnagari script, caste reforms etc.), was revitalised" (quoted from Saffron Brigade). Some of the Hindu Congress leaders such as N.C. Kelkar, a senior Congress figure from Bombay province, Dr. B.S. Munje, a Congress leader in the Central Provinces and a firm believer of Hindu revivalism, Pandit Madan Mohan Malviya, a protagonist of Hindu revivalism in the United Provinces, castigated Congress for its apathy and inertia in protecting Hindus from Islamic onslaught. Thus, a national meeting of Hindu leaders was held at Benares in August 1923, to revive Hindu Mahasabha. In his presidential address to the session, Lala Lajpat Rai said : "We cannot afford to be so weak and imbecile as to encourage others to crush us". According to him non-violence would lead to 'laziness', fake contentment, slave mentality and lack of spirit. Thus the weapon Hindu orthodoxy wanted to use was violence. However RSS was the consequence of imposition of Islam in India in the seventh century itself. Islam appeared in India in the form of Arab traders on the Malabar coast during the seventh century A.D. They resorted to forcible conversion of Hindus. However, it was the fanaticism of Mahmud of Ghazni and the inaugaration of Turkish Sultanate in Delhi in 1192 that a sizeable Muslim community arose in India and a Muslim Army of Occupation consisting of Turkish, Persian and Arab adventurers arose which resorted to forcible conversions. Thus Hindu reaction was bound to emerge at some historical stage. Tara Chand writes: "About the rule of the Mughals Aurobindo said, "when the Mughal ruled, he ruled as a soldier and a conqueror, in the pride of his strength, in the confidence of his invincible greatness..."[1] On the question of Hindu-Muslim antagonism. Tara Chand observes: "Gandhiji's desire to secure permanent Hindu-Muslim unity by co-operating with the Muslims in the Khilafat agitation had little chance of fulfilment. The causes of the communal antagonism were deep. Their roots went down to the foundations of social, economic and political organisation of the Indian society and only a transformation of the whole system could remove them but this transformation was obstructed and slowed by the presence of the third party which wielded political power and used it to retard economic and social growth and communal unity"[2]

Muslim League and Congress co-operated only for six years after the conclusion of Lucknow pact of 1916 by which Congress had agreed to a separate Muslim election list. It was the Motilal Nehru report of India's proposed Constitution which eliminated separate electrol rolls that antagonised Muslims who further went on antagonising Hindus and thus a vicious chain of mistrust arose between the two communities which mistrust and fear have continued to bedevil the relations even now between Pakistan and India.

The roots of the Hindu chauvinism lie in the soil of Maharashtra. It is Maharashtra which produced Hindu Mahasabha, RSS and now Shiv Sena. It is Maharashtra which produced Veer Savarkar. Dr. K.B. Hedgewar who fathered RSS; again it was Maharashtra which produced Nathu Ram Godse, the killer of Mahatma Gandhi.

The ideological framework for RSS was formulated by Dr. Keshav Baliram Hedgewar of Nagpur. He had a fairly lucrative medical practice. He gave it up because of his keen interest in history and politics. It is said that he dreamed of emulating the feats of the Maratha warrior king, Shivaji. Hedgewar read Tilak's *Kesari* avidly. Under the tutelage of Dr. Balkrishna

Shivram Munje he had joined the Indian National Congress. At the 1920 Congress Session in Nagpur he organised a volunteer force of about 1200 youths to maintain order at the meeting. He had participated in Gandhiji's non-cooperation movement and was sentenced to one year imprisonment. Hedgewar was a member of the All India Congress Committee and attended the 1928 Congress Session at Calcutta. He had been in correspondence with Moti Lal Nehru. After 1928, Dr. Hedgewar devoted himself exclusively to building the RSS. Later he left Congress when he felt that Congress was no where near achieving Swaraj.

Dr. Munje and Hedgewar thought of organising Hindus on more disciplined lines because of escalating Hindu-Muslim animosity in Nagpur. During this period Hedgewar began to develop the intellectual foundations of the RSS. A major influence on his thinking was a hand written manuscript of Vinayak Damodar Sarvarkar's *Hindutva,* which advanced the thesis that the Hindus were a nation. However, the most important postulate propounded, by Savarkar, was that Hindus had been unable to ward off domination even by small groups of foreigners because of their mind-set which was bereft of killing instinct. Sometimes in 1924-25, he satisfied himself that he had discovered the cause of Hindus' interminable defeats and humiliations. "The fundamental problem was psychological and what was required was an inner transformation to rekindle a sense of national consciousness and social cohesiveness". Once having created a cadre of persons committed to national reconstruction, he believed, there would be little difficulty in sustaining a movement of revitalization, which, of course would include independence as one of its objectives. The first task was to create a disciplined organisation to train the cadres.

Hedgewar launched his new movement of Hindu revitalisation in September 1925, on Dassera day which commemorates the victory of Lord Rama over the demon king Ravana. The first group had no name. The participants were expected to attend an *akhara* (gymnasium) during the week and take political classes on Sundays and Thursdays. Most of these gymansia were established in the precincts of temples of

Maruti. The youth at such gymnasia were told that the exercises performed were a form of worship of the god Maruti (Hanuman). Maruti or Hanuman is one of the most demanding gods in the Hindu pantheon, requiring physical strength and continence from his young devotees. Swami Ramdas (a 17th century Hindu saint) was himself a devotee of Maruti and he had established Maruti monasteries. During the formative years of the RSS, the members took their oath before the saffron coloured RSS flag and pictures of Maruti and Ramdas. It was in 1926 that Hedgewar chose the name and the uniform of the organisation and the members. The Swayamsevaks in uniform started their training in the use of *lathi* i.e. five foot bamboo stick which can be used as a weapon both for defence and attack. Ever since RSS has continued to expand amongst the Hindu youth.

Hedgewar was acclaimed as the first *Sarsangchalak,* and the Guru model of authority came to govern the leadership body of RSS. Having established the organisation during formative years (1925-31), he embarked on an ambitious plan to make RSS a national organization. Hedgewar kept RSS a non-political organisation. Savarkar was trying to turn the Mahasabha into a political party whereas Hedgewar was seeking to insulate the RSS from politics. The Mahasabha established its own paramilitary youth group, the Ram Sena in 1939. Hedgewar died on 21 June, 1940. He was succeeded by M.S. Golwalkar who had impressed Hedgewar with his ascetic and saintly living. Golwalkar had been functioning as the Secretary of Nagpur's main Shakha since 1934. He was a reluctant leader. The reorientation of the RSS under Golwalkar led to revolts in the organisation in the Marathi speaking districts. K.B. Lamaya, Sanghchalak of the province, resigned. A number of Swayamsevaks defected in 1942, and formed the Hindu Rashtra Dal. Nathuram Godse, the founder of this paramilitary force, had the blessings of Savarkar. In the meanwhile, Golwalkar acted with amazing speed to consolidate his position. He created a new position of provincial *pracharak* (organiser) responsible directly to him. He prevailed upon several local Congress leaders to preside over RSS functions which led to a certain amount of cordiality between RSS cadres and the former. They came to help one another on several occasions.

During World War-II RSS was keen to remain on the right side of the British. However, the British banned military drill and use of uniforms by all the non-official organisations in India. RSS complied even without a demur. Golwalkar was anything but a revolutionary and the Home Department in its official report on the RSS activity said in 1943: "It would be difficult to argue that the RSS constitutes an immediate menace to law and order." Commenting on the violence that followed the 1942 Quit India call of the Congress, the Bombay Home Department observed that the Sangh had scrupulously kept itself within the law, and in particular had refrained from taking part in the disturbances which had broken out in August 1942.

The post-war period saw communal carnage on an unprecedented scale as if barbarism itself had seized this land of sages. Mary Doreen Wainwright writes in *Keeping the Peace in India*: "From the middle of 1946 Ex. INA (Indian National Army) men were busy in Bengal and Punjab and in 1947 in helping to train the Congress volunteers. The RSS membership surged in the period 1945-48 particularly in Punjab, Sindh, North West Frontier Province and Delhi. It was a landmark shift from Maharashtra, the original homeland of Hindu fundamentalism - to the North West."

During World War-II, Punjab was governed by a coalition which included Unionists (a cabal of Hindu and Muslim landlords), Akalis, the Congress and Independents. The Unionist Chief Minister, Sir Khizer Hayat Tiwana, was expelled from the Muslim League before the 1946 legislative assembly elections. In the elections itself the Muslim League in a house of 175, emerged as the largest single party. However, it was denied the opportunity to rule by the clobbering up of ramshackle coalition of Unionists (21) and Akalis and Congress. On 24th January, 1947, the coalition government banned the Muslim League para military outfit namely the Muslim League National Guard and also RSS but left the Congress volunteers and the Akalis (who had been collecting arms feverishly and openly untouched. In protest, the Muslim

League launched a struggle to protest the 'injustice' of denying the largest party the 'right' to rule Punjab. The coalition on 28th January, 1947, lifted the earlier ban order of 24th January on Muslim League National Guard and RSS. It had taken just four days for the Muslim League to make the coalition government of Punjab prostrate before its might. The Lahore correspondent for Allahabad's *Leader* wrote on 9th March, 1947:

"When the League forced coalition government to withdraw its ban on the Rashtriya Sewak Sangh and the Muslim National Guard, the Sikhs realised that private armies had come to the province and that it was high time that they had one such army of their own."

Pendral Moon, a British officer serving in Bahawalpur state, observed: "The hooligan Muslim elements in the big cities perceived all too clearly the weakness of the government; the forces of law and order, not too strong in any case, became puzzled and doubtful of what was expected of them."

He further observed that Muslim police in Bahawalpur state were very unreliable protectors of the Sikh and Hindu minorities. In fact, they sometimes participated in the violence and actively so in an attempt to decimate the minorities. Describing the situation in Bahawalpur state, Moon reports: To kill a Sikh had almost become a duty, to kill a Hindu was hardly a crime and to rob them was innocent pleasure."

This inadequacy of law and order forces is commented upon also by Doreen Wainright as follows:

"Vast quantities of unlicensed arms and ammunition were in the possession of unauthorised persons in Bengal and Punjab. The accumulation was on a scale beyond the power of the executive police forces and the provincial security authorities to check."

The RSS had garnered the goodwill of the Hindu community of Punjab, Kashmir, and other north west princely states. The growing popularity and activism of RSS led many to recognise its strength. On 16th September, 1947, during a visit to a Shakha in Delhi, Mahatma Gandhi pleaded with the volunteers not to take upon themselves the duties of maintaining law and order.

In an interview with Walter K. Andersen and Shridar D. Domle at Nagpur on 19 April, 1969, Golwalkar apprised them that the government supplied the RSS with weapons (as it did with other groups) to protect Hindu refugees. What a government indeed!

Mahatma Gandhi was assassinated on Friday, 30th January, 1948, at 5.30 p.m. by Nathuram Vinayak Godse during a prayer meeting at Birla House in New Delhi. This dastardly murder was perpetrated in pursuance of a conspiracy which had been disclosed by Madan Lal Pahwa as early as January 20, 1948. The assassin Godse had also exploded a gun-cotton slab near the back door of Birla House earlier. Notwithstanding the prior signals, no protective arrangements were made for Mahatma Gandhi. After such an abdication of their duties, were the rulers of that time entitled to continue to rule, history would ask one day.

It was the Hindu revivalism which gave rise to Islamic and Sikh fundamentalism in India. In reality the Indian National Congress in 1920 was the offshoot of Hindu renaissance initiated by Madan Mohan Malviya, Lokmanya Tilak, Bankim Chander Chatterji etc. The personality of Mahatma Gandhi animated Congress with Hindu spirit though the organisation kept the facade of secularism and had a number of Muslim stalwarts in their high echelons but Muslims had started drifting away from Congress with the call for establishment of Pakistan by the All India Muslim League who refused to be swayed by the blandishments of Earl Mountbatten and his family.

We are concerned with Kashmiri Muslims' perception of the role of RSS and its political alter ego Jan Sangh of yore. RSS had insulated itself against political ambition and it was an instrument for renaissance of Hindu cultural values. Kashmir was ruled by interested politicians who wanted to prove their secular credentials. It can be said with confidence that till 1950 National Conference was not only the power to be reckoned with in Kashmir but Kashmiri Pandits and Kashmiri Muslims lived in harmony. Wrote the great Kashmiri poet Mehjoor (1882-1952):

"Mosques, temples, churches, shrines and viharas for all these prayer houses, I will make one door

Muslims are like milk and Hindus like sugar

I mix milk and sugar and make nectar."

One of the patron saints of Kashmir, in the 14th century, Lalla Yogeshwari i.e. Supreme Mistress of Yoga when asked why she went about in her nudity, shot back. "Why not", "I see no men about." According to her, he who lacked God-realisation did not deserve the name of "man". Muslims revered her as Lall Ded. Married at the age of 14, Lalla, because of her miserable marriage, had resorted to penances and Yoga for self-realization. She said :

"Having closed the doors and windows of my body's mansion I caught a thief within who was none other than my life breath. Having bound him tightly in the cell of my heart I flayed him there with the whip of Om."

At some other place she said :

"What acid of sorrow have I not drunk? Countless my rounds of birth and death ho! naught but nectar in my cup quaffed by the art of breath."

She came to be called *Lalla Arif* meaning Lalla the mystic, by Muslims.

However, mysticism and legendary Hindu-Muslim harmony of Kashmir are now as dead as dodo.

Ever since 1950s, the pro-Pakistan elements are active in Kashmir valley, rather to be precise in Srinagar (population 7,00,000) downtown and Sopore of Baramulla district in the north. The southern district of Anantnag (earlier Islamabad) generally remained peaceful. However, since 1984, anti-Indian agitations had not been confined to the downtown of Srinagar, which had always been the flash point for eruptions of violence, but started from south of the valley, that is Anantnag, and spread to Srinagar and the northern-most towns and villages of Baramulla district.

What has followed in Kashmir valley after the announcement of manipulated results of the 1987 elections to 75-member legislature of J & K cannot be described by any other word than armed insurrection carried out by the Kashmiri youth with the help of arms, generously supplied by Pakistan. We had gone in detail into the elections of 1987 to understand the anatomy of Kashmiris' insurrection in the previous chapter.

Again, non-governance of National Conference and the Defectors' Rule from July 1984 to February 1986 left law enforcement agencies floundering and the fundamentalist organisations mushroomed all over the valley.

On the 11th February, 1988, Mahaz-e-Azadi and People's League gave a call for closure of business to observe the death anniversary of Maqbol Bhatt of JKLF who had been hung on that day in 1984. On 11th April, 1988, an army jeep was set on fire and the police dealt with the situation ham-handedly, inviting ire. Police, ill trained and poorly led, resorted to firing when they should have employed other methods to control crowds. On 11th June, 1988, the mob snatched two police rifles after throwing one petrol bomb. Now the militant outfits started calling upon business establishments to down the shutters; thus an era of 'civil curfew' on the call of the militants commenced. In the middle of 1988 an attempt was made to burn a temple at Barbur Shah Sethu the Srinagar. The same month late Maulvi Farooq of Awami Action Committee was placed under house arrest by militants and roads were barricaded on 14th June, 1988. On 31st July, 1988, two bomb blasts took place at Central Telegraph office and at Amar Singh Club near T.V. tower.

The year 1989 saw militant activities reaching a new crescendo. On 27th January an attempt was made to set Kripal Maheshwari temple at Fateh Kadal in Srinigar on fire. JKLF gave a call for a bandh on 11th February, 1989, to mark the hanging of Maqbool Bhatt. Bomb blasts became the order of the day; two blasts took place in Trehgam on 11th February, one at Kailashpur in Srinagar on 16th February, 1989; on 27th February, one person died in bomb blast in Kukar bazar in Srinagar and four civilians were seriously injured in bomb blasts at Badshah Chowk, Srinagar. Another bomb exploded at Fateh Kadal on 3rd April, 1989, damaging a car. The same day, militancy took an ominous turn when militants engaged police in exchange of fire, injuring one policeman and two civilians. Arson was added as a new weapon to terrorist arsenal when on 4th April, 1989, they set shops to fire in Hawal and Maisuma Bazar areas, Srinagar. Bomb explosions occurred simultaneously. April 1989, saw the arrest of the father of JKLF activist Shabir Ahmed Shah and his subsequent death in hospital, triggering a new series of bomb explosions killing some and injuring numerous and damaging a large number of vehicles. Exchange of fire between CRPF and militants started first on 13th July (Martyr's day), 1989, at Zaina Kadal which resulted in the death of two CRPF Jawans and eight Jawans and six civilians received serious injuries. The same month militants fired on police at Handwara on 27th, injuring two of them. On 14th August, 1989, Pakistan Independence Day was celebrated all over the valley and crackers exploded in celebration. CRPF posts were subjected to hand grenade attacks. On 23rd August, 1989, eight National Conference (Farooq) and three Congress (I) leaders resigned from their organisations in compliance with the JKLF call. On 13th September, 1989, the residence of DIG Srinagar Range (Mr. A.M. Wataloo) was attacked, leading to injury to one CRPF Constable and death of one militant Aizaz Ahmed. On 14th September, Vice President of BJP was killed. In protest over the arrest of Shabir Ahmed Shah on 28th September, 1989, extremists fired on CRPF next day and when CRPF retaliated in Srinagar and Anantnag, two civilians died and a number of others were injured.

On 4th October 1989, militants opened a new chapter of killing police officers and their families. At Bankura in Baramulla, they entered the house of ASI Bashir Ahmed of JK police and killed his wife and daughter while injuring the ASI and his son. Bombs continued to explode throughout the month of October. Cross firing between militants and CRPF on 24th October, 1989, led to injury to two CRPF personnel and several civilians. On 31st October rumours spread that Abdul Hamid Sheikh, a JKLF activist, had been arrested. In retaliation, police personnel were fired upon. Arson in banks and schools as well the bursting of bombs continued. A number of CID personnel were killed.

During November 1989, bombs continued to burst. Due to an explosion Gandhi College Srinagar was damaged on 11th November and the same day, National Conference (F) Office at Anantnag was gutted. In protest against Jawahar Lal Nehru centenary, an effigy of Pt. Nehru was burnt on 14th November, 1989. On 18th November, a bomb exploded in LIC building, in Srinagar and at Anantnag in the office of Tehsildar. Militants opened fire in Chhota Bazar, Khanyar, Fateh Kadal, etc.

It is not our purpose to list each terrorist act or outrage. What we have pointed out is that Kashmir Government apparatus was no match to the militant challenge which had assumed the proportions of insurgency. No coherent strategy was evolved either at Delhi or by the Kashmir Government to meet the most formidable challenge of fundamentalist terrorism. In fact, there was complacency because Kashmiri ethos was misread as one of docility. Then there was misplaced euphoric belief that if India could go to the rescue of Sri Lanka and Maldives it would snuff out the guerrilla threat in the valley in a jiffy; let the general elections be over in November 1989. Human beings delude themselves in endless ways. The Congress government had ignored the warnings sent by Governor Jagmohan in the summer of 1989. The new National Front Government at New Delhi had yet to find its ground when Dr. Rubaiya Sayeed, the medico daughter of Mr. Mufti Mohd. Sayeed, Union Home Minister, was kidnapped by JKLF militants from Nowgaon near Srinagar on 8th December, 1989. This kidnapping shook Indian government out of its self–imposed torpor. The whole country, nay the world, woke up to the insurrection in the valley. The agony of the Mufti family came to be shared by the whole country. She was released by the JKLF militants in exchange for release and safe conduct of Abdul Hamid Sheikh, Javed Ahmed Zoragar, Altaf Ahmed Bhatt, Noor Mohammad Kulwal of Srinagar and a Pak agent Sher Mohammad Khan, on the afternoon of December 13, 1989. The swap was a victory for the militants. Bad as it was for the morale of the governmental agencies, the jubilation in JKLF camp was inhumane and barbarous. JKLF supporters, including women and children, came on to the streets, raising pro Pakistan slogans. Banners of JKLF, Islamic Students League and Pakistan were raised atop houses and on street light poles. Militants went on a rampage, ransacking the office of the leading local daily *Aftab* and setting fire to a car and scooters. Cracker bursting has been the imperative ritual for all such celebrations. This was indulged in to their hearts content. People vied with each other in demonstrating their sense of 'triumph' over Delhi.

Evidently after such an outrage no government could hide itself behind lethargic inactivity which had held the Kashmiri government in its thrall for the last two years. Even then no coherent policy was evolved to deal with this armed insurrection, financed and armed from across the border, except putting the entire Kashmir valley under indefinite curfew. In place of going for the guilty, the entire population was subjected to collective punishment. Such measures never succeed. They invite a backlash instead.

Militants took to selective assassinations to drive fear and demonstrate that moderation had no place in Kashmir. On 25th January, 1990, four Air Force personnel were killed at Rawalpara in Srinagar. On 13th February, 1990, Lassa Kaul, Director, Doordarshan, was shot dead while returning home from the office. CRPF patrol was ambushed on 30th March, injuring seven jawans. Former Kashmir Legislator, Mir Mustafa, was kidnapped and his dead body was discovered on 25th March, 1990. He was supposed to have negotiated the release of Dr. Rubaiya Sayeed. The note on his corpse said that the former MLA was 'tried by the Hizbul Mujahideen and was found guilty of being an agent of Intelligence Bureau'.

The exodus of Kashmiri Pandits, who had lived and shared life with Kashmiri Muslims for centuries, became inevitable. Their mohallas looked desolate with homes padlocked and they came in droves to Jammu and Delhi to live under insufferable conditions. Kashmiriyat was dead. More than 90,000 Kashmiri Pandits had to leave their ancestral homes.

There has been tremendous expansion of para-military forces in the last five years. This expansion and their constant deployment resulted in dilution and not unoften, neglect of their training. Thus the fine discipline of these forces leaves much to be desired. Simply because a jawan has an automatic weapon and is fired upon, he does not acquire any right to indulge in indiscriminate firing. He is required to fire only on a 'target' that is the one who has attacked him. CRPF and BSF armed personnel are excellent human material but without periodical re-training they cannot deliver results. Again, they can give superb results if they are led by their officers. In the absence of training and proper leadership, they tend to resort to indiscriminate firing if they come under attack. Such aimless and panic firing had taken place when small pickets were located in areas, inhabited by sympathisers of the terrorists and they came under attack. Finding themselves in a sea of a people whom they perceived to be hostile, they resorted to such firing. On March 29, 1990, CRPF posts at Chhatable, Shamswar, Khanyar, Fateh Kadal and Barbarshah came under fire from militants, killing two of their jawans and injuring five. In retaliation 15 civilians succumbed to the fire opened by CRPF personnel on fleeing militants. CRPF pickets, though suffering casualties, should have fired only on militants and not on civilians. When men are dispersed on isolated posts without proper leadership, they seem to lose their heads.

When Mir Waiz Maulvi Farooq was shot dead at his Nagin lake residence on 21st May, 1990, authorities should have anticipated a mass upsurge. They should have removed penny pickets on the route of funeral procession; nothing of the sort was done. Result was that when those pickets came under attack by the mourners, they opened fire on the funeral procession allegedly killing 57 persons. It again shows lack of leadership. It gratuitously gave an opportunity to the United States to lecture India on the need for restraint and invited ire of the Organisation of Islamic Conference in Jeddah. The result was that Governor Jagmohan had to 'resign' on 25th May, 1990, and the campaign against terrorism suffered a setback.

Changing Governors can prove helpful if they are allowed to formulate and implement a long term strategy. If they are to be changed like dirty liner as had been happening in Punjab, where the tenure of the governors, except for Shri S.S. Ray, had been less than one year, such a change can provide no remedy. A governor would succeed only after laying broad parameters for him, and Central government gives him autonomy to deal with the situation on the spot and provide him help by way of good administrative inputs and well trained and well led police or para-military forces. In Kashmir where civil administration remains at standstill, there is need for re-training and re-locating security forces, and it must be insisted that they are led by officers. If with each major incident or failure the Governor is changed, the change by itself cannot right the neglect of years since a Governor has no magic wand to banish poor motivation of hundreds of officers under him. For a programme to be effective, even for a correct formulation of policy and configuration of alternative approaches, a Governor requires time. Before he settles down, magical results are expected from him. Is it fair?

Jagmohan has called for probe by a panel of two or more judges of the Supreme Court into all aspects of Kashmir militancy—that is, how the militancy had been brought about and which were the forces, personalities and circumstances that brought about the militancy. Jagmohan is an able administrator and he did retrieve the situation, in his four and a half months rule in J&K from a disaster. Evidently his aim was to pin down responsibility on the Chief Minister of J&K. It is unfortunate that both Jagmohan and Dr. Abdullah entertained profound hostility towards each other.

Political leadership cannot go into the nuts and bolts of operations. Neither is it expected to do so. Operations are the exclusive concern of the officer on the spot. However, it must make its policy known to the men who have to execute it. In an interview with Inderjit Badhwar and Prabhu Chawla of *India Today* Prime Minister V.P. Singh said that his policy on Kashmir was 'the seccessionist movement cannot and will not be allowed to succeed. There will be continuous pressure to stop infiltration from both sides. However, it must be sensitive to the human rights of Kashmiris. Third, we must keep our political antenna and develop contacts with the people. Success in any one area helps success in another and we must be sensitive to the human rights'. It is an excellent formulation of policy. However, it is pertinent to ask if the Prime Minister, at any stage, or his representatives, had conveyed to Mr. Jagmohan his concern for human rights. Again is it not a fallacy to say that 'success in any one area helps success in another.' An objective analysis of the situation would show that Mr. Jagmohan had achieved tangible success against secessionists yet his record on human rights side was fautly. Thus success in one area would not by itself lead to success in other areas.

Now what happened was that in his concern for human rights Girish Chander Saxena the successor to Jagmohan, allowed mass demonstrations to take place on 31st May, and on 1st June, 1990. With regard to Fateh prayer of late Maulvi Farooq and installation of Mir Waiz Umer Farooq respectively, the demonstrators raised secessionist slogans. Of course, security forces did not open fire, there was no casualty but secessionism was publicly aired. In reality, in fighting terrorism and secessionism, keeping a proper balance between effective firmness and control on one hand and respecting human rights on the other requires great supervisory skills. To achieve such a balance, we require specialist forces. Every country, faced with the threat of terrorism, has them. The UK has Special Air Services (SAS) and the USA has Delta Force. We created National Security Guards (NSG) in 1985 but its strength has been frittered away in providing personal security guards to the VVIPs. A very insignificant portion of NSG - just a token platoon - was allotted to Kashmir; however sophisticated their equipment, such a small contingent in a city like Srinagar with its labyrinthine maze of lanes and byelanes on the right bank of Jhelum can have no successful impact. During operation Black Thunder in May 1988, NSG had done an excellent job when it had flushed out terrorists from Golden Temple at Amritsar by accurate fire without causing any casualties. Why did not the security forces in J&K show similar combination of firmness and restraint? We have already given the reasons.

India faced a religious crusade in Kashmir. On 21st May, 1990, people did not allow the police to take over the dead body of Mir Waiz Maulvi Farooq. During his funeral procession what did the mourners shout: "*Moulvi Ka Kaya*

Irshad? Al Jehad, Al Jehad' (What did the Moulana call for? Holy War, Holy War). Exactly what India faced was a holy war, a religious war, nothing less and nothing more. India may wax eloquent on economic and political grievances but at the base lies this religious frenzy. Militants are a ruthless arm of the religious crusade. Inter-Services Intelligence of Pakistan under Gen. Gul Hamid had won the ideological war in Kashmir. It had also succeeded in pouring thousands of Kalaskinovs and inexhaustible munition for guerilla warfare; hundreds of crores of rupees had been spent to bring the insurgency to the present state. Commentators have rightly called it a "proxy war" by Pakistan. In 1965 `irregular war' by Pak army guerrillas in civil clothes was met by counter strategy of escalating Indian response by taking the war into Pakistan. This time Bhartiya Janta Party held a rally on Boat Club, in New Delhi on 2nd May, 1990, with the call "Save Kashmir, Save India" and called for destroying training camps for Kashmiri militants in Pakistan Occupied Kashmir. This was the culmination of war hysteria which had been vented from various fora since mid April. Such jingoistic slogans are not going to solve Kashmir imbroglio, when the war is being abjured by most of the world. War mongering is not going to garner India world sympathy. Pakistan has had a long perspective when it started abetting militancy in Punjab and later in Kashmir. She wanted India to be permanently mired in low-intensity war of attrition. Probably aiding Sikh militancy in Punjab was a diversionary tactic of Pakistani's Inter Services Intelligence while they were busy penetrating the police and other services' apparatus in Kashmir and fundamentalising the Kashmiri Muslims. An open war this time cannot solve this problem of militancy. This undeclared war, waged by Pakistan in Punjab and Kashmir, can be defeated only if India defeats the militants without harming the innocent.

Let us study the case of the arrest of Shabir Ahmed Shah, the 37 year old secessionist from Anantnag. He was arrested on 28th September, 1989. Zafar Meraj wrote in *India Today* of 31st October, 1989, that as the news of his arrest spread, violence broke out throughout the valley and police opened fire indiscriminately at various places. Zafar Meraj berated Central and State Govvernment as follows:

"And both the State and the Central Governments have themselves to blame for if a secessionist like Shah has become something of a hero, it is because of complete dis-illusionment with the mainstream leaders, the dismal performance of the State Government, the Centre's repeated bungling on the Kashmir issue, and Chief Minister Farooq Abdullah's obvious ineptitude".

Similarly when Hamid Sheikh of JKLF was arrested on 30th October, 1989, when he had tried to snatch a policemen's rifle and got injured, the militant outfit calling itself Afghan Tigers plunged Anantnag in a bloody riot.

On 5th April, 1990, Kashmiri militants kidnapped Professor Mashir-ul-Haq. Vice-Chancellor, Kashmir University, while he was on his way to a mosque to offer prayers. The same day H.M.T. manager H.L. Khera was also kidnapped and militants demanded release of three leading Kashmiri militants - Ghulam Nabi Butt, the brother of executed Maqbool Butt, Issac Ahmed and Mohd. Altaf Wani—by 3 p.m. on April 9, else the kidnapped were to be assassinated. The same day, JKLF announced its re-organisation Iqbal Gandroo was appointed military adviser to JKLF. On April 9, Mr. Ammanullah Khan, Chairman of the Jammu and Kashmir Liberation Front, announced in New York that Mashir-ul-Haq and H.M.T. Manager H.L. Khera with two others had been executed. India maintains that Mr. Ammanullah Khan's statement was not factually correct as no killing had taken place by that day and this statement acted as a signal or directive to JKLF militants in Kashmir to execute those kidnapped as bullet ridden bodies of the Vice-chancellor Professor Mushir-ul-Haq and his personal assistant Mr. Abdul Ghani were found at Badshahi Bagh on the airport road on the night of 10 April. The dead body of Mr. H.L. Khera, General Manager of the H.M.T., was discovered the same night from Batmaloo area of Srinagar. On 29th April, 1990, B.S.F. was successful in arresting Shaukat Zorgar from Jamia Masjid area. From disclosure made it transpired that Shaukat Zargar had received armed training in Pakistan and the conspiracy was hatched by one Hilal Beg.

A Highly Fortified Hideout of the Militants

It may be recalled that on 25th January, 1990, four Air Force personnel were killed in Rawalpura Chowk, Srinagar. From the disclosures made by the accused in other cases, it transpired that Yasin Malik, Javed Nalfa, Mushtaq Ahmed Lose, Javed Zarger and Nanaji were responsible for these killings. They used a car and motorcycle and sprayed bullets on the Air Force personnel who were standing in three separate groups.

Disclosures made by JKLF militants also led to the working out of the murder of Lassa Kaul, Director, Srinagar Doordarshan, on 13th February, 1990. It came out that he was killed by Shoukat Bakshi and Arif Mohammad, JKLF militants.

Thus all the major crimes, perpetrated by JKLF, have been worked out. Till mid-April, 1990, JKLF was boasting of appointing area commanders for six districts of the valley and the seventh one for Muslim majority district of Doda in Jammu. But by the end of April their highly propagandised organisation had collapsed with the arrest of all their top-notch leaders. Their boast of a sustained guerilla warfare had come to nought that is why Ammanullah Khan had to say that they would henceforth be attacking Indian Army posts on Actual Line of Control - this is the same Ammanullah of Peshawar who in 1966 had sent Maqbool Butt into Kashmir telling him that he, Ammanullah, would be attacking Indian posts on CFL - but he had done nothing of the sort. Having served in the army he has some knowledge of armed forces organisation but otherwise he has been maintaining his leadership by being glib and fattening on Pakistan money. Hizb-ul-Mujahideen was still a force to be reckoned with. Allah Tigers, Zia Missionary and Green Victory groups were miniscule and did not deserve any attention. Hizb-ul-Mujahideen had a large number of activists. Its cadre had 700 trained activists and nearly 500 were said to be under training in Pakistan. Hisbe-Islami is another organisation which was to be watched. In terms of trained manpower it is second to Hizb-ul-Mujahjideen. Hizb-ul-Mujahideen has been ruthless towards what it calls moderates and collaborators unlike JKLF who in the beginning took to dacoities in 1960s and 1970s and later concentrated on kidnappings for release of follow militants on the pattern of Red Brigade of Italy. Hizb-ul-Mujahideen had concentrated on creating terror by the gruesomeness of its acts. It claimed that it had "tried Mir Mustafa, MLA, and found him guilty of being an agent of Intelligence Bureau and hence had executed him".

The daily count of killings in the valley in the last three months of 1990 had been five to six a day.

Another pertinent subject of inquiry is when Ms. Benazir Bhutto replaced Lt. General Hamid Gul by Shams-ur-Rehman Kallu (Retired) as head of Inter Services Intelligence, what role did the latter play? After the death of President Zia-ul-Haq in August 1988 in the air accident, General Hamid Gul had evidently started pouring arms and money from Pakistan to destabilise Kashmir. Militants had already been armed and motivators and guides were in place when Shamas-ur-Rehman Kallu took over. Writes Shekhar Gupta - "Given the Jamait's links with the Kashmiri militants, on one side and the I.S.I. on the other, the nexus is transparent". (*India Today, May* 31, 1990). Exactly I.S.I. used Jamait-e-Islami in Kashmir to subvert the Kashmiri youth and convert them into militants. Camps for Kashmiri Mujahideen were mentioned in shrieking posters seen all over Pakistan. Thus Ms. Benazir Bhutto was deliberately dissembling when she sweet-talked to Indians that she would not use Sikh card; she was aware that Islamic card in Kashmir would soon be ready to be used. The Indian rulers thus proved themselves to be gullible. Was it failure of intelligence? Or did Indians, dreaming the pipe-dream of being dominant regional power, ignore Islamised whiphand in Kashmir as minor incident? Whatever the cause the ruling elite in New Delhi had proved themselves to be amateurish. Once way back in 1983, I had a brief discussion with the late Prime Minister, Smt. Indira Gandhi, on the so-called "peace offensive" launched by President Zia-ul-Haq. I had submitted that in the turbulent history of Pakistan President Zia, though a soldier, had learnt that only sweet treacle will catch the fly. She said India had to be more beware of such sweet, but hollow, talk than threats and bluster. Unfortunately, such insight was not inherited by the subsequent regime which allowed itself to be beguiled by sweet and supplicatory mouthings of the Benazir Bhutto. Then, she talked fire and thunder because she had three to four thousand Kashmiri youth trained in her training camps. She used to fulminate against Zia-ul-Haq but she had eagerly used his terror-machine built by Inter Services Intelligence without any sense of compunction to prove that she was a leader in her own right. She had outdone President Zia-ul-Haq as she had started talking of "Ummah's" support for Kashmir. On her return after victorious tour of Turkey, Syria, Libya, etc., she said:

"Pakistan enjoys the backing of the Ummah in its efforts at economic, social, scientific and technological development" - she told her audience 'Goli chalao, Jehad Jagao'). What a jingoistic Prime Minister? The Muslim leaders believed that as a champion of Islamic issues, Pakistan must maintain its forward march in order to play an increasingly important role in the comity of Islamic countries.

Is she not using the same rhetoric as was used by President Zia? Even during her campaign in Azad Kashmir for elections of 21st May, 1990, she called upon "Azad Kashmirs" to rise for Jehad. She wanted to out pace the rightist parties. However, she was more successful in duping Indian government than President Zia whose subtlety was seen as dangerous. *Times of India* of 10th June, 1990, carried the report of an article in the *United States News and World Report* to the effect that Pakistan got into "the Kashmir act" about two years ago under the late President, General Zia-ul-Haq, but "strangely the then Prime Minister Mr. Rajiv Gandhi did not protest such meddling at either of his two subsequent summits with Ms. Benazir Bhutto. The paper called 1987 elections under Dr. Farooq Abdullah "blatantly rigged, even by debased Kashmiri standards." It further said that Pakistan got into the Kashmir act at about this time. As part of the late President's grand design for a greater Pakistan, he is reported to have diverted some guns and money intended for Afghanistan Mujahideen to help young Kashmiri rebels.

While Indians were euphorically congratulating themselves on Siachin success to the discomfiture of President Zia-ul-Haq, that master of state craft after first planting the fundamentalism in Kashmir through Jamait-e-Islami had struck more grievously by preparing the youth for insurrectionary uprising. The credit for Pakistani success goes to the ate President Zia-ul-Haq. The only credit which Ms. Benazir Bhutto may claim is that by her baby-talk she had made Indian Prime Minister lower down his guard. Now by her talk of "Jehad" and right of "self-determination", she wanted to prove she was the torch bearer of the legacy of her late father. It is not without state patronage that walls of Rawalpindi and Islamabad were pasted with lurid posters calling for Jehad in Kashmir.

Thus the present situation is not only due to neglect of development activity in Kashmir valley - except for H.M.T. factory which came into existence in early 1970s - there has been no industry worth the name in the valley. All the industries have gone to Jammu region. To this monumental neglect of the valley be added the unforgivable neglect of vigilance and security in the face of unmistakable rise of fundamentalism. A volatile place like Kashmir could not, and even ought not be ruled by inept club of buddies come on a picnic.

Now that India had a problem of prodigious proportion at her hands due to her own neglect, it sought solution through rhetoric of war, an escalation of confrontation as happened in 1947 and 1965. The situation in 1993 was radically different from that in 1947 and 1965; in those days' invasion physical infiltration had taken place and Indian counter-strategy of escalation was justified and had proved successful. But in 1993 India had a totally different situation when the population under the spell of militant religion and rebellious youth within the vale had created situation of insurgency. Not war but a mix of steps to disarm and generous help to generate growth-oriented economy are the first imperatives. The government must show its capacity to meet the challenge by being politically innovative and yet incorruptible and accommodative towards aspirations for growth and autonomy of sub-nationalist groups

When militancy reached a new zenith in October–November 1989, Kashmir's life was at the mercy of gun wielding youth. Sanjeev Miglani wrote in the *Statesman* dated November 7, 1989:

"If the law and order machinery has collapsed, it is because that the political masters are dead. There is no one to tell the officers what to do." Thanks to Dr. Farooq Abdullah who must be abroad whenever a crisis descends on the State.

In effect north of Banihal the writ of the government never ran towards the end of 1989. The Director General of Police, Mr. Ghulam Jilani Pandit, found himself a helpless spectator to the collapse of law and order machinery.

The story of the rise of militancy in Kashmir is one of the relentless prevarication and neglect by State and Central Governments in 1989.

Commentators and political leaders bewail the mushrooming of a large number of terrorist outfits in Kashmir. If we are to understand the working of Inter Services Intelligence of Pakistan and the fervour of youth the matter is simple. The oldest terrorist organisation in the valley is Jammu Kashmir Liberation Front (JKLF) under Amanullah. Both Pakistan and Jamait-e-Islami were unhappy with JKLF which avowedly stands for freedom of this state and had called upon both India and Pakistan to vacate J&K. Therefore, when MUF lost elections in 1987, Jamait-e-Islami formed Hizb-ul-Mujahideen that is party (Hizab means party) of crusaders. The name linked the outfit to Iran inspired terrorist outfits in Lebanon and Pakistan's protege in Afghanistan. ISI formed a number of such outfits, namely, Hizb-ul-Islam, Al Umar, Muslim Jan Baz Force, Ikhwan-ul Musalmeen, etc., so that if Indian authorities negotiated peace with one or two organisations, the host of other outfits will not only denounce these negotiations but also continue with the perpetration of their wanton destruction and pillage so that peace was never restored, negotiations or no negotiations. This was done in Punjab and now had been repeated in Kashmir.

The government has shown a woeful neglect in evolving a policy on the abducted/kidnapped individuals, whether it was kidnapping of advocate Shabnam, daughter of Abdul Gani Lone of People's Conference, though she was released within 24 hours due to feeling of outrage expressed by the people of the valley, or the abduction of Mrs. Nahida Imtiaz, a lecturer in the Institute of Management and Public Administration (IMPA) and daughter of National Conference MP Saifuddin Soz (now a Minister of Forests and Environment at New Delhi) by Kashmir Students Liberation Front on 27th February, 1991, from Chhanpura locality of Srinagar and demanding release of five militants. After remaining in the custody of women wing of KSLF for 10 days, she was released in exchange of JKLF militant Mustaq Mohammad Khan. *The Times of India* in its leading article commented as follows on March 12, 1991.

"...... Irrespective of whether only Mustaq Mohammad Khan, a leading KSLF militant, was released as the government maintains, or another four militants were also freed, the kidnapping has once again highlighted the total absence of coherent government policy in dealing with such situations. The release of the KSLF militants has probably conveyed an impression to the subversives that weak government will inevitably capitulate to demands of kidnappers, and the abduction of a family member of a prominent public figure may be the easiest way to secure the release of imprisoned comrades."

The government once again showed its double standards when K. Doraiswamy, an executive of Indian Oil Corporation, allowed himself to be abducted by militants of Ikhwan-ul-Muslimeen. It came under pressure from a lobby and entered into a deal with the abductors whereas it had shown no compunction when it had earlier allowed Mushir-ul-Haq, V.C. Kashmir University, and his Secretary Abdul Gani as well as L.N. Khera, General Manager of HMT to be killed. The freedom of K. Doraiswamy was secured when the government released the killer of Vice Chancellor and General Manager Khera, Javed Ahmed Shalla, in a swap deal. It is no secret that Pakistan was keen on the release of Shalla, and J&K Government, and the Central Government played the role of accomplice of notorious Inter Services Intelligence of Pakistan in releasing this killer. There is no need to go into details of other kidnappings such as of Khemlata Wakhloo, a Minister of State in Dr. Farooq Abdullah's cabinet who had deserted her leader to join the defectors led by G.M. Shah, and her husband, and Tassadaq Ahmed Deva, the brother-in-law- of

Union Minister for Parliamentary Affairs, Ghulam Nabi Azad, because they only demonstrate the way of militants and the need of precise operations such as launched to free Wakhloos. However, militants regained ground, lost in successful freeing of Wakhloos by security forces by kidnapping brother of J&K Adviser Hamidullah.

The most ominous aspect of insurgency in the valley had been that the government machinery was with insurgents. The senior IAS officers made public statements not for just denouncing security forces - this was done more to gain sympathy of their Muslim employees and colleagues - in violation of their service conditions, but that the successful strike by more than one hundred thousand employees, to be precise 1.37 lakh employees, from September to November 1990 was led to success by senior officers of various government owned corporations and Srinagar Municipality and Jammu & Kashmir Bank, etc. They not only secured acceptance of their demands but also had their Chief Secretary R.K. Takkar transferred out of J&K. What governments indeed governed Delhi and Srinagar!

Kidnappings, abductions and inter-gang liquidations continued in 1993. Custodial deaths provoked bandhs and hartals. Alienation of people proceeded. When Major Amanullah Khan of JKLF was arrested in Belgium, hopes were raised that he might be repatriated to India as the latter had apprised Belgium of the charges pending against Amanullah. However, Belgium just deported him to Pakistan.

Militancy continued to rise surprisingly among women. Both Dukhtran Milat and Muslim Khwatooon Mahaz donned off their social aims and lent their unqualified support to militants. In addition, Hizb-ul-Mujahiddin tried to develop their own women wings, imparting arms training to them.

The year 1993 also saw important Kashmiri Muslim personalities coming on one platform called "Hurriyat" i.e. "All Parties Hurriyat Conference." The APHC came into prominence when on 15 October 1993, a number of militants took shelter in the Hazratbal shrine. The authorities tried to starve them out. The Pakistan Government and the Hurriyat leaders mounted a propaganda offensive asking for the lifting of the siege of the militants in the shrine by the Indian security forces. The J&K High Court ruled that the militants holed up in this shrine were entitled to food. Thus sumptuous meals were served to these armed desperados. This order of the High Court was modified by the Supreme Court of India. After 33 days the militants "surrendered" to the Kashmir authorities. Evidently the unstated terms of the agreement were that the militants would surrender their arms and in return the authorities would not oppose their applications for bail and their return to Pakistan. Though the arrests were made under Terrorist and Disruptive Activities Act (TADA) which does not provide for the bailing out of the accused, the militants were allowed to be bailed out and proceed unharmed to their sanctuary in Pakistan.

India Today, of November 15, 1993, described "Hazrat Bal Drama" as "Operation Blunder" by recalling the indecision and rivalries bedevilling the Government operations.

1995 saw the Governor being bombed during Republic Day Parade at Jammu on 26th January, 1995. The Governor, General (Retd.) V.K.V. Rao, had a miraculous escape but eight of the security men died during the bomb blasts close to the saluting dais.

Charrar-e-Sharif is a sleepy town on Srinagar-Yusmarg road. However, the shrine of Sheikh Nuruddin Noorani, the patron saint of Kashmir, is located here. Towards the close of January 1995, a platoon of militants, which included some foreign guest mercenaries, led by one Major Mast Gul, sneaked into the sanctuary of the Dargah. They laid mines inside and outside the shrine. Army laid seige of the town and tried unsuccessfully to deny food and water to the militants holed up in the shrine. The seige, extended over several weeks, failed to break the morale of the militants. In the first week of May, heavy exchange of fire took place and the boom of guns reverberated throughout the town. As a result of this protracted exchange of fire, disaster struck when the wild flames enveloped the town, destroying a major part of the town, rendering 200 families homeless. On May 11, the shrine was burnt and in the fiery turmoil Mast Gul along, with a number of militants, dodged the security forces and reached Srinagar, where he held a Press Conference in which he ridiculed the seige by the army and claimed that he was an invincible guerilla who could break out through any siege. He also appeared on Pak Television to mock the Indian Army. .The suffering of the people of the town was so acute that when the J&K Congress President, Gulam Rasool Kar, visited the town, he was assaulted and received grievous injuries. Army claimed that 20 militants had died in the exchange of fire and the army had suffered two casualties.

1995 saw the emergence of a new militant organisation called Al Faran specialising in the abduction of foreign tourists. On July 5, 1995, they abducted five foreign tourists. On July 11, they abducted another Norwegian tourist. All the abducted tourists were from the West, Europe and USA. The Norweigian, Hans Christian Ostro, was killed by the Al Faran terrorists and his body was discovered at Anantanag.... His head had been severed. One American hostage managed to escape.

Paul Wells (23) of London, Keith Mangen (33) of Middlesex Borough, England, Donald Hutchings (42) of Spokane in Washington and a German Dirk Haracted (26) still remain in their custody. The Organisation of Islamic Countries appealed to Al Faran to release these tourists but Al Faran remained silent to this appeal. Now Al Faran has stated that these four tourists were killed in an encounter with Indian forces on 4 Dec., 1995, at Dabran in Anantnag district. On the other hand, the Indian Army maintains that though an encounter did take place that day, yet no foreign tourist was killed. Only Abdul Hamid, leader of Al Faran, with his four militant companions was killed. In subsequent statements, Al Faran has alleged that the four foreign tourists are no more with them but with the Indian Army. The situation would have been farcical but for the fact that four human lives are involved.

The present lull in the terrorist campaign in Kashmir is not due to political reasons but due to operational constraints. The main being that Kashmiri youth is, for the present at least, disillusioned with Pakistani exploitative tactics. Let us not forget that the Pakistani ISI had yet an inexhaustible arsenal at their disposal. According to a report in the *Indian Express* of

TRG CAMPS OF JKLF ACTIVISTS AS IN EARLY 1990s IN PAK/POK

MILITANT CAMPS IN PAK AREA

1. Sinkari
2. Atlok
3. Abbotabad
4. Jhari Camp near Islamabad
5. Hospital Camp, Jhari
6. Rawalpindi
7. Sialkot
8. Sargoda
9. Gujran wala
10. Gulbarg near Lahore
11. Bandar Road Karachi
12. Peshawar
13. Murree
14. Jobri
15. Chandn Chowk (Rawalpindi)
16. Ojeri Camp
17. Thang
18. Lahore
19. Plamchi
20. Saidagali
21. Alipur Chatha
22. Jhelum
23. Wahshak
24. Koil
25. Kakul
26. Sheikhpura

LEGEND

Militant Camps in POK - 30
Militant Camps in PAK - 26

Total - 56 Camps

MILITANT CAMPS IN POK AREA

1. Kamri
2. Kel
3. Makri
4. Shan Kot Line (Muzaffarabad)
5. Lipa Valley
6. Chinari
7. Aliabad
8. Rawala Kot
9. Hollard Jungle Area (Kotli)
10. Mirpur City
11. Bhimbar
12. Mansor Camp
13. Gilgit
14. Bagh
15. Bhatapore
16. Gojra Fort
17. Madina Market
18. Puni Tander
19. Jari Khas
20. Arza
21. Lahabadpur
22. Nandgali Bagh
23. Leswa
24. Mang Bajri
25. Kotli
26. Siot
27. Dhudnial
28. Palandari
29. Athmugam
30. Hajra

October 26, 1997, World Watch Institute estimated that the Pakistan ISI, the conduit for US arms supplies to fight the then Soviet forces in Afghanistan, had siphoned off three million Kalashnikov rifles and other arms. Only thirty to forty percent arms, supplied to Pakistan ISI, had reached the Mujahidin in Afghanistan; the rest were either supplied to Kashmiri militants and others worth US $ six to nine billions were resold by the ISI. The sale money collected was chanelled into the drug trade to mint more money for the fulfilment of their plans in Pakistan, Kashmir, Afghanistan, and India. Some of the training camps in Pakistan and POK are shown in the map opposite.

The present status of the insurrection and the likely scenarios of militant engagements with Indian security forces are discussed appropriately in the last chapter of the book.

REFERENCES

1. Tara Chand: History of the Freedom Movement in India. vol.III. Publications Division. Page 162

2. Ibid Page 428

10

Al Jehad - The Holy War

The present day Kashmiri youth was not content with mere Islamic resurgence. He had come to perceive himself as a crusader—a holy warrior. He is a fundamentalist who wants to throw off non-Muslim oppressors' yoke. We have to remember that Islam was imported into Kashmir from Iran and what happens in Iran and Afghanistan and Pakistan, profoundly affects Kashmiri youth. We have, therefore, to go through the happenings in Iran and Pakistan in detail.

Does Iran's Constitution Article 10 not provide that "All Muslims are one nation"? On the doctrinaire, level Islamic scholars are divided if Qoran forbids formation of nation-states or not? Ayotullah Khomeini appeared on Iranian political horizon in 1963, but as early as 1940 in Kashf-al Asrar he had not only preached Rule by Islamic clerics but also Islamic Brotherhood. His second book *Hukumat-e-Islami*, published in 1971 from Najaf in Iraq, gave Khomeini's ideas on Islamic Rule all the contours. Islam postulates that sovereign power vests not in the people but in God; this concept negates the modern concept of democracy. It also projects that the people can be guided only by clerics who are masters of Shariat (Jurisprudence). This is what is sought to be done in Pakistan through Shariat Act, passed by the Pak Parliament. In Iran it has already been demonstrated that Islamic clergy can run a government. Thus Muslim Kashmiri youth have started worshipping the photographs of Imam Khomeni. So the Kashmiri perceived himself to be a participant in the Islamic Holy War which had been continuing all over the world, since

1193 when King Saladin who repulsed Christian crusaders, sanctioned by Pope, and died in the cause of Islam. The youth everywhere are susceptible to idealism, however flawed the ideals themselves. Did not the Christian children launch their Crusade against Islam though they could never reach Palestine and were sold into slavery by unscrupulous crooks in the markets of Egypt? How has Kashmiri youth come to this Jehad - this Holy War?

The doctrinaire foundation for Jehad is Quran. It says, "And what reason have you not to fight in the way of Allah and of the work among the men and women and the children who say 'Our Lord take us out of this town, whose people are oppressors, and grant us from Thee a friend and from Thee a helper'."[1] Similarly, Quran enjoins upon the Muslims to fight persecution (Quran 8:39). These Kashmiri youth have come to believe Indians to be oppressors and themselves to be oppressed and derive religious sanction from Quran for their depredations of arson, murder, and hounding out of Kashmiri Pandits. R.C. Martin, a scholar of Islamic religiosity in various connotations, says, "The Muslim term Jihad invokes a large semantic field which connotes `inter alia holy war' but is more broadly understood by the notion of `striving in the path of God' The Quran contains this and related phrases concerning the path or way of God (Sabil Allah) in about 180 verses, clearly a major theme. Striving in the path of God, in turn, is a particular instance of a basic principle implicit in the Quranic cosmology..... the Quranic cosmography correspond to the realms of being and are fundamentally divided between God (Allah) and human kind (Insan). The inherent conflict between angels and satans in the heavenly unseen sphere reflecting those who obey God and those who disobey, gets worked out in the phenomenal sphere of humankind, which is also divided between those who submit and do the will of God, including the performance of divinely prescribed religious duties (literal meaning of Muslim) and those who believe (mu'min) and those who disbelieve and act ungratefully (Kuffar, Kafir). Another aspect of religious analysis of such concepts as `Jihad' is that the events of the Quran framed largely by the mission of the Prophet Muhammad to Mecca and Medina between AD 610 and 632 must be seen as paradigmatic for Islamic history - in the Muslim world view, in some crucial sense one must see and understand "that" history in order to understand "this" history. What happened to the Prophet and his followers places important perspective on what is happening here and now. He further says:

"In Koranic cosmology, as we have seen, this basic group of humans who submit to the will of Allah and believe in his religion (Din) and obey his Messenger must strive in the path of Allah."

"Moreover the term Jihad as such when left unqualified, almost always refers to the Jihad of armed struggle and justified violence. In the broadest conceptual sense, the Jihad is a perdurable state of affairs existing between Muslim society (Dar ul-Islam, the domain of Islam) and non Muslim society (Dar-ul-Harb), the domain of war.

"The Jihad was the first war of Islam God commanded the believer to spread his word and establish his law and justice over the world (Quran 9:5). The Dar-Ul-Islam was the house of the believer where law and justice were given practical expression, and the Dar-ul-Harab was the house of unbeliever and an aspect of the Jihad. Religion, however, was and still is to be carried out by peaceful means as there should be no compulsion in the spread of the word God (Koran 2:257). The expansion of the state carried out by the Jihad, was an entirely different matter."[2]

Above is quoted in detail to clarify the connotation of 'Jihad', a word bandied about but little understood.

On 6th October, 1981, President Sadat of Egypt, while inspecting a military parade held to commemorate the 8th anniversary of the Sinnai War with Israel, was gunned down with fire from automatic weapons. The leader of the assassination squad was Lieutenant Khalid Istumbali - a follower of the Muslim extremist group known as 'Al-Jihad', an offshoot of the Muslim Brotherhood, founded by Hassan al Banna but inspired by the writings of Sayyed Qutab, politically executed in 1966. Qutab wrote for the Muslim Brotherhood (Ikhwan al Muslimin) from prison in the 1950's and 1960's.

First a brief look at Qutab's life. Sayyed Qutab was born in 1906 in the family of a prosperous landowner in Asyet province of Egypt. He had traditional education and learnt the Quran by heart on his own. His father sent him to study at Dar-al-Alum in Cairo. He reduced perception of "otherness" to the categories discussed in Qoranic cosmology-people of the Book converts to Islam and all others must be forcibly brought to Islam.

In his "Signposts Along the Way" written in prison, Qutab adumbrates a radical agenda for action of Islam which was to fulfil its divine mandate. In the chapter "Jihad in the path of God," he refutes the traditional Muslim interpretation that Jihad were to be waged only in defence of Islam. He calls for confrontation against Islam's enemies, that is those who would lead community away from the path of God. He denounced secular powers. Such was the stirring interpretation of Koran by Qutab that it led to the assassination of President Anwar Sadat and the ongoing struggle of fundamentalism was waged in Egypt and other parts of the Islamic world.

A study of Quran in itself yields a number of Ayats to show how Qoran emphasizes the nature and meaning of Jihad and the Mujahideens.

Ayats number 216 and 217 of chapter 2, the cow (Bakarah) read as follows:

Section 13

100. And (as for) the foremost, the first of the Muhajids and the Ansars* and those who followed them in goodness, Allah is well pleased with them and they are well pleased with Him, and He has prepared for them gardens beneath which rivers flow, to abide in them for ever; that is the mighty achievement.

Chapter 8, Anfal , The Spoils of war. The Quran shows fight as a way

216, Fighting is enjoined on you, and it is an object of dislike to you; and it may be that you dislike a thing while it is good for you, and it may be that you love a thing while it is evil for you, and Allah knows, while you do not know.

Section 27

217. They ask you concerning the sacred month about fighting in it. Say: Fighting in it is a grave matter, and enduring (men) from Allah's ways and denying Him and (hindering men from) the Sacred Mosque and turning its people out of it, are still graver with Allah, and persecution, is graver than slaughter; and they will not cease fighting with you until they turn you back from your religion, if they can; and

The Holy Quran extols martyrdom for Ajal 168 in Chapter 3, the family of Imlex 2.

For understanding the doctrinaire foundation of what happened in Kashmir we have to understand the Islamination of Pakistan and Iran.

Article 227 of the Constitution Pakistan had laid : "All existing laws should be brought in conformity with the injunctions of Islam as laid down in the Holy Quran and Sunnah.... and no law shall be enacted which is repugnant to such injunctions", yet nothing was done to Islamise the polity except constituting a Council of Islamic Ideology till General Zia-ul-Huq assumed reins of the government.

President Zia-ul-Haq inaugurated the Shariah Faculty at the Quaide-e-Azam University, Islamabad, on 8th October, 1979, where special arrangements were made for instruction in Shariah Law at postgraduate level for the degree of LLM in Shariah law[3].

Ayatollah Ruhallah al-Musavi al-Khomeini was a crusader of pan-Islamism and worked for the Islamisation of the 45 Islamic countries[4]. He was for export of Islamic Revolution all over the world. Pakistan required no persuasion because to maintain its nationhood, it had to Islamise the country and in Afghanistan Russian intervention was an obstacle but the US arms and money were to take care of it. It is for no mean reason that a large number of Afghan Mujahideen operated from Iran. Afghan Mujahideen had their basis on the soil of both the Islamic republics - Pakistan and Iran. If the Afghan Mujahideen failed in their 1989 offensive of Jalalabad, it was because Afghanistan President Najibullah could create factions among them and because the Mujahideens were based in two countries and not one. Islamic fundamentalists had the vision of Iran, Afghanistan, Pakistan and Kashmir as one theocratic region to be ruled by Islamic Cleric.

Another characteristic of Islamic Revolution in Iran was the use of teenagers to beef up defence on Iraqi front. The teenagers were filled in with such Islamic fervour that even without adequate training they rushed to the front and became either cannon fodder or prisoners of war in the hands of Iraqis.

The same spell was to work on the teenagers and youth of Kashmir. In the words of Salman Rushdie: "People prefer mosques to tanks if a choice confronts them but youth always prefer guns...." Modern westernised elite is given to take Islamic fundamentalism as a passing aberration. It is not so.

Imam Ruhollah Al-Musavi-al-Khomeini was born on September 24, 1902 in a religious family in Qum, a small town 100 kms. to the south-west of Teheran. Imam Khomeini first gained fame as a writer and teacher concerned with devotional and mystical matters. His fame as a revolutionary was to follow. His first statement of a political nature appeared in *Kashf al-Asrar* published in 1943. His fame spread first within Qum and then throughout the country. He confronted Shah's regime when hardly anyone could dare to do so. As a true Muslim, Imam Khomeini held that monarchy in any form was anti-thesis of Islam - only the rightly guided Caliphate could run the Government of the country. Sovereignty vests in Allah and not in his creatures who should joyously and willingly obey all the commands given by God"[5]. In the words of Sayeed Abul Alal Maddudi, the mentor of President Zia of Pakistan, and the guiding spirit of Jamat-e-Islami in India and Pakistan: "The one who rises with the sole purpose of administering and reforming humanity at large cannot help struggling to seize power. For unless one possesses necessary power and authority to enforce one's programme, the proposed system cannot possibly take roots in the world of reality."[6] Iman Khomeini denounced the Shah's regime with fanatic vehemence. During the Moharrum of 1963 Khomeini was arrested at his residence and taken as a prisoner to Teheran. Iman Khomeini was not a person to be intimidated by massive killings of the devout followers and unprecedented repression. On November 4, 1964, the Imam was exiled into Turkey. Of course, he was trailed by the Shah's secret police. In October 1965, Imam Khomeini proceeded to Najaf, one of the Shia shrine cities of Iraq. Najaf became his home for the next thirteen years. On November 23, 1977, the elder son of Imam Khomieni, Hazi Mustafa, was alleged to have been assassinated by the Shah's security police, Savak. Frightened by the popularity of Imam throughout the length and breadth of Iran, Shah's regime requested the Baathist government of Iraq in September 1978, to expel Imam Khomeini from its territory. His fervour for Islamic revolution was considered so charismatic that no Muslim country was prepared to offer him asylum. So Khomeini went to France in October 1978, and took up his residence at the hamlet of Neauphale-Le-Chateau near Paris.

Meanwhile, Iran was in for Islamic ferment. People died in thousands from the police bullets. Yet, the US President Carter on a visit to Teheran in January 1978, lauded Shah as a wise statesman and beloved of his people. After receiving this commendation from the Chief Executive of the US, the government-controlled press attacked Imam Khomeini as an agent of foreign powers. This caused massive demonstrations to break out in favour of Imam Khomeini. His name was constantly repeated in the slogans during country-wide demonstrations. His portraits appeared all over the country and his return from exile to supervise the installation of an Islamic government became the raison d'etre for the revolt. The month of Muharram in 1978 coincided with December 1978, when demonstrations all over the country were held demanding he abolition of monarchy and the establishment of Islamic Republic of Iran. Thousands of unarmed demonstrators were slaughtered. Finding no abatement in religious frenzy of Iranians, the Shah left the country on January 16, 1979, after installing surrogate administration under Shahpur Bakhtiar. Imam Khomeini returned to Iran on February 1, 1979. The Bakhtiar regime committed savage repression to hold on the reins of government but ultimately it collapsed like a house of cards and the Islamic Republic of Iran was born on February

11, 1979, after a decade of struggle by the Iranians. It should be understood that this struggle was not by Imam Khomeini alone but had been waged by his eminent predecessors also. The emergence of an independent socio-economic base had provided the Iranian Shia Muslims strength for fierce protests. For instance the concessions given by Nasir al Din Shah (1848-96) to British for a monopoly over the production and sale of tobacco provided Jamal al Din Afghani to persuade Marje-e-Mutla and Hajj Murza Hussain Shirazi to invoke a religious verdict on the subject. "In the name of Allah the merciful, the compassionate, today the use of tobacco in any form is war against the Imam of the Age", declared Shirazi. Again, Ulema had played a prominent role along with the British and Soviet forces to seek abdication of Raza Shah in favour of his 23-old son, Mohammad Raza Shah Pahlavi, in September 1941. In the beginning, his rule was undisturbed because Ayatollah Mohammad Hussain Bornjerdo and Ayatollah Mohammed Mersani Bebahans, the maraja-e-mutlaq, were moderate. Khomeini's role had been facilitated by the Fedayin founded in 1945 calling for the application of Sharia as provided in the Constitution and a ban on use of tobacco, alcohol, cinema, opium, gambling and wearing of foreign dresses.

The Concept of Islamic State

Unless we clearly comprehend the basics of Islamic state, we cannot understand the barbarism perpetrated in Kashmir valley whose youth had derived their religious enthusiasm both from Islamic fundamentalism of Iran and President Zia-ul-Haq of Pakistan who in turn was inspired by Jamaat-e-Islami whose ideologue was Syed Abul Al Maudadi, an intellectual prodigy and a scholar of profound understanding of Islam. Maudadi was born in the state of Hyderabad (now Andhra Pradesh of India) and provided the ideological underpinnings to Jammat-i-Islami Hind but migrated to Pakistan on the partition of the country. Understanding the work of Jamaat-e-Islami Hind and Jamaat-i-Islami Pakistan is cardinal to the understanding of the present phase of insurrection in Kashmir, carried out in ruthless and gruesome modes of abductions, killings and arson. It is Jamait-e-Islami of Kashmir, which curiously disowned any connection with Jamaat-i-Islami Pakistan, a tool in the hand of astute President Zia-ul-Haq, which turned the verdant and serene vale of Kashmir into a land daily bathed in blood of 'Kafirs' and their collaborators.

Let us first examine the views of Imam Ruhullah-al-Masavi-al-Khomeini on Islamic Revolution and Islamic State since he was not only the charismatic leader who brought Islamic Republic of Iran into existence in February 1979 but also his role is defined by Articles 107 to 112 of the Constitution of Republic of Iran, which incorporates the cardinal principle of the "Governance of Faqih (Vilayat-i-Faqih): vilayat means governance and Faqih is one learned in the principles and ordinances of Islamic law or more generally, in all aspects of the faith; fuquh is plural of faqih; fuquh are not prophets but legatees or successors of the prophets.

According to Imam Khomeini, God has no partner. He is the true monarch. Monarchy and hereditary succession are repugnant to Islam. The Lord of the Martyrs (Imam Hussain, grandson of the Prophet) had to refuse to swear allegiance to Yazid, son of Muawiya and second caliph, since Yazid had succeeded to the caliphate by hereditary succession. The ensuing death of Imam Hussain at Karbala has always been commemorated by Shia Muslims as the supreme example of martyrdom against tyranny. In his book entitled *Hakumat-i-Islami* (since translated in French, Arabic, Turkish and Urdu) Imam Khomeini maintains that monarchy and hereditary succession have no place in Islam.

The Shah of Iran had organised extravagant celebration of two and a half millenia of his dynastic monarchical rule in 1971 for which preparations were begun in the late 1960. Imam Khomeini condemned these celebrations in the following words: "A large number of people had died of hunger. While these tragic circumstances and conditions prevail, millions of Tumans are to be spent on celebrating, in hour of sorrow, on decorating and lighting up Tehran only. Experts from Israel, enemy of Islam, had been invited."[5]

According to Imam Khomeini, Islam is not only a religion of militancy but also militaristic. He avers, "The leaders of our religion were all soldiers, commanders and warriors. They put on military dress and went into battle in the wars that are described for us in our history. They killed and they were killed. The commander of the faithful (that is, Ali Ibn Abi Talib, cousin and son-in-law of Prophet, and first of the twelve Imams of Shi'i belief) himself (upon whom be peace) would place a helmet on his blessed head, don coat of armour, and gird on a sword. Imam Hasen (that is son of Imam Ali and second of the Imams) who died in 50/670 after spending most of his life in seclusion in Medina and the Lord of the Martyrs (Peace be upon them) acted likewise....... Even Imam Baqur that is the fifth Imam) (Peace be upon him) was also a warrior by nature."[5-A]

Now let us examine the views of Maulna Abul Ala Maududi who so influenced President Zia that he went the whole way to Islamise Pakistan's polity and used Jamaat-e-Islami as a vehicle for this purpose.

"Islam is an Arabic word. It is derived from two root words: One salem, meaning peace, and the other slim, meaning submission. Islam stands for a commitment to surrender one's will to the will of God and thus be at peace with the creator and with all that has been created by him."[6-A]

In an address delivered at Shah Chiragh Mosque Lahore in October 1939 Maulana Abul a la Maududi had explained the political theory of Islam. Relevant extracts are reproduced below:

"Islam is not democracy; for democracy is the name given to that particular form of government in which sovereignty vests with the people, in which legislation depends both in its form and content on the force and direction of public opinion and laws are modified and altered to correspond to changes in that opinion. There is no such thing in Islam which, therefore, cannot be called democracy in this sense of the term. A more apt name for it in Islam would be the kingdom of God ..... if I were permitted to coin a new term. I should describe Islamic system of Government as the theo-democracy. That is to say, divine democratic government, because the Muslims have been given a limited popular sovereignty under the suzerainty of God..... No person, clan or group, not even the entire population of the state as a whole, can lay claim to sovereignty. God only is the real sovereign, all others are merely his subjects : Sovereignty belongs to God only. He alone has the right to order others in his own right to do or not to do things. The Prophet himself is subject to God's commands."[6-B]

President Zia-ul-Haq in an interview with Impact International, London, said:

"The first thing..... is to give the nation direction that Pakistan stands for Islam and is totally committed to Islam.'[7]

However, there is controversy whether Islam permits nationalism at all. For instance, Dr. Iqbal interpreted Islamic injunction for Muslims all over to be one nation only. This is accepted by Iran (Art. 10 of the Iran's constitution). However President Zia-ul-Haq has followed Maulana Hussain Ahmad Medani of Darul-Alum-Deoband who maintained Islam does not oppose nation-states.

But the Holy Quran is very explicit. Ayat 213 of Chapter. reads as follows:

213. (All) people are a single nation; so Allah raised prophets as bearers of good news and as warners, and He revealed with them the book with truth, that it might judge between people in that in which they differed; and none but the very people who were given it differed about it after clear arguments had come to them, revolting among themselves; so Allah has guided by His will those who believe, to the truth about which they differed; and Allah guides whom He pleases to the right path."

Kashmiri youth strove to achieve an Islamic State to be merged with Islamic Pakistan. However, their abduction of women and unarmed citizens is counter to Quran which says:

Fight in the cause of God.

Those who fight you.

But do not transgress the limits.

For God loveth not transgressors." 11/90

Ghoulish crimes which Kashmiri youth had been perpetrating make them not crusaders of faith, as they were wont to think of themselves, but "transgressors" as laid down by the Holy Quran.

Towards Islamic Caliphate

The vernacular press of Srinagar is not only pro-militant but full of fervour for establishment of Islamic Caliphate from Kashmir to Central Asia including Pakistan, Iran, Azerbaijan, Uzbekistan and Tajikstan. In February 1992, a two-day summit of the Economic Cooperation Organisation comprising Pakistan, Iran and Turkey was attended by the Islamic republics of erstwhile USSR. Commenting on the outcome of Eco meeting, Pakistani columnist Mushahid Hussain wrote in the *Nation*, "For Pakistan, Eco is a convenient bridgehead for Central Asia, and this element is certainly a plus also for the struggle of Kashmiri people as well, since Kashmir itself is an extension of Central Asia both geographically and culturally."

Earlier the Amir (chief) Jammat-i-Islam, Pakistan, Qazi Hussain Ahmed speaking for Kashmir in Rawalpindi in February 1992 had pronounced "a great Islamic state spreading from Kashmir to Central Asia would emerge after the independence of Kashmir."

Pronouncements, made by militant outfits operating on the insurgent political scape of Kashmir, make an interesting study.

Hizbul-Mujahideen (HM) the militant wing of Jamaat-i-Islami (JI) publically stated that HM stood for:

"Islamisation of socio-political and economic set up and unification of Umma".

It further said:

"The slogan that future of Kashmiri would be decided by Kashmiris has given rise to an evil, which was distorting the Islamic identity of present movement and reducing it to a mere democratic movement. From Islamic viewpoint the people's opinion has no importance. God and Prophets (PBUH) law is the superior and should be obeyed.

(The *Daily Srinagar Times*, 30th April, 1993).

The Kashmiri Muslim women's conglomerate Dukhtaran-e-Milat (DM) in a press conference said:

"This merger of Kashmir with Pakistan was the first step towards the unification of Ummah..... Since we wanted to establish an Islamic Caliphate world over the unity of Ummah was a pre-requisite for this purpose. Caliphate could not be established on merely a part (of the world). The entire Muslim Ummah should have one Caliphate."

(The *Daily Afaq* 16th Nov, 1992).

Thus the insurgency in Kashmir valley was not for the right of self-determination or for establishment of democracy but for the establishment of the Islamic Caliphate. Toynbee in his A Study of History vol.8 page 692-695.

Though Kashmiri Muslims swear by unity of Islam they do not know that the Muslims constituting 1/5th of the world population and 1/7th of world's area are a divided lot. The Organisation of Islamic Countries, comprising sixty seven countries, did nothing to alleviate the sufferings of Bosnian Muslims. If Bosnian Muslims exist today as a political entity, it is due to the intervention of "Kafir" USA and NATO and not the much vaunted Organization of Islamic Countries. More pertinently what has this Organization of Islamic Countries done for Kashmir? The fact is this Organization has done nothing for the Muslims anywhere in the world and it is merely a paper organization. The ineffectiveness of Pan-Islamism is not a recent phenomenon. It is an old malady of Islamic polity and has been noted by Arnold. J.O. The Kashmir aspiration for the universal Islamic Caliphate was no more than a pipe dream.

REFERENCES

1. *A Short history of the Revivalist Movements in Islam* by Syed Ala Maudadi, published by Morkazi Maktoba Islami Delhi, page 25.
2. *Research on Terrorism,* Aberdeen. University Press, 1989, page 54-61.
3. *Pakistan* by Golam W. Chaudhary, Scorpion Public Co., England, page 79.

4. *Islam and Revolution,* by Imam Khomeini, published by KPI, London, Melbourne, Henley, page 35.

5. *Ibid,* page 201 (5A + 5B).

6. *Political Theory of Islam,* by Syed A 'la Maudadi, published by Markazi Maktaba Islamia, Delhi, page 22 (6A - 6B).

7. As reproduced in the *Pakistan Times,* Rawalpindi; 17th Jan. 1979, and as quoted in *Defence Journal of Pakistan,* Feb. 1979.

11

Violation of Human Rights

Human Rights form an integral part of liberal democratic system of governance, adopted by most of the countries. India is one of them.

The General Assembly of the United Nations adopted the Universal Declaration of Human Rights on December 10, 1948. Contained in Resolution No. 217 (iii), which was passed by the Assembly without any dissent; forty eight votes were cast in its favour and eight countries abstained. The absentees were the USSR and her allies of East Europe, Saudi Arabia and the Union of South Africa. The Declaration was recommendatory and not legally binding on member States. This Declaration has influenced the constitutions of various countries framed after 1948. India has incorporated these rights in her Constitution in the shape of Fundamental Rights. Later, the Declaration culminated in the two Covenants - International Covenant on Economic, Social and Cultural Rights adopted by the General Assembly on December 16, 1961. It also formulated and adopted an Optional Protocol to the International Covenant on Civil and Political Rights per its Resolution No 2200 (XXI).

The Covenant on Civil and Political Rights consists of 53 Articles and is divided into six parts. Parts I and II lay down the rights of freedom of the individuals which, inter alia, includes the rights to life, freedom from inhuman or degrading treatment, freedom from slavery, servitude and forced labour;

the right to liberty and security of person and to be free from arbitrary arrest and detention; the right to a fair trial etc.

It is worth mentioning that the rights set forth in the Covenants were subject to certain limitations and were not absolute. By and large, the Covenants provided that rights will be subject to such restrictions as provided by law for the protection of national security, public order or the rights of others, public morals and health, etc. Unlike the pre-modern society where communities, traditional groups, guilds etc., were bearers of rights, the modern concept of rights regards the individual as its primary bearer. Thus in most Constitutions of the world, it is the individual who is protected and assigned rights. No particular group is entitled to a special treatment unless so provided. An individual is considered as endowed with choice and will and is thus afforded his rights.

Article I of the Declaration relates to the right of people to self-determination. However, self-determination has not been defined in the Charter of the United Nations nor under the different resolutions which have been adopted by the General Assembly from time to time. One view is that this right applies only to the colonial people (at the end of World War II, one quarter of the world's population - more than 750 million people, lived in dependent territories) and this right does not extend to sovereign States. Another view is that it applies to the people of territory so annexed by violent means. In 1961, the General Assembly adopted a resolution i.e. Resolution 1664 (XVI) to this effect and the implementation of the Declaration is overseen by a committee which found that by the end of October 1985, only less than four million people remained to be provided the right of self-determination. With Namibia attaining independence, the number of people denied this right must have been further reduced in a major way.

The foregoing introduction was necessary to launch upon a meaningful discussion of alleged violation of human rights in Kashmir. Before we take up the issue of violation of human rights in Kashmir, we have to cognise two more parameters. Any person, violating any law of the land, forfeits certain rights of his. For instance, a murderer has no right to freedom. He is arrested and denied his liberty. The only rights given to him are humane treatment while in detention and the right of fair trial - per process of law. The second is that all these rights belong to non-combatants. That is in war a combatant cannot demand the rights enshrined in the Declaration of the UN or those guaranteed to the citizens of country which is at war. Thus, when a terrorist or militant blows a train or a bus killing unarmed passengers, can he claim human rights as guaranteed by the Constitution? Does he not impinge on the right of the "Group" of peaceful citizens? Again, when an individual or a group wages war against a legally constituted state, what human rights accrue to him then? Again, in its war against insurgents, can the state force resort to torture or fabrication of evidence? These are the basic issues to be kept in mind when we examine the question of human rights in the context of violent insurgency. What is to be considered further is what rights are forfeited when laws are violated? Do rights entail certain duties or obligations? Or rights are to be demanded *per se* without any obligation on the part of the claimant of rights? Human rights constitute the foundation of liberty. But can there by unqualified absolute liberty? Shafesbury has said, "Reason and virtue alone can bestow liberty". Does the road to liberty lie over the corpses of innocent children and women? Pinekard has said, "True liberty consists in the destruction of the rights of others". How can liberty to kill and maim the innocent passengers of bus or those assembled for a festival be defended? That is why Mad. Roland asked, "Men are qualified for civil liberty in exact proportion to their disposition to put chains upon their own appetites; in proportion as their love of justice is above their rapacity. It is ordained in the eternal constitution of things that men of intemperate habits cannot be free. Thus passions forge their fetters". Do looting, abduction, raping and indiscriminate killings of people not connected with the governmental apparatus become benign acts because they are committed in the name of religion and freedom? Montesquieu says, "Liberty is the right to do what the laws allow; and if a citizen could do what they forbid, it would be no longer liberty because others would have the same powers". Atrocity committed by a governmental force is far graver a blow to the government which is supposed to uphold the laws of the land but atrocities committed by the so-called freedom fighters, mujahids or militants are no less abominable because they are committed in the name of religion or freedom or to avenge real or perceived injustice. We have to examine what happened in Kashmir, keeping these considerations in view.

Amnesty International is a voluntary organisation which issues outspoken evaluation on the existence or denial of human rights. The militants in Kashmir refer to the reports of the Amnesty International on the woeful violation of human rights in the insurgency-ridden states of India.

Let us examine the views of Amnesty International in a general way. It may be noted that Amnesty International came into existence in 1961 as a result of the publication all over the world of an appeal by British lawyer Mr. Peter Beneson entitled the Forgotten Prisoners. The publication of this letter aroused concern for human rights all over the world. This led to formation of Amnesty International to seek release of prisoners of conscience i.e. these people detained solely for protests or objections to state's laws or actions. Amnesty International has its affiliates in 150 countries and has now a large budget.

A Conference of World Congress of Human Rights was held in New Delhi from 10th to 15th December, 1990. Mr. Lan Martin. Secretary General, Amnesty International, was in New Delhi in connection with this conference. In an interview with the *Times of India*, New Delhi dated Dec. 19, 1990, he said, "just because someone incites secession does not justify imprisonment. As long as there is no violence, our aim is to seek fair and prompt trial of all political prisoners." Mr. Lan Smith further elaborated: "One has to distinguish between the struggle for a separate land within a peaceful framework and the use of arms... The international covenant envisages as a crime incitement of religious or ethnic hatred. The legitimate question of violation of the right to freedom of expression and incitement is a difficult boundary, and a judgement would have to be made." Thus Amnesty International has no role to play where violence has become a way of life and innocent people are gunned down or kidnapped in the name of religion though the real motives may be ulterior.

However, violence by misguided youth is no excuse for state terrorism. State terrorism in the name of maintaining public order is to be condemned more as it is perpetrated by a disciplined body acting under the cover of law. This brand of terrorism too has ulterior motives, may be graft, may be personal vendetta, may be excessive zeal.

Given the ethnic diversities, the rights of different groups clash. Now when Kashmiri youth claim to work for liberation of the valley by violent means, they have driven out Kashmiri Pandits and Hindus. Kashmiri Pandits are, therefore, justifiably sore that whereas Human Rights groups have highlighted the human rights abuses against Kashmiri militants, such groups have failed to take note of the excesses, committed by insurgents against Kashmiri Pandits who were forced to flee the valley leaving their ancestral heritage and properties. They have started asking for a separate homeland within Kashmir. It is generally true that Human Rights groups ignore the sufferings of peace-loving citizens and concentrate on protecting the rights of insurgents who seek glory through violence and crimes. For instance, there is Jammu & Kashmir People's Basic Rights (Protection) Committee which under Mufti Baha-ud-din Faaruqi, Retired Chief Justice of J&K High Court, has been reporting on violations of human rights committed in the state by security forces. The committee has not dealt with any case of atrocities committed by Islamic terrorists against Kashmiri Pandits. Human Rights organisations should concern themselves both with the victims of state terrorism as well as victims of insurgent violence.

Television in Pakistan and all over the world through British Broadcasting Corporation (B.B.C.) and U.S. networks have been showing people being chased or fired upon by security forces in various towns of Kashmir valley. Cases of children or women killed have also been shown. In print media the draconian nature of laws made operative in J&K have also been severely criticised. It is a fact that there have been violations of human rights in Kashmir valley and this fact is a matter of shame and regret. The National Human Rights Commission has been statutorily established in India, which is trying to bring the culprits to book speedily. No civilised society can countenance torture as a normal means of governance.

The U.S. State Department report on Human Rights in the World for 1992 acknowledges India's commitment to democracy and maintenance of civil liberties. It says (page 1388):

"India is a functioning democracy with strong and legally sanctioned safeguards for individuals and an independent judiciary. A vigorous free press and active civil liberties organisations report extensively on human rights abuses throughout the country. Nonetheless, significant areas of abuse remain, many of them generated by severe social tensions related to violent ethnic, caste, communal and secessionist politics and the authorities' reaction thereto. The catalog of the main problem areas in 1991 varied little from what it has been in past years, and included security force excesses against civilians, particularly in Kashmir, in response to attacks—political murder, kidnappings..."

Whereas criticism for violation of human rights is called for it is at times prompted by ulterior motives. Pakistan's concern for violation of human rights in Kashmir is prompted to divert attention from its active support of terrorism in Kashmir. Being herself a supplier of arms to the insurgents, Pakistan starts crying "foul, foul" as soon as they get killed by security forces. For Pakistanis every encounter in the valley is fake and exodus of Kashmiri Pandits in cruel and humiliating circumstances is a victory of Mujahids. Indeed What logic!

Again, what is the state of Human Rights in Pak and Pak Occupied Kashmir? What about the fate of victims of recurring ethnic conflicts in Pakistan?

The United States has made protection of human rights as a central plank of its foreign policy. They have made U.S. aid and trade dependent upon the state of human rights in the recipient country. But the U.S. has been bowing before the mighty China but would like to browbeat others. In the *Washington Post* of November 18, 1993, Jim Hoagland has questioned the propriety of Bill Clinton shaking hands with President Jiang of China on the occasion of Asia Pacific

Conference. Again, one wonders on U.S. amnesia with regard to its own record in Vietnam. My Lai still rankles as a damning ignominy. Again, what happened in Haiti and Somalia? In Somalia how many were butchered by the U.S. troops in sheer retaliation? Nor can history be devoid of what Americans did in their wars with Spain and Mexico, nay even in their own Civil War.? During the visit of the Chinese President Jiang Zemin to USA in October 1997, the host country warmly welcomed him and not a word was said regarding Chinese contempt for Human Rights simply because a nuclear co-operation agreement was to be signed on October 29, 1997, enabling US energy sector to earn as much as sixty billion US dollars in a period of twenty five years. When money comes, the USA jettisons Human Rights blithely.

There should be no condonation of violation of Human Rights or for that matter of any wrong doing. But those who adopt attitudes, who seek to pontificate on such issues and want to wield their big stick, should examine their own records and understand that whereas wilful violation of Human Rights should not be accepted as a norm but armed insurgency does entitle security forces to act in their own self-defence.

India has to make honest and sincere efforts to ensure that her security forces respect the Human Rights of all, whether insurgents or peaceful citizens. Militant terrorism should not lead to state terrorism. This she should do irrespective of what Pakistan or USA do or say, their own records besmirched with human blood and woes. India should take a firm stand in regard to Human Rights because it is the right thing to do. Every human life matters and everyone is entitled to maintain his dignity, be he a citizen or a member of the security forces. Is it a task impossible to achieve? No, certainly not. India has to inculcate a right attitude with regard to Human Rights in her security forces and she should not only vindicate herself at the bar of international opinion but also show others the way how to do it.

12

Kashmir and the United States of America

With the distintegration of the USSR, and the Gulf war in 1990, the world has become unipolar. The U.S.A. alone reigns supreme in the councils of the world and the U.N. Security Council invariably approves what the U.S.A. proposes. With the end of Cold War, Russia has lost leverage in the formulation of U.N. policies. Some commentators now call Russia third world power in the economic sphere.

The U.S.A has shown keen interest in the resolution of what it calls "Kashmir dispute". It was President George Bush who had sent Gates Mission to the sub-continent in May 1990 when the Prime Ministers of Pakistan (Ms. Benazir Bhutto) and India (V.P. Singh) had engaged themselves in jingoistic threats on Kashmir issue. Mr. Robert Gates, the Deputy Security Advisor, had succeeded in having training camps for Kashmiri militants on Pakistani soil closed but they have continued to flourish in what is called Azad Kashmir by the Pakistanis. Some commentators view Robert Gates mission as phoney and as a ploy to vindicate what has come to be called `American Activism in Kashmir'. However no serious comment is possible on Gates mission at this stage of history.

Clinton Administation claims to have exercised restraining influence upon India and Pakistan when they were moving towards armed confrontation in the spring of 1993.

Clinton Administration regards Kashmir dispute as a potential threat to world peace. In his address to the United Nations on 27th September, 1993, President Bill Clinton made the following remarks which pertain to Kashmir issue:

"The Cold War is over. The world is no more divided into two armed and angry camps.

"Thus, as we marvel at this era's promise of new peace, we must also recognize that the serious threat remains. Bloody ethnic, religious and civil wars rage from Angola to the Caucasus to Kashmir..."

Thus the U.S.A. regards Kashmir as a serious threat to world peace.

Continuing, the U.S. President further said:

"Let me talk more about what I believe we must do in each of these three categories: non-proliferation, conflict resolution and sustainable development...I have made non-proliferation one of our nation's highest priorities."

Thus in addition to Kashmir, he aims at non-proliferation so far as India is concerned. About the U.S. role in promoting peace, President Clinton told U.N.:

"We cannot solve every problem, but we intend to serve as a fulcrum for change and a pivot point for peace."

Thus, the U.S.A. has assumed the role of promoter of peace in what she calls "ethnic, religious and civil wars."

The U.S. and European Community countries have often urged India to improve the state of human rights in Kashmir since Pakistan harps on violation of human rights in Kashmir, whether at the U.N. or the Organisation of Islamic Countries (OIC).

It is, therefore, evident that the U.S.A. would like to promote peace between India and Pakistan by resolving their conflict over Kashmir. As will be shown later from historical documents this has been the U.S. stand since 1948 itself.

Ms. Robin Raphel, who had worked as a counsellor in US embassies both in India and Pakistan, was appointed first

Assistant Secretary of the South Asia Bureau in the US State Department. She told the Senate Foreign Relations Committee early 1993 while seeking her confirmation as Assistant Secretary:

"South Asia - home to one-quarter of mankind faces challenges as ancient as ending poverty, as new as pollution & deforestation, and as tragic as the spread of AIDS and the challenges of terrorism. Moreover, in several places in the region, armed conflict and insurgency continue to take an unacceptable human and economic toll. The proliferation of nuclear weapons and their means of delivery threaten massive destruction in the region..."

"Alongwith democracy, promotion of human rights has become an integral part of our Agenda in the region..."

Thus the U.S. concerns are not only resolution of Kashmir conflict but also non-proliferation of nuclear weapons and promotion of human rights. All these may appear to be separate but, in reality, these strands are interwoven with the 50 year-old Kashmir problem.

On 29th October, 1993, Ms. Raphel told South Asia press correspondents in Washington that the US does not recognise the 1947 Instrument of Accession by which Kashmir had joined India. As such, the US did not consider the state of Jammu & Kashmir as an integral part of India. It has been reported by the *Times of India,* New Delhi (Oct. 30, 1993) that a senior Administration official said: "We view Kashmir as a disputed territory and that means that we do not recognise the Instrument of Accession as meaning that Kashmir's forever an integral part of India."

In India the reaction to above statements was furious and it was alleged that the U.S. had changed its attitude towards Kashmir. The US statements were described as "hostile". Even the Prime Minister of India, Shri P.V. Narasimha Rao was reported to have observed that the latest statement of South Asia Bureau of State Department implied that Indian Independence Act, 1947, framed by the British Parliament, was not valid. Ms. Robin Raphel was pointed being anti-India.

However a study of historical records would show what Ms. Raphel has stated regarding Kashmir has been the U.S. position since 1948 but she had only been undiplomatic in making public what had been confined to confidential files of its Foreign Affairs records. The statements that there had been no departure from the U.S. stand on Kashmir are based on facts as disclosed by historical documents. We quote below relevant portions from published records on Foreign Relations of the United States to show that the U.S. has consistently held the views since 1948 as expressed in 1993. We quote pages 1378-1381 of Foreign Relations (South Asia) Vol. V:

Memorandum by the Assistant Secretary of State for near Eastern, South Asian & African Affairs (McGheet) and the Assistant Secretary of State for United Nations Affairs (Hickerson) to the Secretary of State.

Secret (Washington February 6, 1950

Subject: Kashmir Dispute

Discussion

1. Importance of Settlement

Early settlement of the Kashmir problem is essential to the maintenance of peace and security in South Asia...Lacking some immediate progress, the present uneasy truce may break down, leading to open hostilities between the Indian and Pakistan armies and the outbreak of communal strife throughout the continent.

2. Principal Difficulty

Although both India and Pakistan have proved difficult and recalcitrant, both are far from blameless in the matter...

3. Legal Aspects of Kashmir's Contested Accession to India

India has always insisted that Maharaja's execution of an Instrument of Accession to India in October 1947 was a valid and binding act which determined the legal status of Kashmir. On the basis of this contention, it has been asserted that

Pakistan was an aggressor and has from time to time sought to persuade the Security Council to make a finding of aggression against Pakistan.

In the opinion of the office of the Legal Advisor, execution of an Instrument of Accession by the Maharajah in October 1947, could not finally accomplish the accession of Kashmir to either Dominion, in view of the circumstances prevailing at that time; the question of the future of Kashmir remained to be settled in some orderly fashion under relatively stable conditions; this question is an important element in the dispute; and, in proceedings before the Security Council.

4. "U.S.A. will maintain principle that disposition of the state should be determined in accordance with the will of the people....."

Thus it is clear that the U.S.A. had the same stand in 1948-1950 on Kashmir as was being expressed in 1993 and thenceforth. However Clinton Administration has lent it urgency because both India and Pakistan are nuclear powers and a conflict between them will be catastrophic for the whole of South Asia.

It is time that India takes a more objective view of the stand adopted by the U.S.A. Neither hysteria nor berating any individual functionary of the U.S. State Department will help soften the tensions bedevilling the Indo-Pak relations.

What has been written about the U.S. stand on Kashmir does not absolve it of the charge that she had been following double standards in her dealings with Pakistan and the charge further goes to say that the U.S.A. blinkered at all the Pakistani attempts to acquire nuclear weapons by means of theft and smuggling of nuclear weapon technology and equipment. It has been pouring gratuitous advice on India how to hold elections in Kashmir and not enforce electoral laws requiring candidates to affirm their faith in the Constitution of India, but it has ignored the Pakistani hand in arming and training the Kashmiri youth.

However, there is a silver lining in the fact that the U.S.A. does realise that the Kashmiri Pandits have suffered. With regard to Indo-Pak tensions, Robin Raphel had this to say, "we are also concerned about the perfunctory use of existing confidence building measures between India and Pakistan"

The U.S.A's concern for peace between India and Pakistan will remain unacceptable so long as U.S.A. continues arming Pakistan a la Brown amendment of Pressler Ban on the supply of arms to Pakistan and permitting China to flout the U.N. and U.S. embargo with impunity in the matter of supplying nuclear technology and equipment to Pakistan. Indians ask why the U.S.A. has not taken any real action against China for supplying M-11 missiles to Pakistan whereas she has been frowning upon India for developing "Prithvi" missile. Again, Indians ask while there is pressure on India to sign Comprehensive Test Ban Treaty (CTBT) and Fissile Matter Control Treaty (FMCT) why has China been allowed to defy the U.N. and the U.S. laws brazenly?

The U.S. Congressional Intelligence Committee Chairman Benjamin A Silman has stated that the supply of 5000 ring magnets to Pakistan by China is violative of the U.S.A Nuclear Non-Proliferation Act (NNPA). Similarly, Leonard S. Spector, the proliferation expert at the Carnegie Endowment, has said China's action in supplying magnet rings to Pakistan amounts to violation of the 1968 Nuclear Non-Prolification Treaty which bars transfer by nuclear states of any equipment meant for making nuclear weapons. According to a news despatch by C.K. Arora in the *Patriot* New Delhi of 12 February, 1996, Spector had told *Washington Post* that the U.S. should adopt a strong response since "no one in the world would imagine that Chinese assistance to Pakistani nuclear plan is innocent."

The world is watching what action the U.S.A. takes against Pakistan and China for their flagrant violations of NPT and U.S. Nuclear Non Proliferation Act. Indeed the USA has come to view grave matters affecting peace not on norms of equity and justice but in terms of her brazen commercial interests. During the visit of the Chinese President Jiang Zemin to the USA in October 1997, the USA did not utter a single word against the Chinese supply of missiles and nuclear weapon technology to Pakistan simply because it goes on slobbering over fifty billion $ Chinese market. The USA views its nuclear power sales to

China in terms of prospects of money and jobs than its effect on prospects of peace in Asia. The ideologies in the US Government have made an ignoble bow to the nuclear power industry of their country than serve the strategic requirements of peace in South Asia. Ambiguity marks the US postures since it touts China as second superpower of the twenty first century.

So far as the Indian allegation of US obsession to interfere in Kashmir is concerned, the testimony of Richard Celesti, the new US Ambassador to India, before the US Senate on 28th October 1997, is eloquent. He told the Senate"....... Our mutual interests require us to move beyond the sometimes sterile positions of the past. We need to build a framework of trust......we should have a discourse that is respectful of each other's views." He further argued that Washington must engage seriously with India in the coming years in the same way that "we have done with major nations such as Russia and China"

(*The Indian Express* of October 30, 1997).

The US position has undergone a major shift towards India in 1997. On US relations with China and India, a separate book can be written; it is for nothing that the US pressure on India in regard to Nuclear Test Ban Treaty (NTBT) has not been more than perfunctory and ritualistic?

In passing we may comment on the US reasons for not recognising Kashmir's Instrument of Accesession to India. First, some historians have endeavoured to prove that Indian troops had landed in Srinagar on 25th or 26th October, 1947, prior to the signing of the Instrument of Accession by the Maharaja of Kashmir on 26th October, 1947. Alistair Lamb, who has emerged as a specialist on Kashmir and has written a number of books favouring Pakistan's position, has tried to prove from the movements of the state's Prime Minister Mehar Chand Mahajan and V.P. Menon that the Maharaja of Jammu & Kashmir had signed the Instrument of Accession under mental coercion and even Earl Mountbatten as the first Governor General of India was a party to this fraud. Secondly, it is argued that on 26 October, 1947, most of Kashmir valley as well as Poonch was in the hands of rebels and thus how could the Maharaja accede to India what he did not possess?

A word in passing may as well be said here on the UK's current stand on Kashmir. During the Queen Elizabeth II's visit to India in October 1997, the UK Foreign Secretary Robin Cook, while playing to the gallery in Pakistan and keeping his Mirpuri constituency in England in view, said that because the UK had been the Imperial Power dealing with Kashmir before 1947, she had the duty to mediate between Pakistan and India on Kashmir dispute. He had to retract this statement when he found that by his indiscretion he had embroiled himself in a matter which was too hot to handle. Earlier on October 7, 1997, the UK Envoy to India Sir Gore-Booth had called Indian stand on Kashmir quixotic and called Indian Government as tilting on windmills. However the stand of the UK Prime Minister Tony Blair has been heartwarming for India. He has been celebrating UK-Indo relations with a warmth which goes beyond words.

The visit of the US Secretary of State Madeleine Albright to India on 19th November, 1997, marked a historical watershed in the US perception on Kashmir imbroglio and US relations with India. She declared at her meeting with the Speaker of Indian Lok Sabha, the Opposition and various members of Parliament that the US had no desire to be involved in Kashmir issue, though she hinted that the US was willing to play the role of a mediator if invited to do so. This unambiguous policy statement marks a landmark in the Indo-US relations and should put to rest all the ghosts of misunderstanding on Kashmir issue so far as the USA is concerned.

It may be stated here that Ms. Madeleine Albright is the daughter of Joseph Korbel who was Czech representative on United Nations Commission for India Pakistan (UNCIP) on Kashmir. His name was proposed by India. He wrote the book *Danger in Kashmir* from which we have quoted copiously at various places in this book. This also explains the keenness on the part of Ms. Madeleine Albright to visit Kashmir.

The U.S. decision on declaring Harkat-ul-Ansar operating from Pakistan as a terrorist organisation and Jammu Kashmir Liberation Front as being watched by US State Department for similar declaration would promote better understanding between U.S. and India on the role of Pakistani abetment in promoting armed insurgency in the valley of Kashmir.

It could be feared that the asumption of power in New Delhi by the Bhartiya Janta Party alliance would strain India U.S. relations as the Prime Minister designate had told the U.S. print media that B.J.P. was committed to exercise nuclear option. On relations with the United States Mr. Vajpayee had told Newsweek (March 16, 1998): "we expect the U.S. to be more sensitive to India's security concerns and economic interests. Indo-American relations should be based on mutual respect."

However, it will be unrealistic for India to expect that U.S.A. will ever forsake Pakistan whatever its nuclear crime or terrorist misdeamours. Geography is destiny. Destiny has poised Pakistan in such strategic geographical position that U.S.A. will always be knocking at Pakistan's door to get access to Central Asia which is sandwitched between Russia and China. To restrain the two communist powers, U.S.A. must depend upon Pakistan, however obnoxious its actions are.

Now that India has exploded nuclear devices on 11th and 13th May, 1998, it was inevitable that U.S. must impose economic sanctions per their laws though the anger and sorrow expressed by President Bill Clinton and Republicans are bound to rupture the harmony between U.S.A. and India which had just started emerging.

13

The Growth of Thermonuclearism

On Monday, May 1998, Ironically the Buddha Purnima, India conducted three underground nuclear tests at Pokhran in Rajastan at 1545 hours. The three tests were fusion device, (12 kiloton) low-yeild device (0.2 sub-KT) and the third thermo-nuclear device (43 KT). Thus the sub-continent ominiously entered the era of thermo-nuclearism.

Pakistan was expected to make alarmist noises. According to its Foreign Minister Gohar Ayub, Pakistan had decided to test its nuclear device. However, the decision as to time will be taken later on. It is worth mentioning that the U.S.A. tried its best to restrain Pakistan by sending a high level delegation under Deputy Secretary of State. Evidently it has not succeeded. The real reason for the pendency of Pakistani test is to study the impact of US and Japanese sanctions against India. If these sanctions cripple, Indian economy, Pakistan would defer a test indefinitely because its economy has a narrow base and is fragile as compared to Indian economy. On the other hand, if India can withstand the impact of sanctions without much damage, the Pakistan would conduct its test in the desert of Baluchistan with lot of fanfare and jingoist bravodo. Thus the deferment of Pakistani test is not due to any principle but a matter of economic strategy. Here also there are different readings of the situation. The German Chancellor Mr. Helmut Kohl told the G-8 Conference on Sunday, the 17th May, 1998 that Pakistan had carried out its test. However, Mr. Bill Clinton the U.S. President told reporters that based on their best information it had not happened yet.There have been persistent U.S. reports that Pakistan had been preparing a test site at Chagai in South Western Baluchistan province located only 30 km from the Iran Pakistan border.

The question arises if Shri Atal Behari Vajpayee the poet Prime Minister of India has pushed the sub-continent into the thermo-nuclear catastrophe. A dispassionate scrutiny of facts will show that the sub-continent's plunge into the thermo-nuclear night is not the result of the exercise of nuclear option by India or the stealthy action of Dr. Abdul Quadeer Khan, the father of Pakistani atom bomb, but the Chinese anxiety to keep India on a tight leash to stop 'Indian hegemony' in South Asia as stated by the Chinese Vice-Foreign Minister condemning India's testing of nuclear devices in a formal statement issued on 14th May 1998. Evidently while U.S. is playing the role of Global Policemen, China has taken upon itself to play the role of Asian Policeman. China has arrogated to itself alone the right to possess a nuclear arsenal in Asia. China does not want any other country in Asia to have the status of Nuclear Weapon States.

To arrive at correct array of facts we have to begin with the beginning.

In 1990 and later too, all the leading magazines ran articles to show the relative military strength of India and Pakistan and commented on the possible Indo-Pak War scenarios. They quoted from "Military Balance" to show that India had 1,260,000 men with arms as against 520,000 with Pakistan, India had 10 Army corps and Pakistan 8, India had 3,150 tanks and Pakistan 1,750, India had 20 divisions on western front and Pakistan 15.

One of my colleagues from Border Security Force, Lt. Col. Daljit Singh, who was Assistant Director (Operations) in Punjab when I was Inspector General, B.S.F., Punjab.... told *The Illustrated Weekly* (May 27 June 2, 1990) that Pakistan will stick to 1971 strategy of debouching into Ganganagar, Hindu Malkot, Fazilka, Abohar, Mandi Dabwali, Sirsa and Pakistan - Desert Corps (XXXI corps Bahawalpur) will hit from Rahim Yaar Khan to penetrate towards Jaisalmer. The aim will be to grab maximum territory. Mr. Aditya Chhiber (National Security Doctrine published by Lancer International) averred that during Exercise Brass Tracks in 1987 while India wanted to penetrate Sindh, Pakistan had denuded Sindh of any troops and concentrated to strike in the north and south (a la Daljit Singh) of Punjab. The then Pakistani Chief of Army Staff General Mirza Aslam Beg, claimed that in his massive Exercise Zarb-e-Momin held in December 1989, between Fox Land and Blue Land, which involved half the Pak army, he had evolved a new doctrine of offensive defence. These are all stories. Offensive-defence is much older than Pakistan itself and truly as old as warfare. To clothe it with ideological fervour of Islam was another matter.

We have seen the terrain on Punjab border for six years. Pakistan with its network of Ichhogil canal, Rohi Nala Diversion, Mari Magha drain and Saadiqi canal has made it impossible for Indian armour to penetrate into Pakistan's Central Punjab. Similarly, we have such a series of Dich-cum-Bandh (DCB) defences that Pakistani armoured thrust in Punjab would be slowed and blunted, if not altogether prevented. Therefore, both Pakistan and India concentrate on north and south Punjab where no defensive canals exist, that is north of Gurdaspur and south of Fazilka.

India, by deploying its armoured units in Suratgarh area in1987 has laid bare its strategy. It has prematurely shown its hand.

1971 Bangladesh war had shown two types of operations. Fast moving, rapid envelopments, bye-passing of well-defended locations and torrent like movement. Secondly, there were disjointed ritualistic dog-fight of armour in Shakargarh and Chhamb areas. In case conventional war takes place now, the question is which of the two strategies will be adopted? The same as in Bangladesh or the one which mired Indian and Pakistani armour in Shakargarh?

Both the countries have re-furbished their pile of armaments and have indulged in enough war histrionics with the result that no army can usurp initiative and pre-empt decisive strike. The *Time* magazine May 14, 1990, spoke of alienation of Kashmiris from India and said a war would exact a huge toll in resources and manpower and possibly create political instability. This, indeed, is true. India may have a slight edge in arms and men, yet it is the strategy and operations which would determine if the two countries will stalemate into an indecisive war of 1965 pattern or a decisive war as India did in 1971? But is a war between the two countries probable? We will examine it later.

It must be recognised that both India and Pakistan are nuclear powers though their nukes may be in basements. Only an indecisive war can save the sub-continent from nuclear holocaust. If Indians reach Lahore or Karachi, Pakistan would not hesitate to exercise her nuclear option and the target will not be combat areas but some city say Chandigarh or New Delhi or Bombay. If Pakistani troops make a breakthrough and can capture Amritsar or Pathankot or Samba bottling up Northern Command at Udhampur-Kashmir, India may threaten use of nuclear option. Both the countries have nuclear capability combined with delivery systems (Agni - the Intermediate Range Ballistic Missile (IRBM) reportedly tested since May 1989) and Pakistan has F-16s to carry the atomic bombs from their basement and M-11 missiles from the Chinese capable of carrying 500 kg. payload and now Ghouri with 1500 km. range and the yet to be tested Ghaznavi with 2000 km. range. Neither country has the capability nor political will for the first strike to destroy the other's nuclear facilities.

Thus by allowing Kashmir to become a flashpoint we are allowing the megalomaniac chauvinists in the two countries to subject millions of innocents to nuclear wipe-out or blackmail. Conventional war between the two countries will not remain conventional if a breakthrough is achieved by either of the two adversaries and such a breakthrough does not depend upon the number of tanks and artillery pieces but operational strategy.

Pakistan's nuclear capability was beyond any doubt way back. She crossed the nuclear threshold in 1987 and now in 1978 per Dr. Abdul Qadeer Khan. *The Statesmen* of May 8, 1990, quotes the *Time* magazine as saying that Indo-Pakistan conflict could lead to the first use of nuclear weapons since 1945. The *Newsweek* held that both India and Pakistan are widely believed to have a "bomb in the basement". The ambiguity which Pakistan had maintained earlier on its nuclear capability is no more since the veil has been ripped open. Three Pak Prime Ministers and Foreign Secretary have exultingly proclaimed that they are a nuclear power and they have acquired this capability because of Kashmir dispute. Pakistan has discussed their nuclear capabilities in a debate in their National Assembly on December 2, 1993. Now the statement of the Prime Minister Nawaz Sharif that Pakistan had nuclear bomb and had plans to use it in case of Indo-Pak hostilities should convince everyone where a war in South Asia would lead to. Professor Stephon P. Cohen, who has written authoritative books on Pakistan and Indian armies, has been quoted as saying, "This is the first neo-nuclear crisis that does not directly involve the super-powers." He further said: "I doubt there will be war because both sides know that conventional war will lead to the nuclearisation of South Asia - or worse." Again, the *Statesman* of 28th May, 1990, carried a news item datelined Washington, quoting London *Sunday Times* that the USA and the Soviet Union were alarmed at the possibility of a nuclear war between India and Pakistan over Kashmir and were exchanging intelligence. It said American spy satellites had photographed heavily armed Pakistani road convoys, leaving the nuclear weapons complex at Kahuta near Islamabad and heading for military airfields. The satellites were stated to have also filmed special racks designed to carry nuclear bombs fitted in Pakistani F 16 aircraft. Mr. Leonard S. Spector, Senior Associate at the Carnegie Endowment of International Peace, in an article in the *New York Times* has urged both the super powers "to forestall a nuclear confrontation between their allies in Asia." Spector has also stated "Pakistan has the wherewithal for five to six bombs and India for forty to sixty. And if the bombs have been in the basement they are now getting on to the elevator". Prof. Gary Milholin, Director of the Wisconsin nuclear arms control project, writing in *Washington Post* (10th June, 1990) said that if fighting did erupt between India and Pakistan each side must assume that the other would deploy and possibly use an atomic bomb, and Pakistan no more being conventional but turning nuclear is real. Gary Milholin has now given graphic details of how the USA unwittingly helped Pakistan to acquire nuclear capability. His recent testimony before the US Senate Armed Forces Sub-Committees is eloquent. Writes Gen. K. Sundarji, Retd. Chief of Army Staff, who should certainly be better informed: "Pakistan might, from the outset, decide to degrade, to the extent possible India's nuclear second strike (i.e. retaliatory) capability".

The former Foreign Minister of Pakistan Sardar Assef Ali during his visit to Uzbekistan said that if Kashmir problem was not solved it would lead to nuclear war between Pakistan and India.

Pakistan is reported to have 175-325 kg. enriched uranium, sufficient for 8-16 nuclear weapons. It is estimated that Pakistan had procured 130-200 kg. of weapon grade uranium by the end of 1992. CIA has informed the U.S. Senate: "Both (i.e. India and Pakistan) are producing nuclear weapon components and could assemble a small arsenal of nuclear weapons." The reason for not deploying nuclear weapons in the words of CIA is: "deploying nuclear weapons might prompt international donors to reduce aid beyond what the Pressler Amendment had already imposed upon Pakistan - and both sides probably assess that significant cuts in foreign aid would outweigh benefits of fielding nuclear force."

Through clandestine procurement of foreign spares and know-how, Pakistan has succeeded in constructing an unsafeguarded centrifuge plant which started producing enriched Uranium as early as 1984. Pakistan is in a position to produce 45 to 75 kg. weapon grade uranium and thus produce two or three nuclear weapons every year.

Abdul Qadeer Khan, father of Pakistan's nuclear programme, has said publicly that Pakistan would need five atomic bombs to destroy India, while India needed three such bombs to destroy Pakistan. When there is nuclear weapon capability in both countries, it is an entirely new ball game. The ground realities have changed drastically, as the damage potential of war has gone up astronomically. Leaders on both sides have to understand that any act which threatens the core vital interests of the other side will trigger off responses which may end in a nuclear exchange. Such an exchange may not endanger the planet earth yet would cause horrendous damage to South Asia.

When the Indian Ambassador Abid Hussain presented his credentials, the United States President George Bush had appealed to India and Pakistan to seek "negotiations and conciliation rather than confrontation". He was forthright in describing a war between the two countries a "disaster" for the people of the region, impliedly because of nuclear dimension. Mrs. Margret Thatcher, former British Prime Minister not only joined European Community to encourage India and Pakistan to come to negotiating, table, but also she offered mediation by the UK if India and Pakistan agreed to the same. On 20th May, 1990, she criticised the Kashmir subversives and said Britain had no sympathy with those who used violence for political ends. She said, "We have also been working with our E.C. (European Community) partners to persuade both India and Pakistan to do what they can to reduce tension in the area."

Thus super powers are aware of the shadow of nuclear disaster over the region. In the U.S. State Department, a Bureau of South Asian Affairs has since been created. John Mallot, interim Director of this Bureau told the House Foreign Affairs Sub-Committee on Asia and the Pacific on April 28, 1993:

"The primary U.S. security interest in South Asia is to prevent war, which, in the case of India and Pakistan, could lead to the employment of nuclear weapons..."

"India and Pakistan have advanced programs to acquire weapons of mass destruction and ballistic missile delivery systems. Continuing regional tensions between India and Pakistan, combined with these ongoing programs, mean that the outbreak of armed conflict has the potential to escalate to a nuclear exchange ..." Dei Woosley (Director, CIA) testified before the Senate on February 24, 1993, "The arms race between India and Pakistan poses perhaps the most probable prospect of future use of weapons of mass destruction, including nuclear weapons."

Continuing with his testimony, John. Mallot told the Sub-Committee:

"We believe that India and Pakistan could assemble a number of nuclear weapons in a relatively short time-frame. Both have combat aircraft that could be modified to deliver them in a crisis. Both India and Pakistan are developing or seeking to acquire ballistic missiles capable of striking major population centres in the other country, potentially with nuclear or chemical weapons."

Thus the threat of nuclear war between India and Pakistan on Kashmir issue or "dispute" is more real than we, the people of South Asia, seem to think.

It is this perception which impelled Indian and Pak intellectuals to make a fervent plea for peace. These include Dr. Mubashir Hassan who had been in the Ministry of Z.A. Bhutto as Finance Minister and on the Indian side, B.G. Verghese, Nikhil Chakravarty and Tarlok Singh.

Again shall the two countries be able to save cities and historical monuments from missile war as happened during Iran-Iraq war? India has developed 'Prithvi' surface to surface missile with a range upto 350 kms. and Pakistan is alleged to have HAFT-2 with similar range Pakistan having 41/100 M II missiles imported from China as early as 1992 and now Ghouri with a range of 1500 km.

India must meet Pakistan's 'covert' aggression by an effective counter subversion plan. If India goes on indulging in politics of chicanery, deny people their rights under the Constitution, pursue policies which widen disparities in income and expand para-military forces without upgrading their armament and training, India is just inviting disaster. Can India not fine-tune her counter-insurgency response?

India and Pakistan have the right to strong defense but the combination of nuclear weapons and enduring tension could prove catastrophic to both.

The Assistant Secretary in U.S. State Department, Ms. Robin Raphael, after touring India and Pakistan told *Times of India* Bombay, on October 13, 1994, "There is no popular consciousness in South Asia, unlike U.S. during the cold war, of the devastating effects of nuclear weapons. The idea of nuclear weapons is politically popular in both India and Pakistan. Politicians believe they would suffer tremendously if they gave up the idea of nuclear capability. The option for the bomb is a good vote catching device." This statement shows, as the subsequent events more pointedly, that there has been no capping of nuclear weapons in Pakistan.

Zingoists of the worst order seek stopping Pak patronage of terrorism in Kashmir through a war which will turn vast areas and populations into nuclear waste. Pakistan has been trying to assemble the bomb through extensive smuggling of technology and critical parts in connivance of its nuclear ally, China, and may, in case of war, nuclearise the conflict.

The Sunday Telegraph (London) of 18th February, 1996, says that the supply of 5000 ring magnets by China to the Abdul Qader Khan Nuclear Research Laboratory of Pakistan points out that Pakistan is going ahead with its uranium enrichment programme and is now involved in putting together a nuclear bomb. These rings, supplied by China, would replace the worn-out rings at the Kahuta nuclear plant, thus increasing its capacity to enrich uranium. The detection of the attempted smuggling of laser equipment at Heathrow airport shows that Pakistan has embarked upon a major expansion of its nuclear weapon programme. According to *Sunday Telegraph* (February 26, 1996) whereas Chinese expertise has been instrumental in developing Pakistan's nuclear programme Pakistan has resorted to extensive smuggling and theft of nuclear technology and equipment from the international market with the help of funds from Saudi Arabia and Libya.

Thus Pakistan is preparing for a nuclear confrontation with India, of course, in collusion with its nuclear ally China. With the Islamic nuclear bomb dangling in the north west and the Chinese nuclear arsenal in the north east, India is sandwiched between the two nuclear allies and the nuclear flash point lies in Kashmir. This is because of the intractable problem and the unmitigated antagonism between India and Pakistan.

A state of perpetual conflict prevails since the birth of Pakistan itself in 1947, and India and Pakistan have ever since remained locked in hostile postures. Various confrontations and armed clashes between them have settled no dispute and these confrontations have only proclaimed the futility of war for settling any dispute. Russel Brines writes: "The indecisiveness of the first Kashmir war (i.e. 1947-48) had perpetuated the unsettled position of that State, making it a magnet for an almost continual Pakistani political offensive which led to war (of 1965). The indecisiveness of the second greater conflict left open a broad new range of problems and objectives with both the belligerent powers still strong to pursue them." (*Indo-Pakistan Conflict* by Russel Brines - Pall Mall Press, London, page 64).

The state of continual belligerence between two nuclear powers glaring menacingly at each other is fraught with the seeds of mutual destruction.

United News of India in a despatch from Washington datelined February 23, 1996, has reported that the Director, Central Intelligence Agency (CIA) John Deutch, testifying before the US Senate Intelligence Committee, on 22nd February, 1996, has confirmed that Chinese nuclear technology and M-11 ballistic missiles have been shifted to Pakistan. So far as the supply of missile M-11 is concerned, CIA had obtained information in 1992 itself and for this the USA had applied very mild sanctions against China and Pakistan in 1993 for one year only since the transfer was in violation of Missile Technology Control Regime (MTCR).

About the tension between India and Pakistan the CIA Director told the Senate Sub-Committee as follows:

"The Kashmir dispute is not easily susceptible to resolution and remains a possible flashpoint for regional war with the potential to escalate into a nuclear exchange.... Nowhere in the world are the stakes for the global proliferation regime higher than in South Asia... India and Pakistan stand at cross-roads in their history—if they are prepared to cap their nuclear and missile programmes, they can become a force for progress in the global effort to negotiate a Comprehensive Test Ban Treaty (CTBT) and a Fissile Material Production Ban Treaty....."(FMPBT).

Thus if armed hostilities break out between India and Pakistan this war will have the potential of degenerating into a nuclear war of mutual destruction!

Even if war is averted, the danger of nuclear disaster is not so easily avoided. Dr. Qadeer Khan, retired General Aslam Beg, the Prime Minister Mian Nawaz Sharif and the present Pakistan Chief of the Army Staff General Jahangir Karamat may gloat over Pakistan being a nuclear power with hundreds of missiles borrowed from their master China. But they do not know that a nuclear disaster can overtake Pakistan, and also India, due to mechanical failure in their equipments or human error. Do they not know that suicidal megalomaniac pilots in some countries had tried to play nuclear havoc and the disaster was averted because those countries had fail-safe technologies to deal with such menaces or failures. Has Pakistan acquired similar technologies? Certainly not. Thus in the event of such human or mechanical errors, will Pakistan not be committing nuclear harakari? We from India can wish Pakistan adoption of all the safety measures as Pakistan's failure in this regard will mean disaster for India also.

On 19th March, 1998, Bhartiya Janata Party assumed the governance of India along with its alliance parties. The assumption of power by the Bhartiya Janata Party was proceeded by a variety of declarations on the party's determination to exercise nuclear option on behalf of India as well as the development of Intermediate Range Ballistic Missile 'Agni'. The posture of Bhartiya Janata Party and its allies on the issue of nuclearisation of weapons deserves to be examined in detail if we have to form an accurate picture of the current nuclear stand off between India and Pakistan.

Bhartiya Janata Party Election Manifesto 1998 makes the following observations relevant to the subject:

"In the recent past we have seen a tendency to bend under pressure...

"The BJP rejects the notion of nuclear apartheid and will actively oppose attempts to impose a hegemonistic nuclear regime by means of CTBT, FMCR and MTCR. We will not be dictated to by anybody in matters of security requirements and in the exercise of the nuclear option.

"...The BJP rejects all forms of political and economic hegemonism and is committed to actively resisting such efforts:

"...We expect the United States to be more sensitive to India's security and economic interests: [1]

"Re-evaluate the country's nuclear policy and exercise the option to induct nuclear weapons

Expedite the development of the Agni series of ballistic missiles with a view to increasing their range and accuracy"[2]

On the eve of taking charge of the government the BJP and its allies issued a National Agenda for Governance on 18th March, 1998. On the subject of India's Nuclear Policy the Agenda said:

"Preserving India's Unity and Integrity is our prime concern and for this we are prepared to exercise all our options, including the induction of nuclear weapons."

Elaborating Shri Atal Behari Vajpayee said:

"All our options are open. There is no time frame for exercising the option which India is now keeping open...My government will give importance to national security and for that whatever is needed we will do. We will not bother about the annoyance of others nor is it necessary for anyone to get annoyed"[3].

On 20th March, 1998, India's new defence minister George Fernandes told the press that the induction of nuclear weapons as also further testing of the Agni intermediate range missile was subject to a Strategic Defence Review (SDR) to be undertaken by a soon-to-be stabilished National Security Council (NSC). He further elaborated that it was difficult to set a time for establishing NSC and thus evolving SDR". Significantly he added: "It is not our purpose to start an arms race. India's policy is defence oriented and not war oriented"[4]. He candidly acknowledged that he was a "pacifist" but further qualified his pacifism by asserting "Pacifism does not mean surrender and not caring for national security"[5].

It is known in all the well informed circles that Mr. Mohan Guruswamy is the defence and international affairs expert in the BJP and that he spearheads the lobby in the party which wants India to go nuclear. In an interview with the Times of India defence correspondent Mr. Dinesh Kumar in answer to question "Is the BJP serious about inducting nuclear weapon?" Mr. Mohan Guruswamy answered "It is very clear we will induct nuclear weapons. The government however has to decide on what kinds of nuclear weapons to induct after understanding our capabilities and requirements". With regard to coping with negative international fall out arising out of India's exercising its nuclear option, Mr. Mohan Guruswamy stated "We will do whatever is required for India's security interest. We will not be dictated to by outsiders in this matter...".[6] By exploding three nuclear devices on 11th May, 1998 and of more tests of 13th May, 1998, Shri Atal Behari Vajpayee has dared the world to show that India's security is paramount for his government.

The interview given by Shri Atal Behari Vajpayee to the News Week (USA) and published on March 16, 1998 is very significant. The following observations of Mr. Vajpayee deserve to be reproduced:

"As we have already stated in our manifesto we propose to review India's nuclear policy and exercise the option to induct nuclear weapons. I would like to mention here that we believe in a nuclear-weapon-free-world. But the nuclear-weapon powers do not believe in it: they would rather practice nuclear apartheid, which we are totally opposed to".

Reactions to Shri Vajpayee Government pronouncements in Pakistan and USA were bound to raise apprehensions about India's future plans on the issue of nuclear weapons. At its weekly briefing Pakistan Foreign Ministry's spokesman Tariq

Altaf told the press at Islamabad on March 19, 1998, that the National Agenda of Shri Atal Behari Vajpayee government was a "worrisome document". He further criticised the earlier statement of Mr. Vajpayee, when he was the leader of opposition seeking to wrest control of "Azad Kashmir" and said that such misadventure would receive a matching swift and telling response from Pakistan".[7]

After test firing Ghauri, the Pakistan's IRBM, Mr. Nawaz Sharif the Prime Minister of Pakistan observed on 7th April, 1998, "the public statements by the BJP that the country would keep its nuclear option open is a source of great concern for us". According to the press report published in Times of India of April 8, 1998 he charged the international community of adopting "double standards by turning a blind eye to India's nuclear programmes". Pointing out reasons behind what he called "Washington's discriminatory policy the Pakistan Prime Minister said; "It is India's size and the overall global perception of its economic potential, the attempt to build new Delhi as a counteravailing force to China, and a general hostility towards Islamic countries, are the primary reasons for this". In the same report of Times of India, the press correspondent reported from Karachi "The worsening of ties between India and Pakistan will provide an opportunity to the United States to play a more dominant role in South Asia. In the ensuing swirl of events, both India and Pakistan might end up losing much control over their destinies". The report further clearly portrayed the jubilation sweeping Pakistan in the wake of successful test firing of Ghauri on 6th April, 1998.

The US reaction was on expected lines. A U.S state department official said on March 19, 1998 "Our long standing view is that the introduction of nuclear weapon in South Asia would be destabilising and is an issue of deep concern". US Ambassador to India Richard F Celeste said in Calcutta on 1st April, 1998 according to the Times of India of the next day that there was no ground to believe that India was going nuclear...to believe that the new Indian government is going to exercise the nuclear option immediately is like crossing the bridge even before coming to it...we do not believe this is going to happen". It may be noted that there is no condemnation of the Vajpayee government in the US comments. They are guarded.

The Indian government policy on exercising of nuclear option is designed to wait for some time. It is one of mature caution. The government has announced the formation of panel under the previous MOS for Defence Shri K.C. Pant to recommend modalities for the constitution of a National Security Council. After the National Security Council comes into existence it would undertake a security defence review and only after such a review the question of exercising the nuclear option would arise. It is, therefore, clear that notwithstanding the brave words used in the BJP Election Manifesto, the BJP stand after the formation of the government has become pragmatic and is informed by mellowness than by bravado and flambuoyance. Inspite the firing of Ghauri by Pakistan India's response is that of self confidence and not of panic.

Here we need not discuss the various missiles developed by Pakistan and India. India established Indian Guided Missile Development Programme (IGMDP) in 1983. The project was entrusted to Defence Research & Development Organisation (DRDO). It developed Nag, an anti tank missile, with a range of 5 kms, a surface-to-air missile named Akash, with a range of 5 kms and the surface to surface battlefield missle Prithvi capable of carrying a conventional payload of 500 kg with the maximum range of 350 km. The most criticised IGMDP missile has been 'Agni' (fire) first tested on May 22, 1989 and the last test was held on Feb. 19, 1994 whereafter the Govt. of Shri P.V. Narsimha Rao froze further development allegedly under U.S. government pressure. It is maintained that the Agni has a range of 1250 miles. On the Pakistani side Pakistan developed Hatf-I and Hatf-II. Haft-II has a range of 200 km and was built with the help of Chinese technicians. The Pakistan's Space and Upper Atmosphere Research Commission (PSUARC) at Sonmiani near Karachi with the help of the Propellant Factory in Havellian and the A.Q. Khan Research Laboratory produced Hatf-III.

During all this period Pakistan continued to receive advanced missiles from China in addition to the technical assistance by way of expertise and components from China. US slapped Pakistan and China perfunctory penalties in, 1993 for the transfer of Missiles M-11 from China to Pakistan: the penalties were mild on the plea of lack of foolproof evidence that the entire missile systems had been transferred. It deserves to be noted that M-11 missile is nuclear capable unlike any missile developed by India.

With the test firing of Ghauri by Pakistan on 6th April, 1998, all thresholds in the development of lethal missiles in the sub continent have been crossed. Ghauri has a range of 1500 kms. Dr. Abdul Qadeer Khan told Pakistan TV on 14th April, 1998. "We have a series of such missiles and their production is going on in full swing". He told Urdu Daily usafthat Pakistan had acquired nuclear capability way back in 1978. Dr. Qadir Khan went on to say that Pakistan's "defence is invincible". Nothing can hit Ghauri. Pakistan's President Muhammed Rafiq Tarar on pilgrimage to Saudi Arabia said that test firing Ghauri was an achievement not only for Pakistan but for the whole Muslim world. Dr. Abdul Qadir also told Ausaf that another missile Ghaznavi with a range of 2000 kms was also ready for test firing. He further said that Pakistan could explode a nuclear device the day the Pakistan government gave him the necessary permission.[9]

While addressing a workshop on "Vision of Iqbal and Pakistan 2010" at Islamabad on 18th April, 1998, Pakistan's President, Muhammad Rafiq Tarar urged Pakistan scientists to develop a series of new missiles which should be named after the Muslim rulers of the sub-continent. He said that "Ghouri, Ghaznavi, Babri and Abdali missiles should be developed to make the defence of Pakistan impregnable." He went on to say: "We should rekindle the concept of Islamic Ummah (world). We should keep in view the collective interests and resources of the Islamic world while making any future planning."[10]

All the secular forces in the world should thank the fundamentalist President of Islamic Republic of Pakistan for his candidness and having put them on notice for the malignant and destructive schemes of the Islamic Pakistan.

Pakistan claim to have carried out five Nuclear Tests on May 28, 1998 to even account with India. Thus the terrible Nuclear Arms Race gets into full swing.

The economic an other implications of Pakistan's nuclear power and its defence being invincible will be examined in the next chapter.

REFERENCES

1. Bharatiya Janta Party : Election Manifesto 1998; page 29.
2. Ibid; page 31.
3. *Times of India,* March 19, 1998.
4&5. *Times of India,* March 21, 1998.
6. *Times of India,* March 26, 1998.
7. *Times of India,* March 27, 1998.
8. *Times of India,* March 28, 1998.
9. *Times of India*, April 16, 1998.
10. *Times of India* and *Hindustan Times,* April 20, 1998.

14

Kashmir - The Nuclear Flashpoint

Late Shamim Ahmed Shamim of Shopian in South Kashmir was a brilliant Urdu writer and he uncompromisingly exposed the hypocrisy and lust for office of the rulers of Kashmir, India and Pakistan in his weekly *Aiana*. I was an avid reader of the weekly as his journalism was of its own genre: informative, caustic and uncompromising. Once he visited Pakistan towards the close of 1960s. On return he published vignettes of the characters he had encountered in Pakistan and his impressions of Pak polity. One of the episodes he described was that at one gathering, he was asked, `What about Kashmir problem!' Before Shamim could answer, a Pakistani wit intervened to say: "Kashmir is theirs, and the problem is ours;" it was so till early 1980s. Kashmir is Indian even now but it has turned into a festering sore for India as well as Pakistan.

After India-Pak war of 1971, which led to dismemberment of Pakistan, India thought that the two-nation theory, which had been the raison d'etre for Pakistan, had been demolished and buried for ever and Pakistan had accepted Actual Line of Control in Kashmir under Simla Agreement 1972. Kashmir problem had ceased to exist on ground though it might be pending in the United Nations archives. At the same time it was felt that if an opportunity came Pakistan's way, it might try to wrest Kashmir militarily and avenge its defeat of 1971. This scenario appeared so credible in 1972 that I too was of the opinion that militarily alone we must strengthen ourselves in the valley. This I happened to discuss with late Shri D.P. Dhar, Minister without Portfolio in Union cabinet at that time who was of the same view. Thus Mr. Dhar agreed to press for the creation of a separate army corps for Kashmir valley. Without any delay a Corps was sanctioned and we came to work with XVI corps in the valley. However the heady victory of 1971 also bred in all of us a sense of smugness, a sense of complacency that Pakistan had been put in its place.

With this sense of complacency, New Delhi came to neglect the developmental activity in the valley. Though Five Year Plan allocations were regularly raised, funds went into improvement of tourist facilities, horticulture and construction of buildings only. There was generation of jobs too but the improvement in this sector was marginal. Beautiful hotels came up. The number of house-boats increased. A number of tourist lodges, generally ugly, came up all over Srinagar, but nothing was done to de-congest the downtown areas below Budshah bridge - this is the area which festers with agitation, with terrorist hideouts and communal virus. Paper schemes never took a concrete shape. The downtown areas Habba Kadal to Idgah and Khanque-i-Maula and Khanyar remained ghettos and several inhabitants came to acquire ghetto's siege mentality. Development on the outskirts of Srinagar was impressive but the downtown area was neglected and it continued to breed discontent and militancy. Bansi Parimu, a Kashmiri artist of repute, writes about the area as "a dirty and drab slum" and that there used to be a park in the area which "has been buried under ugly and stinking slums. Not only that this vandalism has reduced the historic city of Srinagar to a lungless one, but has deprived Kashmiri youth of any facility of recreation."[1] The Planning Commission approved whatever the State government proposed and the State Government proposed only that which could be added to the architectural glitts or the coffers of those who were close to the corridors of power. There were macro-plans but no micro-plans.

Thus New Delhi came to be identified with nouvou riche and the neglect of larger bodies of the poor and rural Kashmiri population. The root-cause was complacency which transformed itself into blinkers, while Kashmiri Jamait-e-Islami under Pakistani JEI's direct influence and aid embarked upon fundamentalism. Complacency also means lack of coherent policy evolved with inputs of ground reality. Unless India establishes her objectives clearly in Kashmir and provides inputs to secure the same, the wound, a gaping wound that Kashmir is at present, would continue to fester. India has to create conditions so that migrants return.

Observed Jagmohan, erstwhile Governor of Kashmir, "Each and every component of the power structure had been taken over by the terrorists. Subversive elements had infiltrated the police.... Many government officials took arms training, met Amanullah Khan and continued to draw salaries from the Government". He wrote in the *Hindustan Times* (Feb, 17, 1995), "the Spirit of Munich had seized the people and the Government of India ....The lapses of the politicians and administrators are the natural corollaries of this social phenomena." Therefore, to create conditions so that the government apparatus, is cleansed of murky elements and becomes a self-sustaining, efficient instrument of governance, a new vigilance and a new awakening are required. Else it will remain a wound causing atrophy for Kashmiri society and a catastrophe for India and Pakistan.

Though clear evidence is available of Pakistan's abetment in Punjab and J&K, yet India needs to examine where she herself has faltered. Wrote *India Today,* "It is perhaps a singular Indian trait to look for scapegoats whenever the need is for brutal self scrutiny. The last decade, in particular the Indira-Rajiv Gandhi period, was characterised by facile invocation of political demonology and mindless xenophobia"

In place of dealing with terrorism systematically, which cannot be done in a short span, the Government wants to revive political process in the hope of restoring status quo ante. Never will it be status quo ante now in Kashmir. It is self-defeating to seek status quo: New Delhi wants to pass the buck to local satraps.

Again, it is meaningless to seek to talk with terrorists. Indian efforts for such a dialogue failed in Punjab and are bound to fail in Kashmir too. First a terrorist is a psycho-path who cannot see reason. Secondly, he is a puppet in the hands of Pakistan. India has to embark upon long term planning and not fall a prey to political cretinism. There is no short cut. No pat solution. India should show no more mendacity of thought. S.B. Chavan, the then Union Home Minister, visited Jammu and Kashmir on September 25-26, 1991, in the august company of Rajesh Khanna, the actor of Bombay's tinsel world, and invited the extremists to the negotiating table, to sort out Kashmir problem. *The Times of India* reported the next day that all the militant organisations had rejected his offer. Earlier whenever Kashmir issue was raised in the Parliament Chavan's stock reply was that due to one reason or the other, he had not been able to visit Kashmir and that he would soon be visiting the troubled valley, implying that he was a political magician and his visit alone would solve the problem! Now the two Prime Ministers of United Front have toured the state but no political solution has surfaced.

Opposed to this school of revival of political process is that school of thought which calls for destroying training camps in Pakistan as if Pakistan would sit back and let India do it - such an act means war, definite war. The present low-intensity, undeclared war would erupt into a full scale war with both countries employing the most lethal weapons. This war will be most destructive as the lethality of weapons with both the countries is enormous. The feasibility of hot pursuit does not exist - it is a chimera and the question is whether the bombing of training camps and pursuit of terrorists in POK shall not be *cassus belli*? And is India so superior in military strength as to inflict reprisals without inviting counter measures from Pakistan? Pakistan's perception of India is that of a country without hope. *Globe* of Karachi said, "India's democracy and India's polity is only deceptably stable."[2] Once India crosses into Pok, large scale hostilities are likely be unleashed. The Time's correspondent Edward W. Desmord wrote: `Against the background of separatist surges elsewhere in the world, particularly in the Soviet Union and Eastern Europe, Indian political observers have begun to wonder whether the union can survive. Not that anyone is predicting fragmentation at least not yet."[3] Says a western diplomat in New Delhi, "India's political and economic system is much too strong to break up and the democratic set up is resilient enough to accommodate dissent."[3] But wrong perceptions lead to war. The reprisal theory or pre-emptive, self-defence theory succeeds only when a giant power initiates action against a tiny state such as the United States action in Grenada in 1982, in Libya in April 1986, in Panama, and in Iraq (the Gulf war) in January-February 1991. The only country which has got away with reprisals against terrorists is Israel. Her success is primarily because she has been fighting for self-survival and also because the adversaries arrayed against her have been too weak.

Regarding the future of Kashmir, terrorism will ultimately fail the way it has failed in Punjab. Unless Pakistan relents in her efforts to train and arm insurgents no orderly progress in this area is possible. Cacophony of political parties in India will be raised ritualistically to arrange or create consensus without any meaningful result. India will continue to look for scapegoats rather than seek genuine solutions. India should seek fresh ideas and scientific inputs. Till 1996 Indo-Pak relations had touched a new bottom line. At present Pakistan has closed her consulate in Bombay and India was asked to close hers at Karachi. Both the countries expel diplomats on trumped up charges.

Dileep Padgaonkar visited Pakistan and he shared his impression with the readers of *Times of India* in its issue of 16 January, 1996, as follows :

"A category of Pakistanis regard India to be a natural enemy of their country. In an article in The News Moonis Ahmar of the University of Illinois, states that his perceptions are shaped by a deep rooted belief that India has not been reconciled to Pakistan's existence. India, according to these hard-liners, (who are to be bound in the military establishment, the clergy and large sections of the political class and the bureaucracy), engineered Pakistan's dismemberment with creation of Bangladesh and is now involved in the disturbances in Karachi.

In their eyes, India's growing military might, especially its missile progammes and nuclear ambitions, its handling of the Kashmir insurgency and its inability or unwillingness to settle bilateral problems with its other neighbours, constitute clear proof of its hegemonistic designs. Much in the same way, the destruction of the Babri Masjid, the treatment of the Muslim minority in general, the burgeoning aggressiveness of the Hindutva forces indicate that India's secularism is a sham.

These hard-liner elements make no bones of the fact that India cannot be trusted and that, as Prof. Ahmar writes, "the only way to ensure the security of Pakistan is by desintegrating India (and) the insurgency in Indian-controlled Kashmir is to seize an opportunity to initiate the process to that effect."

The above is the general line of mistrust of India on the part of lay Pakistanis.

The agony of Kashmir will end when the undeclared war between India and Pakistan ceaselessly going on since 1947 itself comes to an end. Not crossing of borders or ceasefire line by the armies of the two countries is not peace. Absence of open hostilities is not peace. True peace will dawn only when hatred ceases.

Change is the law of life. All living organisms are in a state of constant change and flux. Only fossils do not change. India should decide if it will abide by the living or fight for the fossils of her follies in Kashmir. Marcus Aurelius, the Roman Emperor, wrote : "you are afraid of CHANGE? but nothing can happen without change; it is something that is of the essence of the nature of the Universe".

T.S. Eliot says :

"We cannot revive old faction.
We cannot restore old policies.
Or follow an antique drum..."

The great Mao-tse-Tung said :

"The world rolls on,
Time passes
Ten thousands years are too long!

Seize the day—seize the hour."

Even the non political Beatle John Lennon sang of peace on earth as follows:

"You may say I'm a dreamer
But I'm not the only one
I hope some day you'll join us
And the world will live as one."

The above prophecy has almost been fulfilled as globalisation is at present the prevailing philosophy in the political and economic world. Thus both India and Pakistan must shed their rigid postures on Kashmir. The world does not want any serious war. Whether it is Palestine or Ireland or Korea global forces are for change from hostility to peace.

If India agrees to change in Kashmir some solution can be found which will satisfy India, Pakistan and the Muslims as well as Kashmiri Pandits of the valley. The possible options can not be spelt out here because the parties have not accepted that change is the necessary catalyst for resolving the existing conflictual situation. If India and Pakistan remain locked in a ceaseless conflict they would be inviting outside powers to intervene in Kashmir. They will not be allowed to render the planet Earth into a radioactive inferno. The world will not stand by as a mute spectator if Indian and Pakistan rulers nuclearise their civilisational conflict of ages past. Normalcy in Kashmir will be restored only if the two countries earnestly negotiate.

Pakistan's use of arms, supplied by USA ostensibly to meet the communist threat from the North, against India in violation of solemn assurances to the contrary has eroded faith in Pakistan's professions of peace. So when Pakistan made an offer of peace during the rule of President Zia-Ul-Haq, Prime Minister Indira Gandhi observed, "you can't talk of peace and prepare for war." The fact is that Indo-Pak relations have never been peaceful, not to speak of their being ever friendly. People of both the countries share several cultural values and extend warm hospitality to the sports teams and delegations and even other visitors, yet Islamabad and New Delhi governments have shown grave mistrust of each other, plunging the sub-continent into serious bouts of tension.

The Times of India of March 23, 1998 reports : "Just days after assuring the new Indian Prime Minister Atal Behari Vajpaye that Pakistan is ready to go an extra mile for establishing good neighbouring ties with India, Pakistan premier Nawaz Sharif has said normalisation with India is not possible without settlement of Kashmir issue".

The refrain of Pakistan's stand is that Kashmir is the only source of tension between the two countries and this may lead to a nuclear war because the two countries which are nuclear powers and they have developed delivery systems. However, there is no guarantee that even if Kashmir issue is settled to the satisfaction of Pakistan, Indo-Pakistan tensions will be buried. We may, therefore, go into some historical facts. Russel Brines writes: "Pakistan was built from a vague concept into a nation by relentless pressure on the Hindu majority. Jinnah and his successors used every victory to press for a further expansion of the Muslim state. The Indians have frequently said, with justice, that they can never be sure where Pakistan will stop; the acquisition of disputed Kashmir might lead to fresh pressures elsewhere. On the other hand, the Pakistan may perpetually be unsure of themselves until their borders are readjusted and the state is by some by means geographically united. In the meantime, Kashmir by 1954 had become for both nations a symbol of national unity which, if yielded, could threaten the disintegration of the home countries themselves...". The struggle (over Kashmir) rose from the basic fear and mistrust of the two nations. If these were eliminated, Kashmir might assume its proper place as a secondary objective; if not, a solution of Kashmir would not settle the fundamental controversy".[5]

The above, though quoted in extension, epitomises the causes of Indo-Pakistani conflict. According to Pakistan Kashmir is the only root cause of non-peace between India and Pakistan whereas India and all other preceptive observers blame the fear and mistrust between the two countries and hold that Kashmir is a mere expression of the same fear psychosis. In the words of Russel Brines again : "Centuries of bloody history had built up mutual fears and suspicions between the Hindus of India and Muslims of Pakistan.[6]

Centuries of antagonisms can be thawed by confidence building measures and not by a knee-jerk solution of Kashmir. The relations between the two countries have been bedevilled by Pakistan seeking foreign crutches. First it was Baghdad Pact, than came CENTO and then SEATO and a perpetual flow of American arms to maintain Balance of Power between the two countries. The outdated concept of Balance of Power was evolved for maintaining peace between city states of Central Europe in Medieval times. It played hell with the peace of Europe for hundreds of years.[7] It is unfortunate that USA has shown itself an enthusiastic proponent of the pernicious doctrine of Balance of Power. Apart from the periodic bouts of infusion of modern American arms into the anaemic body politic of Pakistan is the question of the bilateral defence agreement of 1959 between the USA and Pakistan and now is the no more secret military-cum-nuclear Sino Pakistan nexus.

In addition to the dangers inherent in the doctrine of Balance of Power is the throwback of parochialism from which both India and Pakistan suffer. The anti-dote to parochialism which kept the world in chains for centuries, is science. Pakistan might have acquired the technology to manufacture weapons of mass destruction and can gloat on success in test firing Ghauri and further being ready to fire Ghaznvi, the fact remains that the masses in the sub continent have not acquired a scientific temper. This is why innocent lives are lost everyday at the altar of superstition and sectarianism. Do we realise where is this perochial, dehumanisation is leading us to?

Writes Arnold J. Toynbee: "The essence of the institution of the parochial state is the custom that calls on its citizens to give their lives for it in war."[8] Such states have war as their raison d'etre. But should millions perish in the nuclear cauldron in answer to the megalomaniac war cries of the militarists.

Pakistan's successful entry into nuclear era has always been dependent on furtive support. Now that it is going to serially produce Ghauri and Ghaznvi the question is from where it would get the money for its insane plans. Soviet Union was a military super power till 1990 when it dawned upon it that it could not "afford" a super power military establishment.

Pakistan's budget is peanuts as compared to USA where it was 335 bl dollars in 1986 and 255.4 bl dollars in 1994. The USA's budget for research and development alone is placed to be more than 42 bl dollars. Now if Pakistan has to acquire a superpower stature it has to scrounge for funds. Obviously it is depending upon the bounty from Muslim countries that is why Pakistan's President has called Ghauri an achievement of muslim countries. Even then, will the extent of financial aid from Muslim countries be such that Pakistan will be able to tide over the expenditure involved in the nuclear race embarked upon by it in the Indian sub continent or before there is an exchange of nuclear war heads between the two countries they will fall under the weight of their financial misadventure and meet the fate of Soviet Union? By calling its atom bomb the Islamic Bomb and Ghouri a Muslim delivery system Pakistan can wheedle money from oil rich Saudi Arabia and Libya, yet how long? The fiscal deficit is rising both in India and Pakistan. The GDP in India is down from 7.5 per cent in 1996 to 5 per cent in 1997. Pakistan's entire budget is not enough to service even the interest on loans due from her. Then how long can it depend on Islamic bounty to rescue it from bankruptcy?

The only solution is that the two countries should work for amity between them than try to work for the destruction of the other which will also mean its own destruction. The choice is either friendship or destruction. Should millions die excruciating death in the nuclear inferno and millions be incapacitated to satisfy the ego of warmongers? Statesmanship requires that two countries should shed their distrust and fears. Unless their insecurities are buried, their neurotic race for arms would result in self destruction. A paradigm of win-win solution is required for which compassionate statesmanship, and not gun totting generals and party bosses who thrive on manipulation alone, has to emerge.

The risk of war between India and Pakistan is not a figment of paranoid imagination. Write Alvin and Heidi Toffler: "A related set of assumptions is still widely held in the affluent West. It include the liberal idea that no one really wants war...and that all differences can be negotiated peacefully if opponents will only keep talking to one another because in the end, the global system is eventually rational. Yet none of these assumptions apply today. At times some governments do, infact, want war in the absence of external threats (The Argentianan Generals who started the Folkland/Malvinus war in 1982 did so for purely for internal political reasons in the absence of any external threat whatsoever).[9]

Pakistan has a civilian elected government according to their constitution of 1973 but everyone knows that power in Pakistan vests in Pakistan Army. Whenever a solution by compromise on Kashmir is in sight the Pakistan Army steps in to block the same. This recalcitrance of Pakistan Army is born of its unspoken desire to teach India a lesson for what India did to Pakistan in 1971. So long as Pakistan Army is not prepared to let the past be past and think of the future of Pakistan, the danger of break out of war between the two countries and its further degenerating into a nuclear exchange between the two neighbours, who were one people 50 year back, who are even now one in several facets of their lives, is real. Pakistan and India are "crazy states" in the terms of characteristics laid by Israeli political sciences Yehez kel Dror referred to by Alvin Toffler. In the end one can not help quote Trotsky as quoted by Tofflers "You may not be interested in war, but war is interested in you". So far as India and Pakistan are concerned we may say nuclear war seems to be interested in the sub continent. The chauvinistic myopic generals and politicians seem to be out to plunge the sub continent into nuclear holocaust in order to satisfy their egos, though commit a sacrilege because the scripture says : "God that made the world and all things therein...hath made of one blood all nations of men for to dwell on all the face of the Earth".

If India and Pakistan have to survive, they should fervently pray along with Joshiah Gilbert Holland (1891-91) and act on the contents of his poem "Wanted."

> "God give us Men! A time like this demands
> strong minds, great hearts, true faith, and ready hands;
> Men whom the lust of office cannot kill;
> Men whom the spoils of office cannot buy;

Men who possess opinions and a will;
Men who have honour......who will not lie;
Men who can stand before a demagogue;
And damn his treacherous flatteries without winking.

Indians and Pakistanis would have to opt for rulers who are compassionate and dedicated to peace if the Kashmir problem has to cease to be a cause for mutual hatred and destruction. Else missiles hitting cities in India and Pakistan will compell them to opt for use of nuclear option wiping them out off the face of the earth.

At present, Pakistan aided militancy in Kashmir is about to die, notwithstanding the sporadic killings of Hindus in Kashmir (17 killed near Ramban in June 1996, 23 killed in Wandhama village on January 25, 1998 - Republic day eve and nearly 29 killed in Prankhote in Udhampur district on April 17/18 1998.) Reliable estimate is that seventy-five percent of the Kashmiri youth who had taken up arms feeling frustrated on the failure are roaming various cities of India in search of jobs; twenty percent of the militant youth feeling frustrated are in search of employment in Kashmir valley itself. Only five percent of those who had taken to arms are still working as militants. They are working along with the Afghan mercenaries. According to some reports these five percent Kashmiri youths are held ransom by the Afghans and were they freed these youth would have laid their arms. However their accompanying the Afghans is keeping some vestige of militancy alive in Kashmir. The Afghans do not want or seek any set-piece battle with the Indian security forces, but are content to indulge in sporadic bombing and other outrages. The number of Afghan mercenaries operating at present (November 1997) in Jammu & Kashmir is said to be two thousand five hundred. The mercenaries have been claiming responsibility for the killings of innocent Hindus - the latest being the claim of Lashkar-i-Taiba for the Prankhote massacre in Udhampur district. Subsequently this has come out that this outfit is patronised by the Pakistan Government.

However the more ominous scenario is what is being cooked up between ISI and Taliban forces of Afghanistan. The

Talibans are being told by ISI that the former have been able to capture Kabul and power in Afghanistan because of the massive assistance given by the ISI to them. Now that the ISI is meeting failure in Kashmir, the Talibans should come to their assistance in Kashmir. One report is that Talibans have promised to come to the aid of ISI in Kashmir at on appropriate time. If Talibans actually mount an attack on Kashmir they are bound to be drubbed because Indian Army is a professional force and not the rag-tag the Talibans have been accustomed to fight and overcome in Afghanistan. If the Taliban gets sound beating, will the Pakistan Army not intervene as they did in May 1948, to help the frontier tribes men? What is the guarantee that the Pakistan Army will succeed to stem the Taliban rout and if Pakistan Army faces a stark defeat in Kashmir will they not be tempted to use their much touted nuclear option?

The people of India and Pakistan have to ask themselves and their rulers if people of the subcontinent should perish under the thermonuclear shroud for a small piece of land though it may be divinely beautiful like Kashmir?

REFERENCES

1. Kashmir Let Down Through the Ages, By Bansi Parimu- *The Statesman,* June 22, 1990.
2. *Sunday* September 25-October 5, 1991. "As the Pakistanis See us" by Khushwant Singh.
3. *Time,* Dec. 24, 1990, captioned India at War with Itself.
4. *India Today,* March 31, 1990.
5. Russel Brines: The Indo-Pakistani Conflict; Pall Mall Press, London, page 103.
6. Ibid, page 3.
7. Arnold J. Toynbee: Study of History, Vol. 5, Annex I to V C (i) (d) (y).
8. Ibid.
9. Alvin and Heidi Toffler I: War and Anti-War Survival at the Dawn of the 21st Century, Warner Books (1994), pages 330-331.

Index